PEREGRINE BOOKS

THE KNIGHT, THE LADY AND THE PRIEST

Georges Duby was born in 1919 and educated at the Lycée de Mâcon and the University of Lyon. One of France's greatest medieval historians, he is Professor of Medieval History at the Collège de France in Paris. He has received the Ordre du Mérite Agricole and is an Officier, Légion d'honneur. Georges Duby is the author of many distinguished works on French and European history including, *The Age of the Cathedrals*, *The Chivalrous Society* and *The Three Orders: Feudal Society Imagined*.

GEORGES
DUBY

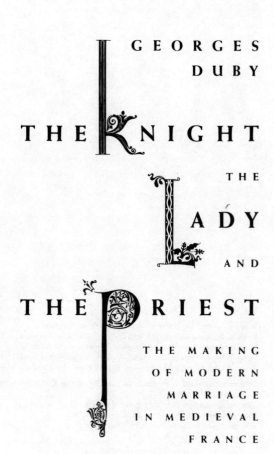

THE KNIGHT

THE

LADY

AND

THE PRIEST

THE MAKING
OF MODERN
MARRIAGE
IN MEDIEVAL
FRANCE

Translated from the French by Barbara Bray
Introduction by Natalie Zemon Davis

PENGUIN BOOKS

Penguin Books Ltd, Harmondsworth, Middlesex, England
Penguin Books, 40 West 23rd Street, New York, New York 10010, U.S.A.
Penguin Books Australia Ltd, Ringwood, Victoria, Australia
Penguin Books Canada Ltd, 2801 John Street, Markham, Ontario, Canada L3R 1B4
Penguin Books (N.Z.) Ltd, 182–190 Wairau Road, Auckland 10, New Zealand

Originally published in France as *Le Chevalier, la Femme et le Prêtre* by
Librairie Hachette, Paris
This translation first published in the United States of America by
Pantheon Books, a division of Random House, Inc., 1983
First published in Great Britain by Allen Lane 1984
Published in Peregrine Books 1985

Made and printed in Great Britain by
Richard Clay (The Chaucer Press) Ltd, Bungay, Suffolk
Set in Garamond

CONTENTS

AROUND ELEVEN HUNDRED

THE TWELFTH CENTURY

INTRODUCTION

In *The Knight, the Lady and the Priest* Georges Duby gives a masterful treatment to marriage, a subject that has woven in and out of his writing for thirty years. In the 1950s, he tracked the marriages of chatelains and knights in the Maconnais region to show how they strengthened family position and local class lines. His work in the sixties revealed the characteristic paternal strategies used in the eleventh and twelfth centuries to keep seigniorial land intact, such as allowing only one son to wed and marrying off all the daughters, often downward; the military and amorous escapades of the knights, young and not so young, became much more comprehensible when one learned what their authoritarian fathers were up to. Then in the 1970s, Duby focused on the medieval family and sexuality. Out of all this has come an innovative book in which marriage serves to reveal changes not only in aristocratic values and behavior but also in religious concepts and liturgy, in perceptions of the sacred and profane, in the relations of laity and clergy, and in the nature of power and the social order.

That marriage should link so many features of social life is not surprising, so Duby assures us; it is after all an institution that defines much about our present and our future. Yet it is his conceptual framework that makes it possible for us to see this: he places aristrocratic marriage within a system fraught with conflicts—between pope and king and priest and seignior in the first instance, but also between young men and old men, married priests and celibate priests, disaffected heretics and the evil world, and finally between men and women. The range of sources used is appropriate to the task, from papal letters and monastic cartularies to religious drama, from saints' lives to genealogical histories. If some of them have been exploited before by writers on courtly love and specialists in canon law, they have rarely been joined together and read with such sensitivity to what they could yield for the theory and practice of marriage.

Or rather we should say theories and practices, for it is this multiplicity that is the main argument of the book. In the tenth and early eleventh centuries, the marriages of warriors and kings were made by abduction as well as by arrangement, and might join a couple incestuously, that is, related within the many prohibited degrees of kinship; varieties of concubinage existed openly; and husbands repudiated their wives and took new ones. Most of this was done not with a sense of wickedness but out of rightful concern for dynastic and family alliance and for children who would carry on knightly virtue in their blood. Simultaneously the ascetic-minded clergy were reminding everyone (including men within their own ranks) of the sinfulness attached to the uncontrollable passions of sex and were urging on the laity the Church's rules for the lowly state of marriage. Marriages should come about by peaceable betrothal and never by abduction; they should extend amity by allying people outside the seven degrees of kinship; married men should not commit adultery (though the fornication of the unmarried was not terribly serious), and they should not repudiate their wives. If dissolution of marriage was required, it should be done only at the bishops' hands. As for the rituals of marriage, priests had little to do with making them sacred beyond occasionally blessing the marriage bed.

By the beginning of the thirteenth century, the picture was very different and many of the features of what we think of as the traditional Christian marriage system were in place. Whatever divergences there were in behavior, marriage was at least conceived of in the same way by knight and priest, king and pope. It was an estate open only to the laity (not even subdeacons could have wives) and competing forms of concubinage had lost their earlier legitimacy. Marriage was now a sacrament with its own theology of consent and bodily union, the priest playing a role at the solemn pledges and gift exchange of the betrothal and at the nuptial blessing before Mass. The abductions of the young had become domesticated into the games of courtly love and jousting; their fathers had accepted the principle of monogamy and, if a marriage had to be dissolved, were now willing to take the case to the Church in hopes that the unwanted spouse would be adjudged a cousin. Meanwhile the Church, showing itself more understanding of the strategies of aristocratic families, reduced the prohibited degrees of kinship from seven to four.

What is at the heart of this accord, Duby demonstrates, is the notion of hierarchy. The husband has authority over the sexuality and property of his obedient wife; the Church has authority over the laity in regard to marriage and other spiritual questions. It is no coincidence that this vision of marriage carried the field at the same time that the image of the three orders was taking hold, an image that (as the author has shown elsewhere) justifies the obedience of the men who work, the superiority of the men who pray, and the overall—and new—power of the king above the men who fight.

Thus Georges Duby suggests that the construction of a marriage system and a sexual economy was connected with the construction of political and ecclesiastical systems and an economy of feudal property. Each step toward the reconciliation of knight and priest on the marriage question he explains by a cluster of economic and cultural changes. For the chatelains and knights whose wealth was drawn not from war booty but from seigniorial properties, marriage had to ensure more than blood and alliance. Fathers took firmer control of family matters to prevent a divided inheritance and too many male marriages; wives were given smaller bride-gifts and daughters smaller dowries, where the latter had begun to be used; husbands tried to merge their women's property with their own. The significant kin network was no longer conceived as the maternal and paternal cousins and uncles stretching out on either side, but was defined "agnatically," back through the male line to a single distant founder. The consequences of all this were paradoxical: at first they reinforced the knights' indifference to the Church's incest prohibitions and the rest as still interfering with their marriage strategies; but then, concerned to have legitimate heirs, fathers came to appreciate some of the advantages of the monogamous ideal.

For the priests there were other paradoxes. They were caught up in defending the clergy's privileged status—indeed in defining it anew—against married priests who mixed the sacred and the profane too freely and against heretics who went too far in separating them. The spokesmen for Church reform had to reaffirm more strongly than ever the purity of the ascetic life while demonstrating that marriage is after all not polluting. This turned out to be good preparation for the body-spirit issues central to twelfth-century theological reflection on the incarnation of Christ and the motherhood of Mary, and ultimately for Peter Lombard's classic definition of the dual nature of marriage: consent at its heart—but copulation following fast afterward.

Georges Duby has offered a time frame and an important web of connectedness for "the making of modern marriage in medieval France." How does it fit with what American and English scholars have been telling us about that institution and the role of women within it? An impressive study of *Women in Frankish Society* by Suzanne Wemple deals with similar issues in the years 500 to 900 and describes the "ascent of monogamy" already in the ninth century: "the continuance of aristocratic lineages could no longer be entrusted to a succession of wives or to simultaneous wives" (p. 96). While agreeing on an early collaboration between Carolingian kings and bishops on this matter, Duby would argue that its fruits were precarious, easily undone by the political disarray of the tenth century. Clearly the transformation of this cultural pattern, so rooted in the everyday decisions of small groups, took a very long time and required favorable circumstances for its completion. Meanwhile recent work on the appearance of the dowry in Western Europe and on the role of aristocratic women in land transactions is at least consistent with Duby's time frame and chain of explanation.

Other scholars, while sharing Duby's view of marriage as part of a total social system, are suggesting new elements be added to the system. In *Christianity, Social Tolerance and Homosexuality*, John Boswell has documented the remarkable degree of homoerotic expressiveness found in the writings and behavior of monks and priests—and in some lay aristocratic circles as well—reaching a height in the late eleventh and early twelfth century. And it was tolerated. The early penitentials took sodomy much less seriously than adultery. Bishop Yves of Chartres, whose *Decretum* is analyzed by Duby for its elaboration of the canon law of marriage, had almost nothing to say about homosexuality; and when Yves protested to Pope Urban II against the installation of a certain John as bishop of Orleans on the grounds that he was the lover of the archbishop of Tours, it was especially because he feared John would be under the archbishop's thumb. In any case the pope did not intervene and John ruled his diocese for forty years. Boswell notes that this laxity toward homosexuality was concurrent with the Church's energetic actions to stamp out clerical marriage: "Leave us alone and chastise yourself, sodomite!" wrote one married priest. The tide turned against Ganymede only in the thirteenth century, when the victory against the married clergy had been won and when, as Duby tells us in his last chapter, changing economic and political structures were also encouraging aristocratic fathers to let more of their sons marry.

Yet another complexity has been introduced into the picture by David Herlihy. He urges us to think of the agnatic kinship system, with its exclusion of women from the family lineage, as something superimposed upon but not wholly obliterating the bilineal system that preceded it. Rather, the two remain in permanent tension with each other: kinship on the distaff side, being called up any time one had to consider incest prohibitions, and responsibilities to one's daughters and younger sons always tempering an absolute commitment to the father's line. This image of the aristocratic family in the eleventh and twelfth centuries adds interesting depth to the quarrels and calculations described by Duby in the houses of the lords of Amboise and the counts of Guines.

As both of these examples suggest, current American and English research has been giving a slightly different reading to the potentialities of

the religious life and to the situation of women in the centuries that concern Duby. He warns that the sources for research on medieval society
have virtually all been written by men, and by members of the clergy to
boot. His goal has been to "demystify" their discourse, which he hears as
variously hostile, disrespectful, and fearful of women. For the seigniors
and princes, women were instruments of the male lineage, at their best
when they sacrificed all their energies to serve the family's interest, but
ever to be feared for their insatiable sexual appetite and propensity to
stain male honor by adultery. Under an overlay of compliments and con-
ventions, courtly literature is "a male morality, based on a primal fear
of women and a determination to treat them as objects." For priests and
monks women embodied the sin of sexuality and were praised only for
heroic obedience even to evil husbands (Saint Godelive) or for saintly
detachment from the flesh (the married but ascetic Saint Ide). The privileged figure was the lost mother whom unwed men had left behind,
sought within the frustrations of the monastery in the figure of the Virgin
and perhaps too among the mysterious fairies met by young knights in
their wanderings.

Duby ends his book with the moving query, how much do we learn
about women from all this? He suggests that the multiplication of nun-
neries and the swelling of the ranks of the more egalitarian heretical
groups were signs of women's dissatisfactions with aristocratic marriage.
Scholars especially interested in the history of women have been trying to
devise strategies to answer Duby's question. These include reading every
scrap of writing left us by medieval women, religous and lay, and also,
with proper attention to context and comparison, reading texts by men
for clues to the female experience. Thus Caroline Bynum finds twelfth-
century visionary Hildegarde of Bingen reformulating Paul's "Neither
was the man created for the woman; but the woman for the man" (1
Cor. 11:9) as "Thus it is written: Woman is created for the man and
man is made for woman." And Joan Ferrante shows that in the lais of
Marie de France some marriages are spoiled by jealous or faithless husbands, but love is as much a resource for a woman as for a man, "freeing
the lover's imagination from the bonds that society imposes upon it."

In the absence of much direct evidence of how aristocratic women viewed their lot, social historians have tended to interpret their situation as a mixed affair. Subject to the authority of fathers and husbands though these women were, no one has been tempted to see them only as victims. Rather, one asks about them—as about any group with limited access to power—what options did they have and how creatively did they use them? Suzanne Wemple talks of the consequences of monogamy for women in terms of a series of trade-offs: on the one hand, women lost the sexual freedom, right to choose, and social mobility that went along with the system of successive marriages and of unions other than marriage; on the other hand, wives were more secure in their position and had an enhanced and respected role in the domestic administration of the family. Their scope was largest, she suggests, when feudal decentralization allowed political power to devolve on the monogamous family unit; then "women were equipped to act with authority as helpmates and *dominae* in both economic and political affairs" (p. 122).

From the vantage point of this mixed vision, Duby's Saint Ide emerges from the Clunaic hagiography as a woman of considerable independence, in control of that powerful female sexuality, growing from mother to miracle-worker, living on her own in the world. Emerging from the Amboise genealogy and shining in more than reflected male glory, is Elisabeth de Jaligny, an heiress who fights for her rights and her sons' rights, a tough widow remembered for berating her son in asking, "Why did you get involved in this war without consulting me?" The answer to Duby's question is that we learn much about women from this book on medieval marriage. Out of his dissection of male discourse—sensitive, humorous, and beautifully expressed in the lively and flowing translation of Barbara Bray—come any number of wives, daughters, widows, and concubines, clamoring to be heard in their own right. Georges Duby gives to medieval marriage not only its complex system and historical dynamic —but also both its sexes.

The following are publications referred to in this Introduction and/or recommended as further reading

Baker, Derek, ed. *Medieval Women: Dedicated and Presented to Professor Rosalind M. T. Hill* Oxford: Basil Blackwell, for the Ecclesiastical History Society, 1978.

Benton, John. "Clio and Venus: An Historical View of Medieval Love." In *The Meaning of Courtly Love,* edited by F. X. Newman, pp. 19–42. Albany: State University of New York Press, 1968.

Bloch, Marc. *Feudal Society.* 2d. ed. Translated by W. A. Manyon. Chicago: University of Chicago Press, 1962.

Boswell, John. *Christianity, Social Tolerance, and Homosexuality: Gay People in Western Europe from the Beginning of the Christian Era to the Fourteenth Century.* Chicago and London: University of Chicago Press, 1980.

Bynum, Caroline Walker. *Jesus as Mother: Studies in the Spirituality of the High Middle Ages.* Berkeley, Los Angeles, and London, 1982.

Donahue, Charles, Jr. "The Canon Law on the Formation of Marriage and Social Practice in the Later Middle Ages." *Journal of Family History* 8 (1983): 144–158. Special Issue on Religion and the Family in European History. Includes important bibliography.

Duby, Georges. *The Chivalrous Society.* Translated by Cynthia Postan. Berkeley and Los Angeles: University of California Press, 1977.

———. *La Société aux XIe et XIIe siècles dans la région mâconnaise.* Paris: Librairie Armand Colin, 1953.

———. *The Three Orders. Feudal Society Imagined.* Translated by Arthur Goldhammer. Chicago and London: University of Chicago Press, 1980.

Ferrante, Joan M. *Woman as Image in Medieval Literature: From the Twelfth Century to Dante.* New York and London: Columbia University Press, 1975.

Hajdu, Robert. "The Position of Noblewomen in the *Pays des Coutumes,* 1100–1300." *Journal of Family History* 5 (1980): 122–145.

Herlihy, David. "The Making of the Medieval Family: Symmetry, Structure and Sentiment." *Journal of Family History* 8 (1983): 116–130. Special Issue on Religion and the Family in European History. Includes important bibliography.

Hughes, Diane Owen. "From Brideprice to Dowry." Papers from the Shelby Cullom Davis Center for Historical Studies. *Journal of Family History* 3 (1978): 262–298.

McNamara, Jo Ann and Suzanne F. Wemple. "Sanctity and Power: The Dual Pursuit of Medieval Women." In *Becoming Visible: Women in European History* edited by Renate Bridenthal and Claudia Koonz, pp. 90–118. Boston: Houghton Mifflin, 1977.

Sheehan, Michael M. "Marriage Theory and Practice in the Conciliar Legislation and Diocesan Statutes of Medieval England." *Mediaeval Studies* 40 (1978): 408–460.

Soliday, Gerald L. *et al. History of the Family and Kinship: A Select International Bibliography.* Millwood, NY: Kraus International Publications, 1980.

Stuard, Susan Mosher, ed. *Women in Medieval Society.* Philadelphia: University of Pennsylvania Press, 1976.

Wemple, Suzanne Fonay. *Women in Frankish Society: Marriage and the Cloister, 500 to 900.* Philadelphia: University of Pennsylvania Press, 1981.

Natalie Zemon Davis

PREFACE

I n autumn 1973 I decided to devote my seminar at the Collège de France to the study of kinship and sex in the West during the tenth, eleventh, and twelfth centuries. My ambition being to understand how what is called feudal society functioned, I had already examined its economic relations, the evolution of its chain of command, and the development of its ideas of social order, i. e., those aspects that were best known and most clearly illustrated by available sources. It was now time to look into those fundamentally important mechanisms that ensure the reproduction of any society and the perpetuation of its structures. This new field of research was relatively untilled and very large, but it proved fertile—and may still produce further yields even after the eleven years of intensive work that has already been done, though we hope to have finished by 1984.

Our most substantial sources have been the texts the great princely houses of northwest France commissioned, in the twelfth century, for the glory of the heads of their respective families: these texts traced each house's genealogy and celebrated the memory of its ancestors. Especially important for us were the history of the counts of Guines, written around 1200 by Lambert of Ardres, and the history of the lords of Amboise, which its author—probably a canon of the cathedral at Tours—presented to King Henry Plantagenet in about 1155. Marriage, of course, at once emerged as the keystone of the structure that gave the aristocracy its preeminence. But we also discovered that, while the institution of marriage had been very thoroughly studied by historians of law and morals on the basis of normative writings and theoretical treatises, great uncertainty still prevailed about practical realities, about how people reacted to the models set before them and to what extent the prescribed rules were obeyed. At the very first glance there seemed to be a great discrepancy between practice and theory, including the principles laid down by the leaders of the Church. We therefore set about trying to discover what that practice was, and what married life meant in the daily life of the nobles, the only class available for observation.

In April 1976, I gave an account of our early findings in an inaugural address at a conference on marriage studies organized by the Medieval Institute at Spoleto. During the academic year 1976–1977 my seminar at the Collège de France focused on marriage customs between the year 1000 and the beginning of the thirteenth century, as exemplified by the line of the kings of France, the family group placed in the spotlight by its position at the top of the hierarchy of power and prestige. In May 1977, when I was invited to deliver the James S. Schoules Lectures at Johns Hopkins University, I naturally chose to give a three-part account of the results of our latest investigations, which was published with some additions in 1978 by the Johns Hopkins University Press as an elegant little volume entitled *Medieval Marriage: Two Models from 12th-Century France.*

At that point I was as yet scarcely halfway through my research, so *Medieval Marriage* was bound to be just an interim and provisional report on the work in progress. I waited another two and a half years before I ventured to assemble what we had gradually found bit by bit and to organize it all into a coherent argument. That first synthesis was the subject of a series of lectures I delivered at the Collège de France between

November 1979 and March 1981, and provided the basis for the book presented here in translation.

It bears little resemblance to its predecessor, for, while recapitulating the contents of *Medieval Marriage*, it also presents them in a revised form that takes into account, for example, comments contained in critical reviews of the earlier book. Above all, as well as containing new material making it four times as long as the text of the Baltimore lectures, *The Knight, the Lady and the Priest* embodies a completely different approach. *Medieval Marriage* was chiefly based on the history of the counts of Guines and on the writings that arose out of the conflict between the ecclesiastical authorities and the kings of France—Robert II, Philip I, Louis VII, and Philip Augustus—over the monarchs' marriages. New sources, much more numerous and varied, have made it possible to multiply the case studies tenfold: they include the list of penances drawn up by bishop Bourchard of Worms, the marriage contracts preserved in the archives of Burgundy, the correspondence of Yves of Chartres, lives of saints, the narratives of Chrétien de Troyes, the theological treatises of Hugues of Saint-Victor, the genealogical texts concerning the counts of Anjou and the lords of Amboise, the autobiography of Guibert of Nogent, and so on.

Our previous research had brought out the coexistence of two matrimonial moralities, one imposed by the priests and the other put into practice by the warriors who then formed the ruling class; also the conflict between these two models, which grew more acute during the eleventh century and then gradually died down, ending in the compromises that were to govern Western marriage practices for centuries. Setting out from these same facts, the present study went deeper and drew finer distinctions. The approach to the subject was diversified by fresh hypotheses, many of them suggested by those who had for years been attending my weekly seminars: Maurice Accarie, Francesco Chiovaro, Guy Lubrichon (to whom I refer in the following pages), and others too numerous to mention individually. More characters made their entrance on the stage. The tone changed too: what was addressed to specialists at Johns Hopkins was now aimed at a much larger public, at all educated people who would like to understand how the structures and rites at present disintegrating before our eyes came into being almost a thousand years ago, and thence why those rites and structures are falling apart today. The results of a lengthy program of research suddenly became topical.

The book concludes with a question: what do we know about the women? For my study of medieval marriage brought me to the frontiers of an unknown realm: the world of women. I had been hearing about women all along, but the speakers were always men representing members of the other sex as objects at once contemptible, terrifying, and tempting.

What I want to do next is try to demystify this male discourse and find out what the position of women really was in the period with which I am concerned. And as research in this field is not nearly so advanced in France as in the English-speaking countries, I shall await with great interest the comments of those who are about to read this book in English, and who may be able to help me in the next stage of my quest.

Beaurecueil, June 1983

THE KNIGHT
THE LADY AND
THE PRIEST

CHAPTER I
THE MARRIAGES OF
KING PHILIP I

I n the autumn of 1095 Pope Urban II was at Clermont in the
Auvergne, on the southern border of the Capetian sphere of influence.[1] After being driven out of Rome he had spent some months
traveling in great pomp, escorted by his cardinals, through southern
Gaul. He felt at home in that part of the world. He had once been grand
prior of Cluny, and the region was full of priories belonging to that
congregation. It was here that for the last twenty years and more the
papacy had been most successfully pursuing a policy of Church reform
—a policy designed in fact to purify the whole of society. The aim was
to prepare men and women for the tribulations awaiting them at the
expected end of the world; to bring them back, whether they liked it or
not, to the paths of righteousness; to define, in terms of their station in
life, their individual duties. The overhaul inevitably began with a purge
of the ecclesiastical hierarchy, for it was up to the servants of God to set

an example. They needed to be cleansed of two kinds of corruption. The first was simony, the name applied by contemporary scholars to the intrusion of secular power, and especially the power of money, into the choice of Church leaders. The second was Nicolaitism: immorality and the love of worldly pleasures, first and foremost of these being, of course, the love of women.

But now the time had come to deal with the laity, to make them too conform to ways of living that the priests said were pleasing to God. At this point the Church's task became more difficult. For on all sides men rebelled, and the princes of this world backed up their resistance. The emperor himself did so, and after him the other kings, each in the territory heaven had given into his power. For these temporal rulers saw themselves—like Charlemagne, whose heirs they claimed to be—as charged by God to maintain the social order. And they were loath to let others meddle in it, upsetting the rules prescribed by custom and telling their soldiers how to behave.

No kings came to Clermont. But there were many bishops and abbots, together with the aristocracy of the surrounding regions—enough people of quality for the pope to feel he was presiding over Christendom itself, acting as supreme guide, and occupying an emperor's place as the head of all earthly sovereigns. From this position Urban II spoke as if to the whole world, legislating, judging, punishing. Of all his decisions the most famous was his call to the First Crusade: all the knights of the West were to set forth and prepare the way for the great migration through which the whole company of the faithful were to see Jerusalem. There, when the Holy Sepulchre had been set free, they would wait by the empty tomb for the Last Judgment, the great transition for which the reform had been a preparation, the resurrection of mankind amid a blaze of glory.

That grandiose rallying cry has overshadowed another of Urban II's decrees, part of the same overall policy: the excommunication of King Philip I of France. Philip was the first ruler of the western Franks to disgrace himself so badly in the eyes of Church authorities as to call down this dread punishment. Excommunication cut him off from the very community of the faithful he was supposed to rule. It brought down God's curse upon him. And it doomed him to eternal damnation if he did not mend his ways.

Philip had already been excommunicated once, a year earlier. On October 15, 1094, thirty-two bishops had met at Autun under the papal legate Hugues of Die, archbishop of Lyons, to pronounce sentence on him. At the same time they quashed the decisions arrived at by a council the king had recently presided over in Reims. There was conflict between the two parts of the kingdom of France: the north, which was controlled by the king, and the south, which was not. But above all there was a clash between two irreconcilable conceptions of the Church: on the one hand, the traditional Carolingian view, which saw the prelates of each nation gathered together under its divinely appointed king; on the other, the disquieting vision of reformers like Urban II, according to which the spiritual was above the temporal and kings were therefore subject to bishops, and bishops themselves subject to the unifying authority of the bishop of Rome. If these new structures were to be acccepted, kings must be made to yield. To force the king of France to bend the knee, the leaders of the reform excommunicated him, first at Autun and then at Clermont.

The minutes of the Council of Clermont have not survived. We know of its proceedings only through references in the works of contemporary historians, monks who noted down year after year such events as had made an impression on them. Nearly every one of them mentioned the solemn assembly at Clermont, but almost all referred only to the expedition to the Holy Land, which greatly appealed to their imaginations. Some, however, did say in passing that the king of France had been punished, and why. Philip I had not, like Emperor Henry IV, been excommunicated for rising in armed rebellion against the Holy See. The pope had chosen to chastise Philip for his morals, and in particular for his behavior in regard to marriage. According to Sigebert of Gembloux his offense consisted in having, "while his wife was still alive, taken as an additional wife [*superduxerit*] the wife of another, he also being still living." Bernold of Saint-Blasien gives more detail: "Having dismissed his own wife, he united himself in marriage to the wife of his vassal"; the grounds for his punishment were "adultery." To this crime the *Annals* of Saint-Aubin d'Angers adds the further one of incest.[2]

But all this does not tell us very much. Fortunately we learn more from what Yves of Chartres, a bishop in northern France, had to say on the matter some fifteen years later. In order to prevent a proposed marriage between two cousins of the king of France, Yves sent the archbishop of Sens a genealogical chart showing that they were related.[3] He knew this family tree well, he said. With his own ears he had heard it recited twice at the court of Pope Urban II, the first time by a monk from the Auvergne and the second by the envoys of the court of Anjou. In the course of the argument Philip I was accused of "having carried off the wife of the count of Anjou, she being his cousin, and having wrongfully kept her. . . . The king was excommunicated by the Council of Clermont because of this accusation, and also because of proof of incest."

This was what an intelligent man with a good memory and who had been closely involved in the affair remembered fifteen years later. What had shocked people was not bigamy—the fact that the king had married again while his first wife was still alive. Nor was the scandal caused by adultery—the fact that the king had taken another man's lawful wife. No. The trouble was that the woman he stole was related to him. She was not even related to him by blood; she was the wife of a very distant cousin, the great-grandfather of the count of Anjou being the great-great-grandfather of the king. But this had been enough to bring down excommunication and anathema upon King Philip.

And as he would not give in, but "returned to his commerce with the said woman, he was excommunicated [again] at the Council of Poitiers [1099] by cardinals Jean and Benoît."

Philip I was just as concerned about his own salvation and just as afraid of sinning as anybody else. But his beliefs about right and wrong were different from those that the reforming clerics were trying to impose. He thought differently from them about marriage. And he was sure he was guilty of no wrongdoing.

Philip had married Berthe de Frise when he was twenty. His first cousin, the count of Flanders, had given him her hand: she was his wife's daughter by a previous marriage. This arranged marriage set the seal on a reconciliation between the king and his vassal and father-in-law.

For nine years Berthe remained barren. But she prayed, and at last a son was born: Louis, later Louis VI. Heaven had answered the entreaties of Arnoul, a reputedly holy hermit of Saint-Médard de Soissons whom people came from far and near to consult on family problems. Arnoul, who like Berthe was from Flanders, had interceded for her lest she be sent away for not producing an heir. But despite the birth of Louis, Berthe was repudiated, though not until 1092, twenty years after her marriage.

Her husband then installed, or rather imprisoned, her in the chateau of Montreuil-sur-Mer. This fortress was part of her dower, i.e., the settlement made by the husband on the wife when they exchanged vows, and which came in handy if he wanted to get rid of her later: he could leave her in possession of the property but keep her sequestered there.

Having thus disposed of Berthe, the king took up with Bertrade, who belonged to the Montfort family and was married to the count of Anjou.

Did Philip seduce Bertrade or she him? Did he take her by force or did she come to him? Or—and this seems most likely—did he have an arrangement with her husband?

And what did what we call love have to do with it all? I must say at once and emphatically that we do not know, and no one ever will. We are almost entirely ignorant about the men and women who lived in France nearly a thousand years ago: their mental imagery, how they spoke and wore their clothes, their feelings about their own bodies. We do not even know what they looked like.

What was it about Bertrade that attracted Philip? What was the nature of his desire? We can guess at the answer to such questions in the case of Charles VI and of his uncle the duke of Berry at the end of the fourteenth century. But the paintings and sculptures that survive from three hundred years earlier give us no female form to contemplate except the stylized image of the Virgin Mary, a symbol or theological argument rather than a woman. Apart from this there remain only the lurid, frenzied, broken puppets representing the damned, which priests made use of in their sermons to illustrate the fate awaiting the lustful.

So my investigation of marriage during this period is necessarily restricted to what was on the surface both of society and of institutions; to facts and to events. About the passions that moved body or spirit I can say nothing.

Philip's remarriage caused a sensation, as can be seen from the allusions to it in the few written records that survive. The best chroniclers of northern France—Clarius of Sens, Hugues of Flavigny, Sigebert of Gembloux—all bore witness to ceremonies as solemn and holy as for a real marriage. The lord of Beaugency, issuing a document at that time, did not date it, as was the custom, in terms of the birth of Christ or of the reign of the ruling sovereign; he dated it "the year when Philip took to wife Bertrade, wife of Fouque, count of Anjou."[4] So people were surprised. But there was no sign of disapproval. It would all probably have passed off quite peacefully had it not been for the reformers. Had it not been for Yves, bishop of Chartres.

Yves was fifty years old and had just managed, not without difficulty, to establish himself on his episcopal throne. He replaced one of the prelates dismissed by Urban II in his purge of the superior clergy. The Roman Curia's interference in local affairs had shocked many clerics, including the metropolitan archbishop of Sens, who refused to ordain the new bishop of Chartres. So Yves got himself ordained in Capua by Urban II himself. This was taken to be an infringement of the powers of the king, and in 1091 the interloper was deposed by a synod. But Yves held out, relying on legates and on the Holy Father himself, insisting on the supremacy of papal decisions. Brought up as a rigorist, Yves was already inclined to sympathize with the reformers, and his present difficulties threw him into their camp. He joined them in their confrontation with the old school of prelates, his allegedly simoniac and Nicolaist colleagues, and with their accomplice the king. The see of Chartres became an outpost in the struggle, a wedge driven into the traditional structures of the royalist Church.

Philip's second marriage provided Yves with a good opportunity to launch an attack. The king, wishing the wedding to be an impressive occasion, summoned all the bishops to be present. But the bishop of Chartres declined the invitation, and tried to persuade others to do the same. He argued, in opposition to his enemy the archbishop of Sens, that it was the archbishop of Reims who had the right not only to crown the kings of France but also to consecrate their marriages. He wrote to the archbishop of Reims[5] that he would not go to the wedding "unless you yourself celebrate and perform it, with your suffragans assisting and cooperating." But he also gave a warning: "This is a dangerous matter. It could do great harm both to your reputation and to the honor of the realm." Moreover, "Other and secret reasons of which I may not speak at present prevent me from approving this marriage." He addressed another, more outspoken letter to Philip himself: "You will not see me in Paris, with your wife of whom I know not if she may be your wife."[6] The wording is important. Men like Yves were skilled in rhetoric and practiced manipulators of language. When he used the word *uxor*, Yves was recognizing that Philip and Bertrade were already husband and wife: for him the nuptial ceremony was merely an additional celebration. "I shall not come," he went on, "until I know if a general council has found that you and your spouse are legitimately divorced, and that you and her you wish to wed may legitimately be married."

What Yves was saying here was that only churchmen were competent in such matters, that the authority of bishops was subordinate to that of councils, and that the matter in question turned on two separate issues. Did Philip have the right to repudiate his first wife?—a question that carried an imputation of bigamy. And had he the right to marry the second?—a query that raised the issue of incest. And until the matter had been cleared up there could be no marriage, only concubinage. But was it decent for a king to live in that state? Yves insisted on this point in order to justify his not going to the wedding. He was not failing in his duty; on the contrary. On the temporal plane he was acting as a loyal counselor when he declared this marriage to be detrimental to the crown. On the spiritual plane he was acting as a vigilant director of conscience when he declared it to be detrimental to the king's salvation.

The letter ended with a little sermon on lust, illustrated by Adam, Samson, and Solomon, all of whom were ruined by women.

Philip took no notice. The union was celebrated in due form and blessed by the bishop of Senlis in the presence of all the bishops in the royal domain. The archbishop of Reims had given his approval, and so apparently had Cardinal Roger, papal legate to the north of France. But Yves persisted. He assembled a file on how to "bring about a divorce between Philip and his new wife."[7] He sent it to the pope, who replied with letters and a circular to the prelates of France forbidding them to crown Bertrade queen. There was also a reprimand to the archbishop of Reims and a warning to the king. If he did not cease all relations with the woman he had "by way of wife," he would be excommunicated.

The bishop of Chartres had already decided to break with the king. He withheld vassal service and did not bring his knights to the great assembly at which the king arbitrated a quarrel between the sons of William the Conqueror. This made him guilty of a felony, and he fled. By the end of 1093 he was to be found among the retinue of the pope. At this point the whole matter might have been smoothed over, for Berthe died, and so Philip was no longer committing bigamy. But we must not forget that Philip was anxious about the salvation of his soul. It is more uncomfortable for a king than for an ordinary man to be told he is living in sin. Philip gathered together in Reims as many prelates as he could—two archbishops and eight bishops. They all confirmed the royal marriage. They went further and talked of trying Yves of Chartres. The Council of Autun was the answer.

The excommunication of the king of France was a very serious matter, but it was part of an overall plan: the Roman Curia's all-out offensive aimed at carrying through the reform. The pope was to tour southern Gaul, but to win the day in the north it was necessary one way or another to deal with the king. Yves of Chartres, who had reliable sources of information, declared that help could be looked for in two quarters. First perhaps, in the king's own family, in the person of Prince Louis, who was thirteen and would soon attain his majority. When Philip remarried he had set his son up in an appanage, but like all aristocratic heirs at that time Louis champed at the bit and was impatient to come into his inheritance. And behind Louis there probably already lurked Suger, the same age as the prince, and the reformed monks of Saint-Denis. The second and more certain source of support was Anjou, the reformers' trump card.

Little attention has been paid so far to Fouque Réchin, count of Anjou, the husband in the case. Or to Bertrade herself. For what was in question, on trial, was the behavior of one man: Philip. Bertrade was just as guilty of adultery as he, but her case did not concern the state. It was up to the betrayed husband to seek revenge if he wanted to. But all Fouque did was look around for women to replace his wife. He was, however, in the pope's power.

Nearly thirty years earlier a papal legate had disinherited Fouque's elder brother for violating the rights of the churches in Anjou, and "on behalf of Saint Peter" had handed the principality over to him. It was strange that a representative of the Church of Rome should dispose of a French earldom. Strange, but not inexplicable. In 1067 the king was very young and the Capetian dynasty was weak. Moreover Fouque had bought Philip's agreement by giving him the Gâtinais. In any event, since then Anjou had been subject to a sort of apostolic sovereignty, and the count's hands were tied. They were tied all the more tightly because he too had been excommunicated. He had taken his brother prisoner, refused to free him, and kept him in such confined captivity for so long that he had gone out of his mind. So Fouque could be made use of. In June 1094, a few months before the Council of Autun and at the same time as the Council of Reims, the legate Hugues of Die came in person to Saumur to rescind the excommunication. Hugues, after checking that the brother really was insane, reconciled Fouque with the Church and confirmed him in his possession of Anjou, though at the same time making him promise "not to remarry again without the advice of the legates."[8] True, he had already overstepped the mark in the matter of polygamy. But the real reason behind the interdiction was that by preventing him from taking another wife the legate ensured that the case of his current legal spouse, Bertrade, would be kept open.

Through Fouque, then, it was possible to revive the question the death of Berthe had resolved. Fouque meekly did what was expected of him. Up till then he had not opened his mouth; now he became vociferous. On June 2, 1095, when making a deed of gift to Saint-Serge d'Angers, he had it dated "at the time when France was defiled by the adultery of the unworthy King Philip."[9] In November he sent evidence of the kinship between himself and the king to Clermont, thus supporting the accusation of incest. During the winter, Urban II, steering clear of the areas firmly under Capetian control, arrived, in the course of his journey, at Anjou. In Angers he presided over the dedication of the Church of Saint-Nicolas, where the count's father was buried. On March 23 he had himself crowned in Tours and, during the procession to the Church of Saint-Martin, presented Fouque with the golden rose, which might be interpreted as a rite of investiture.

It was at this point, while groups of Crusaders were beginning to form, that the count of Anjou dictated, in learned Latin, a strange document setting out his hereditary rights.[10] He recalled that his ancestor had received Anjou from the king of France, but from a Carolingian king "not of the race of the impious Philip." Did not Philip's impiety, a stain spreading from the person of the king over the whole of the kingdom and bringing down plagues upon it, justify Fouque's breaking the bond of vassalage and placing Anjou entirely under the fief of the Church of Rome? The Curia's strategy was obvious: to remove the excommunication from Bertrade's first husband and transfer it to the second. So letters were sent by the pope from Tours to the archbishops of Reims and Sens, condemning any prelates who maintained relations with the king or who dared to lift the anathema from Philip unless he broke with "the woman for whom we excommunicated him."[11] The meaning of all the remonstrances, protests, and fulminations becomes clear when we restore them to their true context at the heart of the great political question of the age: the fierce struggle of the spiritual power to dominate the temporal.

Philip, growing old, was more and more uneasy under the anathema. In 1096 he pretended to yield and "abjure adultery." Urban II immediately pardoned him. But, when it turned out that Bertrade had not left the royal bedchamber, in 1099 the zealous cardinals summoned the bishops to Poitiers, where they renewed the king's excommunication. They had to do so in haste, because the count of Poitiers, who was also the duke of Aquitaine and the "William" who wrote the love songs, was an enemy of the Angevins and a vassal of the king, and he broke up the council bent on dishonoring his lord. This is further proof that to most people Philip did not seem particularly culpable.

But at last, with the passage of time, the business came to an end. The Capetian king was no longer an enemy to be undermined. The conflict known as the War of the Investitures[12] was dying down, and Yves of Chartres himself was working for reconciliation. In 1105 the archbishops of Sens and Tours and the bishops of Chartres, Orleans, Paris, Noyon, and Senlis met in Paris in the very place where the suspect marriage had been celebrated. Since it was necessary to go through the motions of recognizing the superior authority of the papacy, pontifical letters were read out. The bishops of Orleans and Paris asked Philip if he was ready to "abjure the sin of carnal and illicit copulation." In the presence of the abbots of Saint-Denis, Saint-Germain-des-Prés, Saint-Magloire, and Etampes, the king, barefoot and dressed as a penitent, swore an oath: "I will never again have relations or converse with this woman except in the presence of trustworthy persons." Bertrade made a similar promise. So the anathema was lifted. But could anyone possibly have been taken in? The two continued to live together and in 1106 were given a warm welcome in Angers by Count Fouque of Anjou.

The story stuck in people's minds. Half a century later, between 1138 and 1144, Suger wrote a biography of Louis VI, an apologia that was to have a lasting effect on the collective memory of the French. When they think of Louis they see him as "the father of the common people," a good king flanked by mediocrities: on the one hand his son Louis VII, and on the other his father, Philip I—both debased by women. Suger, to enhance his picture of his old friend Louis, discreetly disparaged Philip, who was unpopular at Saint-Denis for having chosen to be buried not there but at Saint-Benoît-sur-Loire. Suger explained that

Philip had forgone the honor of being interred at Saint-Denis[13] as a penance, because he was ashamed of his behavior.[14] The remarriage itself is scarcely mentioned, but Suger is careful to distinguish Louis, born of the "most noble spouse," from his two brothers. He affects not to regard them as true heirs, nor to accord the title of queen to their mother, "the countess of Anjou, *super ducta* [supernumerary wife]."

At this time the mainstream of historical writing was Anglo-Norman and hence anti-Capetian. William of Malmesbury presents Philip I as a man of pleasure, saying he dismissed his first wife from his bed for being "too fat." He was attracted and corrupted by Bertrade, an ambitious woman and faithless wife. He then abandoned himself to "consuming" passion, forgetting the maxim that "majesty and love do not go together."[15] *Amor* meant male desire. Philip's fault was that he could not control this weakness and thus, because of a woman, failed to live as a king should.

Orderic Vital is more severe on Bertrade, whom he describes as lascivious and fickle, ensnaring the king of France. "So the unruly concubine left the adulterous count and clung to [*adhesit*] the adulterous king until he died." Philip was not another David, the sort of seducer a king might boast of being, but a modern Adam, Samson, or Solomon, "led astray" (as women may be but men should not) and sunk in fornication. Deaf to the admonitions of the bishops, "hardened in crime," and "persisting in his wickedness," he was "eaten up with adultery" and died driven mad by toothache.[16]

The chroniclers of Tours, anxious to preserve the reputation of Frankish virility, painted the king as a less feeble character. The chronicle of the lords of Amboise suggest that it was Philip who took the initiative. True, he was "libidinous" and "lewd," but it was he who tempted and inveigled Bertrade and finally carried her off by night. In short, he abducted her.[17] All subsequent historians, however, have seen Philip merely as a lustful middle-aged man wallowing in the pleasures of the bed.

But that is only one side of the story. All the contemporary judgments that survive have come down to us because they were recorded in writing—and the writing was done by priests or monks. In those days the Church had an exorbitant cultural monopoly. It alone could create enduring objects capable of lasting through the ages. The men who provided our only sources of information were among the best educated of their day—the best, that is, in terms of what the academic and ecclesiastical culture of that age had to offer. And they were all men putting forth accepted opinions; the texts that were preserved and copied over and over again were texts that toed the line. We know, from his carefully kept correspondence, the thoughts of the bishop of Chartres on this topic. But about those of the bishop of Senlis, who officiated at Philip I's remarriage, we know nothing.

What chiefly concerns us, the way the knights lived and thought, can be seen only through the eyes of the priests, and of the most conformist among them, those who were canonized by the Church like Saint Yves of Chartres.

How many others, we might wonder, felt as these men did and in the name of the same principles? How many regarded the king's behavior as wicked and sinful, harmful to both his soul and his body, and ultimately injurious to his kingdom? For we must not forget that the rigorists were not condemning a single case of profligacy between a man and a woman (or rather the profligacy of one man, for they were concerned only with him). What they were considering was the joining of a man to a woman in a way that enabled the two to present themselves as man and wife. They were considering a union everyone thought of as a kind of marriage, permissible or otherwise. Their judgment would have been less severe if they had not been dealing with a solemn and official union necessarily subject to laws that must not be broken. If those laws were broken, the culprits must be solemnly reprimanded.

In these circumstances the very partial sources on which we have to rely reveal only one thing: the precise rules laid down by the rigorist Church to determine what constituted a *legitimum matrimonium*, or lawful marriage.

Clearly these requirements were not insisted on by the majority of churchmen at the time and in the region of which we are writing. We have only to look at the bishops, all of whom except one turned up for the king's second marriage in Paris. They cannot all have been adventurers, toadies or timeservers. Consider too how little store they later set by the sentence of excommunication, and how ready they were to annul it despite the pope's threats and remonstrances. The fact was that their moral values were different from those of the rigorists, and did not require their moving heaven and earth to separate Philip and Bertrade.

As for the nobility, we know practically nothing about what they thought. But is it really likely that where their own interests were at stake they took the sterner view? We have only to look at William of Anjou driving the reforming cardinals out of his capital, and the attitude of Fouque of Anjou before he became an instrument of papal intrigue.

When we come to Philip I himself, can we really imagine he was "impious," or even inattentive to the gaggle of priests who were always snapping at his heels? Can he really have been negligent of the king's "majesty," when he never stopped struggling against his rivals, the feudal princes? He held out for twelve years, keeping up appearances but never abandoning the woman he regarded not as his concubine but as his wife. Can we not assume this was because he also had principles? They might have been different from those of Yves of Chartres, but they were no less exacting.

I do not say that *amor* did not enter into it at all, but I do suggest that when Philip dismissed his first wife, then took and kept another, he was not giving way to senile passion but applying a set of moral standards. These rules were related to lineage; he was responsible for a patrimony. This of course included his "domain," the lordships that had belonged to his ancestors. It also included the "crown," which had been incorporated into these. But first and foremost it included the glory of his race—and all that had come down to him from his father and was his duty to hand on to his lawful son.

In 1092 Philip had only one son, a boy of eleven. In those days eleven was a vulnerable age, and the child was delicate. Suger hints at this in his life of Louis VI, where he says that William Rufus, king of

England, "hankered after the kingdom of France, if by some mischance the sole heir should die."[18] Philip could hope for no more children from Berthe: it was time for her to go. Robert le Frison, count of Flanders, who had given Philip Berthe's hand twenty years before, was preparing himself for death in the monastery of Saint-Bertin, and the danger posed by the "hatred"[19] a repudiation would incur in that quarter was for the moment diminished. And indeed it proved to be of short duration. Philip married Bertrade.

It was a good choice. At a time when the Capetian monarchy was much depleted, the king's first priority was to consolidate the reduced territory he was ruling as best he could from Paris and Orleans. The need was not to make brilliant alliances with great families of royal descent, but to lessen the power of the political groupings growing up around the chateaux of the Ile-de-France.

Montfort was a key fortress on the approaches to Normandy, the king's most vulnerable flank. And it was held by Amaury, Bertrade's brother. She herself was descended through her mother from Norman princes and from Richard I, the "pirate" count. She had already proved her fertility by giving sons to the count of Anjou, and she bore Philip three children, two of whom were boys. But it was necessary for those two sons to be legitimate, so the fate of the king's whole line depended on the status accorded to his consort.

If Bertrade were regarded as a mere concubine, her sons would be bastards and Philip's rivals could indulge in all kinds of hopes. These rivals included, as we have seen, William Rufus, who according to Suger "set at naught the rights of Bertrade's sons to the succession." But if the second marriage were held to be legal, then the danger of escheat receded. So it was natural that Philip, who might easily have found another way of satisfying whatever desire he felt for Bertrade, should do all he could to make their nuptials a striking and duly solemn occasion, and that, until his eldest son had proved his virility, he should refuse to estrange himself, even if only for appearance's sake, from the mother of his younger sons. It may have been love that made him decide not to part with Bertrade. What is certain is that his duty as king obliged him to keep her, come what might.

Philip, in his fifties, a time of life at which all other French kings had died, was bound to have been haunted by fears of hell. He must have hoped that the bishops might intervene and officially cleanse of sin the physical intercourse he indulged in, no doubt with pleasure. The fact was, he did not think, and other people did not think, that he was doing anything wrong.

The story I have just told by way of the early historians interests me not in itself but for what it reveals. As often happens with events causing such upheaval, it throws light on elements frequently left buried beneath the surface. In the case in question, commentators often mentioned what was considered unusual, thereby suggesting indirectly what was considered usual and what, because it was not written about, would otherwise remain out of the historian's reach. And so the story of Philip's second marriage brings us to our main question: what did marriage mean, how was it arranged, in the Christianized Europe of eight or nine centuries ago?

My aim, by approaching this question from various angles, is to find out how what is called feudal society worked. This brings me naturally to marriage. For the role of marriage is fundamental to every social formation, and in particular to the one I have been studying for many years. It is through the institution of matrimony, through the rules governing marriage and the way those rules are applied, that human societies control their future—even those societies that claim and even believe themselves to be the freest. Through marriage, societies try to maintain and perpetuate their own structures, seen in terms of a set of symbols and of the image they have of their own ideal perfection. The rites of marriage are instituted to ensure an orderly distribution of the women among the men; to regulate competition between males for females; to "officialize" and socialize procreation. By designating a father, marriage adds another form of affiliation to the only self-evident one, through the mother. It distinguishes lawful unions from others and gives their progeny the status of heirs—i.e., it gives the offspring ancestors, a name, and rights. Marriage establishes relations of kinship. It underlies the whole of society and is the keystone of the social edifice. So how can one understand feudalism without first acquiring a clear idea of the rules and standards according to which a knight arranged his marriage?

Marriage, which is necessarily overt, public, ceremonious, surrounded by special words and deeds, is at the center of any system of values, at the junction between the material and the spiritual. It regulates the transmission of wealth from one generation to another, and so underlies and cannot be dissociated from a society's "infrastructures." This is why its importance varies according to the place of inheritance in production relations; why its role is not the same at every level of the hierarchy of wealth; and why it plays no role at all for the slave or peasant with no patrimony, who mates but does not marry.

Also, because marriage also regulates sexual activity, or rather the part of that activity concerned with procreation, it belongs to the mysterious realm of vital forces and drives; in other words, to the realm of what is numinous and sacred.

The codes by which marriage is governed therefore belong to two different orders: the profane, and what we may call the religious. Normally the two systems adapt to and reinforce one another. But there are times when they are in conflict, and such temporary discord causes marriage practices to change and evolve toward a new equilibrium.

The story of Philip I shows how two conceptions of marriage clashed in Latin Christendom about the year 1100. It was the climax of a conflict resulting in the introduction of customs that have lasted almost up to our own day, up to the new phase of debate and change that we are currently going through. In King Philip's time, as in our own, a new structure was emerging, with difficulty, and I have tried to find out how and why.

Because the crisis in marriage practices grew out of the same general movement that was causing all social relations to change, both in people's everyday lives and in their dreams; and because this present inquiry of mine is a direct continuation of and complement to my previous study of the three "orders," or functional categories, of society,

I have set it in the same context as that earlier study: northern France, in the eleventh and twelfth centuries. But this time I have limited my field of observation to high society, the world of the kings and princes and knights. It is probable that the behavior and perhaps also the rites of ordinary town- and country-dwellers were different from those of the gentry. But practical considerations force me to limit my initial approach to the subject. For as soon as the historian leaves the thin upper crust of the society of this period, he enters impenetrable darkness.

Even at his chosen level there is not as much light as he would like. Knowledge of the rules and customs surrounding marriage is very difficult to come by for three main reasons. First of all, writing—at least in the deliberate form designed to resist the erosion of time—was still the exception rather than the rule. It was used mainly to prescribe rituals, set out the law, and define moral principles. Almost all of what is visible on the surface, therefore, is the toughest part of the ideological carapace, justifying the actions people admit to but concealing those they prefer to hide. What I am able to see is restricted entirely to what people were willing to own up to.

The second obstacle to a more complete view of medieval marriage is that all the witnesses are, as has already been noted, ecclesiastics. They are men, males, either celibate or trying to pass themselves off as such; men professionally obligated to express repugnance toward sex and particularly toward women; men either without experience of marriage or else saying nothing of what they knew, advancing a theory designed to strengthen their own power.

Their testimony is thus not the most reliable evidence on the subject of love or marital theory and practice, or in general on the different set of moral standards observed by the laity in the matter of marriage. They either depict these other standards as being identical with their own, or else, when castigating aristocratic immorality, deny that they exist. So I have had to resign myself to relying on the outsiders' view of marital behavior, a view that usually takes the negative form of condemnation or exhortation. Fortunately, between the year 1000 and the beginning of the thirteenth century, relevant documents become more plentiful and more informative. Because of the gradual secularization of the upper-class culture, an ever-increasing amount of what the knights thought and did was recorded. So this study will develop chronologically, with the picture it seeks gradually emerging more clearly and more colorfully, though I cannot hope to provide more than a general framework enlivened with a few specifics.

The third obstacle in obtaining a true knowledge of the marital theories and practices of this period is the danger of anachronism. Anyone trying to interpret the uncertain vestiges of times gone by must be careful not to fill the gaps by giving reign to his imagination, not to import into the past what he has really learned from the present. The men I am studying are my ancestors, and the models of behavior I am tracing have survived into my own lifetime. The marriage I speak of is my own marriage, and I am not sure if I can free myself from the ideological system I am trying to analyze, demystify. I am involved; can I really be impartial?

I must never forget the differences, the hundreds of years that separate me from my subject, the great stretch of time that hides almost all I am endeavoring to see behind a veil I cannot pierce.

CHAPTER II
MORAL VALUES:
PRIESTS AND KNIGHTS

Since I am forced to see everything through the eyes of the priests it seems as well to begin with the screen on which the image I seek must be projected, i.e., the Church's conception of the institution of marriage. At first this conception might appear complex, for no single attitude was common to the entire Church: we have already seen discordant voices raised among the prelates during the reign of Philip I. In fact the theory was built up slowly, by a meandering process feeling its way along for centuries during which layer upon layer of contradictory texts were piled up. But the theory did rest on one foundation, on God's message, on just a few words which none of the eleventh-century bishops ever forgot.

Some of the words came from the Old Testament, from the second account of the Creation in the Book of Genesis. They set forth four propositions:

1. "It is not good that the man should be alone." God decreed that the human race should be of two sexes, and that there should be a union between them.
2. But he created the sexes unequal: "I will make him an help [*adjutorium*] meet for him [*simile sibi*]." Man came first, and kept that precedence. He was made in the image of God, while woman came second, a reflection of his image. Eve's body was flesh of Adam's flesh, made from one of his ribs, and thus inferior.
3. The two bodies were designed to merge into one: "A man shall leave his father and his mother, and shall cleave unto his wife: and they shall be one flesh." Marriage led to unity.
4. But marriage did not do away with inequality. Woman was inferior, weak; it was because of her that man fell and was driven out of Paradise. Henceforth husband and wife were doomed to imperfect couplings, to love that must be mingled with shame. The woman was awarded an additional share of punishment, having to suffer the domination of the man and the pains of childbirth.

The teachings of Christ were based on this original text. Some words recorded in the Synoptic Gospels provide answers to two questions about the practical side of marriage. The disciples were puzzled at the custom by which a husband was allowed to repudiate his wife. Jesus, referring to Genesis, declared marriage to be indissoluble: "What therefore God hath joined together, let not man put asunder" (Matt. 19:6). Repudiation was categorically forbidden—save in one case: "except it be for fornication" (on the part of the wife).

These words, as reported by Matthew, suggest that Jesus, like all the men of his own day, regarded adultery by the wife as of crucial importance. But if we refer to Mark 10:12, we may argue that in Christ's view the two partners were equally responsible.

After Jesus had laid down the principle of indissolubility, the disciples demurred: "If the case of the man be so with his wife, it is not good to marry" (Matt. 19:10). This seems to raise a very precise question, but its implications are boundless. Since the kingdom of heaven was identified with Paradise regained, should not anyone wishing to work toward redemption while still on earth simply subdue the prompt-ings of the flesh, repress his sexual activity, and renounce marriage? The Master's reply was ambiguous: ". . . There be eunuchs, which have made themselves eunuchs for the kingdom of heaven's sake. He that is able to receive it, let him receive it" (Matt. 19:12).

The early leaders of the Christian sect remembered these words. But obeying Christ's instruction to render to Caesar that which is Caesar's, they adapted themselves to the world as it was: ". . . As God hath dis-tributed to every man, as the Lord hath called every one, so let him walk"; "Art thou bound unto a wife? Seek not to be loosed. Art thou loosed from a wife? Seek not a wife" (1 Cor. 7:17, 27). But Paul, dismissing arguments for and against ritual observances such as circum-cision, declared that all that really mattered was "the keeping of the commandments of God" (1 Cor. 7:19).

A rule drawn from these commandments was established in the prim-itive *ecclesia*, derived from the original and necessary subordination of women as evidenced by the account of the Creation. Peter and Paul both kept telling women to "be in subjection to your own husbands" (1 Pet. 3:1; Eph. 5:22; Col. 3:18). One of the functions of marriage was precisely to regulate this inequality. Just as the relationship between God and Adam was transposed at lower levels into the relations be-tween superiors and inferiors in the hierarchies of heaven and earth, so it was to be transposed in the relationship between husband and wife. The man dominated the woman: he was to "cherish" her, she to "revere" him. Husbands were urged to deal with their wives sympatheti-cally, "according to knowledge," giving honor to them "as to the weaker vessel" (1 Pet. 3:7). Men ought "to love their wives as their own bodies. He that loveth his wife loveth himself" (Eph. 5:28). In a married couple the workings of *caritas* should reach perfection; *caritas* was that full circle of love flowing out from and back into the divine source that called the whole universe into existence. Marriage would thus mirror the link between the Creator and His creation, the Savior and His Church.

Saint Paul says: "Wives, submit yourselves to your own husbands, as unto the Lord. For the husband is the head of the wife, even as Christ is the head of the church. . . . Husbands, love your wives, even as Christ also loved the church" (Eph. 5:22–23, 25). This is not so much a metaphor as a sublimation, and lends more rigor to the precept of indissolubility. Again, speaking in the name of the Lord, Paul commands: "Let not the wife depart from her husband: But and if she depart, let her remain unmarried, or be reconciled to her husband: and let not the husband put away his wife" (1 Cor. 7:10–11).

But "the time is short," and man must prepare for Christ's second coming. So "It is good for a man not to touch a woman" (1 Cor. 7:1). To celibates Paul says, "It is good for them if they abide even as I" (1 Cor. 7:8). Widowers will be happier if they stay as they are (1 Cor. 7:40). "He that giveth his daughter in marriage doeth well; but he that giveth her not doeth better" (1 Cor. 7: 38). It is good for a man to be a virgin "in the present distress" (1 Cor. 7:26). At a time when a man should be attached wholly to Christ, "he that is married careth for the things that are of the world, how he may please his wife" (1 Cor. 7:33). Marriage is not actually forbidden, but it is treated as the lesser of two evils, a "permission" (verse 6) or concession granted "to avoid fornication" (verse 2) to people who "cannot contain": "But if they cannot contain, let them marry; for it is better to marry than to burn" (verse 9). For Satan tempts through incontinency (verse 5). But while man is allowed to marry in order to avoid sin, he must treat marriage with care. Let them "that have wives be as though they had none" (verse 29). And let husbands and wives abstain "with consent for a time, that ye may give yourselves to fasting and prayer" (verse 5).

Such was the teaching of the Scriptures.

In the primitive Church, growing up in the context of Hellenic culture, the tendency toward asceticism increased, influenced at first by the sacrificial rites practiced by other sects. As soon as the Eucharist came to be seen as a sacrifice, it became necessary for the participants to be purified beforehand and for the officiant to be chaste if not actually virgin. What was merely advised in the First Epistle to the Corinthians was now insisted upon. Philosophy also came into it. Philosophers were allowed to make use of women for occasional satisfaction but were dissuaded from marriage because it interfered with contemplation and troubled the soul: a prostitute was better than a wife. Finally, and above all, Christian thought was caught up in the strong current that led urban intellectuals in the East to see the universe as a battlefield for the struggle between spirit and matter, and all that was physical as belonging to the kingdom of evil. Copulation, the bodily humors, procreation, and consequently marriage—all were regarded with deeper repugnance than before. Could a man rise toward the light without detaching himself from the body? Small groups of *perfecti* went to live as monks in the desert, secluding themselves from the world and professing a horror of women. The writings attributed to Andrew the Apostle and to Titus, one of Paul's disciples, also spread this ethic of rejection. They praised the purity of Saint Thecla, and promoted the dream of incorporeal union, spiritual coupling as practiced among the angels.

The Fathers of the Latin Church inherited these attitudes. Saint Jerome had no doubt that Adam and Eve remained virgin in Paradise. Their bodies were not united until after the Fall, under God's malediction. So all marriages were accursed. The only justification of matrimony was that by bringing virgins into being it repopulated heaven. "If there were no marriage there would be no virginity." But in itself marriage was evil. A husband was necessarily a fornicator and became an adulterer into the bargain if he came to love his wife with too much warmth. If that happened he also turned her into a prostitute.

In his *Adversus Jovinianum*, in praise of virginity, Jerome used every possible weapon in his frenzied fight against women and marriage. Gregory the Great took up a similar position, but his influence was incomparably greater. His works were constantly read and reread both in the monasteries and in the courts of the bishops. In Gregory's view human society, guided by the "prelates," was divided into two parts: on the one hand the elite, consisting of the "continent," who resisted the temptations of the flesh; and, on the other hand, the "conjoint," the rejects, who had not spurned marriage. These latter were inferior, an object of contempt, because marriage was unavoidably sullied—by pleasure. Ever since the sin of Adam, and because man cannot control himself and lets his spirit lose its mastery over his body, there had, alas, been no copulation without pleasure. That being so, the original law of marriage was "broken."[1] To marry was a sin. The boundary between good and evil ran between the "continent" and the "conjoint," between chastity and wedlock.

Saint Augustine was less severe. He too believed that man was the scene of a constant battle between the drives of bodily desire and the will, which illuminates the mind. When he meditated on Genesis, Augustine, like Ambrose, saw Adam as the spiritual aspect of the human condition and Eve as its sensual side. Satan triumphed by winning over the spirit through weakening the flesh. One whole line of Augustinian thought is dominated by dualism: evil comes from the body, and therefore from the woman, who is inferior and carnal.

But though, like Jerome and Gregory, Augustine ranks husbands and wives a long way below the "continent," at the bottom of the hierarchy of virtue, he does admit that man, while delivered over to lust by original sin and so ineluctably wicked, still has the power to resist the encroachments of evil. He does this through marriage, the least imperfect form of copulation. The sexual act is a sin, but while it is mortal in fornication it becomes venial in marriage and can be redeemed. Thus Augustus shifts the boundary separating good and evil, so that now, instead of lying between chastity and wedlock, it lies between wedlock and fornication.

There is some good in marriage. In the first place it enables mankind to multiply, thus making it possible for Paradise to be repopulated and the fallen angels replaced. Above all it is a way of restraining sensuality, i.e., women. In Paradise, wrote Augustine, evil arose because desire entered "the part of the soul that should have been subject to reason, as the wife to her husband." Marriage could restore the original heirarchy, the domination of flesh by spirit. But only on condition that the husband ruled over his wife, and was not weak like Adam.

The feeling that evil arose out of sex became a rooted obsession, a fixed idea that explains many of the prohibitions introduced by the heads of the Latin Church. What was penance if not first and foremost the renunciation of sexual pleasure? The first duty of a penitent—one of that special "order" as members of which Philip I and Bertrade walked barefoot before the bishops in Paris in 1105—was to practice abstinence. Quite apart from such distinguished sinners, ordinary couples were always being exhorted to continence. If they disregarded the admonition, they were threatened with begetting monsters or at best children who were sickly. Husbands and wives must of course keep away from one another during the day. They also had to do so on the nights before Sundays and holy days, out of respect; and on the nights before Wednesday and Friday, by way of penance. The same applied to the three forty-day periods of fasting before Easter, before Holy Cross Day in September, and before Christmas. Nor might a husband approach his wife during menstruation, nor during the three months preceding or the forty days following childbirth. Young couples were called upon to learn self-control by remaining chaste for the first three nights following their nuptials. The ideal couple, of course, was a pair who remained totally chaste by common consent.

In the early centuries of the Church, its leaders nearly all looked on marriage as something repugnant and did their best to keep it as far away as possible from all that was sacred.

In the area I have chosen to explore, the Carolingian era was a time of great cultural fertility. Study of the writings of the Church Fathers was approached with new vigor, and in the year 1000 was still absorbing the best of their successors. The libraries that Yves of Chartres and his colleagues made use of had been built up under the Carolingians. The same period also saw a reordering of society through close cooperation—closer than at any other time in French history—between the spiritual and temporal powers. By his coronation the king of France became a member of the college of bishops, and he felt obliged to apply their principles. But in so doing he modified them, making his ecclesiastical colleagues keep their feet on the ground. The conjunction of temporal and spiritual powers stemmed the tide of asceticism and softened its aversion to the institution of marriage. Scholars still read and copied Jerome and Gregory, but they neglected the *Adversus Jovinianum* and concentrated their attention on Augustine and the positive aspect of marriage.

The bishops realized they could not lead the laity to virtue by inculcating loathing of the married state. The way to achieve their object was rather to extol marriage and put it forward as a possible framework for a good life. And so to strengthen the foundations of secular society they set about improving the moral standing of marriage.[2]

In 829 the leaders of the Frankish Church gathered in Paris around the Christlike figure of the emperor Louis the Pious, son of Charlemagne. Ten years earlier Louis had endeavored to reform the ecclesiastical hierarchy; now he proposed to organize the less lofty part of society. Taking as his model the Rome of Constantine, which it was the current ambition to revive, the emperor would listen to the counsel of the learned, intending to pass their instructions on to the "men of power," those who wielded the sword in his name and who would force the people to behave as they should. In this way society would be regenerated and brought back into an arrangement pleasing to God. The bishops spoke as the spirit moved them, and, as their main discourse concerned the laity, they naturally spoke of marriage.

A summary of their propositions[3] has survived, under eight headings:

1. "The laity must know that marriage was instituted by God." From the outset the institution of marriage is associated with religion by reference to the Book of Genesis.
2. "There must be no marriage by reason of lust, but rather by reason of the desire for offspring." Here the reference is to Saint Augustine: marriage is justified by procreation.
3. "Virginity must be preserved until the nuptials."
4. "Men with wives must not have concubines." But clearly unmarried men might do so.
5. "Laymen must know how to cherish their wives in chastity and honor them as they would any weaker being."
6. "A man must perform the sexual act with his wife not for pleasure but in order to beget children, and a man must not come to his wife when she is with child."

7. "As the Lord has said, except in cases of fornication, a wife must not be set aside, but must be put up with; and those who, having set aside one wife for fornication, take another, are held, according to Christ's words, to be adulterers."
8. "Christians must avoid incest."

The conjugal morality taught by the priests to the laity, i.e., to the great of this world, was one preached by males to males as the only responsible parties. It could be reduced to three precepts: monogamy, exogamy, and the repression of pleasure. All the rest—the need to remain virgin until the wedding ceremony, the duty of cherishing and honoring one's wife—seemed secondary.

This very simple text was immediately worked up by Jonas, bishop of Orleans, into a treatise *On the Institution of the Laity*. This book was one of the mirrors held up to princes that they might see and correct their own faults, and thus be better able to perform their duty of setting an example to the people. It was a clever piece of pedagogy. Addressing the *bellatores*, whose vocation was war, Jonas depicted life as a battle against vice, promising them the joys felt after victory. Marriage was one of the weapons to be used, the most useful because it was to be directed against the worst adversary, which was sexual desire. Marriage was a medicine instituted to cure lust, an effective remedy but a dangerous one needing careful handling; a knight who was self-indulgent with it grew soft. Jonas was discreetly preaching a morality adapted to a certain social class. It did not prescribe the abstinence required of monks and priests; merely moderation. It dealt with a matter of physical and therefore of spiritual hygiene.

Jonas of Orleans had read Cicero as well as Augustine, and he included among the values of marriage *amicitia*: friendship or fidelity, that virtue of the good subject on which the strength of the state is built. From friendship he went on to nuptials, to love, seeing marriage as an image of the mystical union between God and his creation. But he did not forget that it was also an image, as well as the foundation, of the political order. Pastors like Jonas were realists, cooperating with princes to hold down unruliness.

So the married state was a virtuous one. But virtuous to greater or lesser degrees. Jonas distinguished three degrees. At the lowest level, marriage was a mere concession to sinful nature, disciplining man's basic instincts, and thus just something to be tolerated. On the next level, when its object was procreation, it was actually recommended. At the third level, if the sexual element were removed altogether and it became a "fraternal association," it would be praised to the skies. But such a perfect form of marriage was unattainable: in this wicked world, lust could not be entirely banished from the act of procreation, and marriage could not be "without sin." The transgression referred to by Gregory the Great was inevitable. But at least the sin could be redeemed by suitable penance and limited by the exercise of restraint. A virtuous prince, helped by the exhortations of his bishop, should get the better of himself and approach an *honesta copulatio*. He should learn from this book to make his marriage conform ever more closely to the divine will. It would thus be an increasingly useful instrument in the maintaining of public order.

Thirty years later public order was tottering. In northern France the cultural revival was at its height but the political edifice was crumbling. Both revival and disintegration gave churchmen food for thought, but the mounting danger was the greater spur to philosophy.

When Hincmar, archbishop of Reims, wrote about marriage, and he did so at length, he presented it first and foremost as a bulwark against violence. His works included one treatise *On Divorce* and another *On the Stamping Out of Abduction*. The latter is a discourse on peace, that earthly reflection of the heavenly Jerusalem the king and bishops were jointly charged with restoring. Everywhere it was being shattered by greed and the desire to possess. This was a typically male fault, a distortion of the masculine virtue of strength. Man was a natural plunderer of property of all sorts, and above all of women. To restore order it was necessary to strengthen the "marriage pact," which allowed women to be shared out peacefully among men, and so to lend as much prestige as possible to the civil and secular rites by which this agreement was concluded.

According to Hincmar these crucial rites were the formalities of betrothal: the *desponsatio*, or first stage of the matrimonial procedures, consisting of the agreement between the betrothed pair—or rather between their respective families.

Hincmar declares, and with particular emphasis in the other treatise, *On Divorce*,[4] that the bond is forged in accordance with the "laws of the world" and in conformity with "human customs." He sees marriage as what it actually then was: a social institution governed by natural law, an "association" in which the two partners are unequal. "Between husband and wife there is established an affective relationship [*dilectio*], which is primordial and excellent, except that in this conjunction the direction [*praelatio*] belongs to the man, and the submission [*subjectio*] to the woman." The man is the "prelate"; it is he who gives the orders. But out of hierarchy comes complementarity: just like sun and moon, water and fire, the masculine and feminine principles, in coming together, remedy one another's deficiencies. In marriage, woman's cunning and man's roughness are both mitigated. Out of this comes harmony, whence the offspring who at once perpetuate their parents and bring them happiness. Here we see again the religious and ethical attitude of Saint Augustine, but inside a completely secular framework.

According to this typically "renaissance" concept, full of reminiscences of ancient Rome, marriage still remained within the jurisdiction of civil law. Hincmar recalls[5] an incident he witnessed in the palace at Attigny during the reign of Louis the Pious. Before the assembly of nobles a woman accused herself of having sinned, but called for justice from the emperor in the matter of the "unseemly things"—Hincmar does not enlarge on what they were—which had passed between her husband and herself. Louis thought it his duty to submit the case to the bishops then sitting in council, but they decided not to proceed, leaving such matters "to the laity and the husbands. . . . This pleased the nobles," said Hincmar, "because the right to judge their wives was not taken away from them."

In northern France in the ninth century, marriage was still something in which priests were not closely involved. There is no mention of nuptial benedictions in the texts, except in the case of queens, where it was still only one element in the ritual of coronation. Two examples: the marriage of Judith, daughter of Charles the Bald, to a Saxon king in 856; and that of Ermentrude, who in 866 married Charles the Bald himself. Hincmar conducted the service on the first of these two occasions.

The bishop of Bourges forbade the priests in his diocese to take part in nuptial ceremonies. These "ceremonies," it is true, came after the *desponsatio*, or betrothal, and celebrated the physical union with laughter and carousing. But even at the much more sober ceremony of the *desponsatio* there is no evidence that priests were required to be present, except in the sees of Orleans and Bâle.

The rites surrounding the nuptials themselves belonged to the "level of the common people," or rather to the secular side of contemporary culture. Descriptions of princely marriages in the Carolingian chronicles speak only of the rejoicings and of the procession that conducted the bride to the marriage bed. Hincmar, an excellent jurist, defined marriage in terms of its civil forms, referring to the classical Roman tradition. The *copula* of lawful marriage, he said, is formed "between two persons who are free and of equal rank . . . the free woman being given to the man by the decision of her father, dowered in accordance with the law, and honored by public nuptials." The union was completed by the *commixtio sexuum*, or fusion of the sexes.[6] There is no mention of prayers or of any other kind of ecclesiastical participation.

Now at this period in the history of Christianity, theology derived directly from liturgy and so had a lot to say on the subjects of baptism, the Eucharist and penance. But on the subject of marriage it could only be silent, for there was no liturgy connected with it. Neither Hincmar nor his contemporaries gave any space to the need for consent, attributing no superior importance to the exchange of vows as distinct from the physical union. But one senses in their writings a desire to fill this gap, and the scholars who forged the *False Decretals*[7] included passages on nuptial benediction, which they attributed to Popes Callixtus and Evaristus. And we see Hincmar groping beyond what he calls the "lawful nuptials" uniting the bodies of husband and wife and making their union a part of "natural" society, toward something else: the "mystery" that occurs in other "mystical" marriages, which are "signs" or symbols of the spiritual relationship between Christ and the Church.

Hincmar seeks but does not find. The vocabulary and the mental apparatus at his disposal will not let him go any further. He is paralyzed by the weight of a long tradition of rejection.

In Carolingian France the institution of matrimony was still relegated to the margins of what was considered sacred. But because it was the main foundation of public peace, and because, through the structures of the State, the bishops were closely involved in the preservation of that peace, the leaders of the Church had to pay more attention to it than had their predecessors, and they had to do so with a lesser show of repugnance.

It was then that the gradual sacralization of marriage began. The way had been prepared by the sacralization of kingship, i.e., of the power to order earthly society. The ritual trappings of marriage remained completely secular, but now it began to acquire an ethical content. The prelates, asked to promote the values of marriage, seized the opportunity to emphasize two rules. First, "the evangelical law concerning one sole wife,"[8] as Remi of Auxerre put it, was loudly proclaimed by way of protest against princes like King Lothair II and Count Etienne, both of whom had changed wives. Secondly, a stricter emphasis was laid on the prohibition of taking to wife a cousin within the seventh degree of consanguinity, or blood kinship. The degrees were calculated in the Germanic manner, a primitive physical count *per genicula*, starting from the shoulder and proceeding in a straight line from one joint to another down to the last phalanx.[9]

When spread out over seven generation and linked to the notion of incest, the field of consanguinity was literally beyond measure, with so many people excluded from availability that it was almost impossible to observe the prohibition. The rule surprises us; and it obviously surprised contemporary scholars. They sought in vain to find a basis for it. There was nothing in the Scriptures to justify it: the prohibitions in chapters 18 and 20 of Leviticus were much less stringent. Roman law did refer to the sixth and seventh degrees, but only in relation to inheritance, and the Roman way of counting the degrees in both directions[10] resulted in the barring of only about a twentieth of the number of cousins forbidden under the system now proposed. At the Council of Paris in 829 the prohibition was promulgated without explanation. No one, not even Isidore of Seville, consulted as a last resort, was able to provide a satisfactory explanation. It should also be noted that the second rule, requiring exogamy, was in outright contradiction of the first, which insisted on indissolubility. For a presumption of incest not only made divorce permissible, as in the case of fornication, but actually made it compulsory.

The fact that the bishops had to keep on repeating both that a man must not repudiate his wife and that he might not marry a relative shows that on both counts their exhortations met with opposition. They came up against different conceptions of marriage in theory and in practice. The resistance did not arise, as the priests pretended to believe, out of deliberate disobedience or unruliness. It derived from a different quarter altogether, from another set of rules and principles that, instead of being imported, like Christianity, were time-honored and indigenous. We know nothing about them except what we learn from the resistance they offered, for they were preserved not in writing but in people's memories, and revealed themselves only in ceremonial customs, words, and fleeting gestures.

Any historian trying to feel his way through the darkness to guess at the shape of the knightly system of ethics must be on guard against seeing its relation to the ecclesiastical system in terms of black and white, then or now.

One morality was not opposed to the other as barbarism would be to civilization, or even, more simply, as matter to spirit. The set of symbols from which lay morality and marriage customs were derived was not based solely on material values. Production, money, and market forces were not the keys to that system as they are in our own culture. The men whose marriages I am trying to investigate did not think primarily in terms of economic interest. At the end of the period we are concerned with, i.e., at the beginning of the thirteenth century, this kind of consideration still occupied only a marginal place in a knight's consciousness. Nevertheless, through the infiltration of attitudes that had grown up on the lower edge of aristocratic society among the nobles' recruits from below who rose to be government officials, court purveyors and the like, that *cupiditas*, or desire to possess, common to all wielders of power, tended to change imperceptibly into *avaritia*, or the love of money.

The key to the aristocratic system of values was probably what twelfth-century Latin texts referred to as *probitas*, a valor of body and soul that produced both prowess and magnanimity. In those days everyone thought this supreme quality was transmitted through the blood. The function of marriage was to ensure that the manly virtue of valor was passed on in honor from one generation to the next, that blood was propagated in such a way that it did not, as they said then, degenerate, i.e., lose its genetic virtues. The purpose of marriage was to unite a valiant progenitor to a wife in such a manner that his legitimate son, bearer of the blood and name of a valorous ancestor, should be able to bring that ancestor to life again in his own person. But all depended on the wife. She was not regarded as a mere passive terrain, as she is even today in some black African cultures. In Carolingian and post-Carolingian Europe people believed that women produced sperm, or at least that both the man and the woman contributed to the act of conception, and that the immediate effect of sexual intercourse was to mingle indissolubly the blood of the two partners.

Though none of their ideas have come down to us directly, such seem to have been the fundamental premises underlying the knights' moral attitude to marriage.

But at least we know a little of what the kings thought, and each king was half warrior too. Their edicts have come down to us in writing, which enjoyed a revival because of the sacralization of the civil power. And as the kings, intermediaries between the spiritual and temporal powers, usually extracted from the bishops' instructions only those parts that did not conflict too sharply with secular morality, the royal decisions recorded in the capitularies tend to reflect such features of the lay ethic as best accorded with what most churchmen demanded. This can be seen particularly in the case of the prohibition against what was then called abduction.

It was the duty of the king to pursue abductors in the same way as he pursued arsonists, murderers, or thieves. In feudal times, abduction was one of the four crimes involving blood law,[11] a direct legacy of Carolingian royal justice. The sovereign, backed up by the bishops, was bound to put asunder couples who had not been joined together peacefully and in accordance with the prescribed rites. Such unions were not marriages, and it was necessary to dissolve them and to restore the kidnapped woman to the family from which she had been violently snatched. This had to be done so that the tissue of society should not be torn, so that the one initial disturbance should not through a concatenation of family feuds spread throughout the nobility.

This preoccupation is very evident in the capitularies of the early ninth century. They maintain that a union between an abductor and his victim is illegal. If the girl was already promised to another man, that man was still entitled to take her and make her his lawful wife. If he no longer wished to do so, the girl's relations still had the right to give her in marriage to anyone they liked, with the exception of the man who had abducted her. The essential thing was to prevent the defrauded family of the intended bridegroom from attacking the family of the abductor.

If, on the other hand, the girl was not already spoken for; if she had not been previously bestowed on another by the ceremony of the *desponsatio*, then all that was needed was her father's consent and a trifling penance, and the unlawfully formed couple could become a lawful husband and wife. The meaning is clear: marriage was a matter of free choice—not of the bride and groom, but of the bride's relations.

The few ninth-century texts that survive are full of cases of abduction. Widows, nuns, wives, daughters, whether betrothed or not, all appear as so many quarries pursued by packs of young men. We must suppose many of the kidnappings to have been shams, ways of getting round the demands of the law or of convention. Arranged abductions could be used by husbands to get rid of their wives, by brothers to deprive a sister of her inheritance, and by fathers to avoid the burdensome expense of a wedding. But the cause of such violence must sometimes have been the unbridled greed and desire to possess so deplored by Hincmar.

Lastly there was what seems to have been the determining factor of social ritual. For was not abduction a sort of young men's game, as Jacques Rossiaud's studies show collective rape to have been in the towns of pre-Renaissance France?

Georges Dumézil, investigating marriage in Indo-European cultures,[12] distinguishes four ways of taking a wife, which can be reduced to two basic and contrasting forms. In one a girl is the subject of a legalized exchange, given by her father or bought by her husband, the transaction being carried out quite openly, ceremoniously, and with solemnities designed to uphold public order. In the other form, this order is flouted and broken by a free and individual act that eludes all control: the girl gives herself to or is seized by the epic hero.

The distinction between these two types seems to me to correspond to the distinction that operated in the period I am concerned with, and which can be observed very clearly in the twelfth century, when secular culture was emerging from its former obscurity. Here one of two models was available to male members of the aristocracy, according to whether they were "old" or "young," as long as one understands that the distinction then referred *not* to two different age groups but to the impact on social behavior of two different sets of values, one prizing order and good behavior and the other boldness and energy.

When William of Malmesbury reproached Philip I with forgetting that "majesty" and "love" did not go together, he was alluding to two ways of behaving toward women, one suitable to men who were sedate and settled down, the other appropriate to the young. In his fictionalized account of what happened he makes the nub of the story the unseemliness of a nocturnal abduction carried out by a king already in his forties.

In the high society of Europe in the eleventh century, or in the ninth for that matter, the most important split was probably that between the younger and the older males, and the code of conduct followed by the "younger generation" may be supposed to have grown out of this conflict. The code required them to seize women by violence in the teeth of husbands and matchmaking families. There is an obvious parallel here with hunting, which of course figured largely in the education of young noblemen.

Ritual rapine gradually became largely symbolical. By the twelfth century it had been reduced to the carefully controlled game of courtly love. But from all appearances rites of abduction were practiced quite literally by the Carolingian aristocracy.

We have already seen that at the end of the eleventh century not all churchmen shared the same idea of what constituted a good marriage. The knights were not unanimous either. The rules against abduction laid down by the Carolingian kings satisfied only one segment of their noble subjects—the *seniores*, or fathers of families, who, like the bishops, had an interest in the preservation of law and order, and wanted to protect their own power against youthful intrusion.

If we examine this power and that law and order, together with the established part of society and the socially recognized, stable couples, formed peacefully and soberly, we see that there was more than one way for a man and a woman to live together. Hincmar describes one of these, giving a brief account of the rites involved, the dowry, and the procedure by which the girl was handed over; he applies to it the specific phrase "coupling in legal marriage," "legal" meaning in conformity with Roman law. In doing so he distinguishes this form of conjugal association from others the existence of which he thus admits implicitly.

As early as 829 a report presented to Louis the Pious by the bishops took into account this diversity, distinguishing "spouse" from "concubine." The scholars of the ninth century, who claimed to be raising ancient Rome out of its ruins, exhumed from the codes promulgated by its emperors a model of marriage, the *connubium legitimum*, which specified among other stringent requirements that the consorts should be free and of the same status. But in the same texts the researchers found traces of another kind of union, also perfectly official but simpler and infinitely more widespread: concubinage. The Church had once regarded this very common kind of union as valid, giving it formal recognition in the year 398 in canon 17 of the Council of Toledo.

In 829 the Frankish bishops, while remaining intransigent on monogamy, declaring that a man might have only one partner, were prepared to tolerate concubinage as a poor substitute for full marriage. They could hardly do otherwise if they did not want to destroy society. And there were advantages to this dual system. Precepts could be applied more flexibly. A priest might be refused a wife but allowed to keep a concubine. A noble might drop his concubine in order to contract a "lawful marriage," and yet not commit bigamy. All that was needed was to quote another canonical text, a letter from Pope Leo I: "A man who is married after having put away his concubine is not remarrying: the former was not a full marriage . . . not every woman united [*juncta*] to a man is his wife [*uxor*]."[13] These words made it possible to leave custom undisturbed.

Though we are largely ignorant of Frankish marriage laws, we do know that they recognized, somewhere below the *Muntehe*, equivalent to the Roman "lawful marriage," but far above a mere liaison, the *Friedelehe*. This second-class kind of marriage was used to impose some discipline on the sexual activities of young men without involving family "honor"[14] in the long term. The offspring of such unions had a weaker claim to inheritance than the offspring of legitimate marriages; if the father later contracted a lawful union, the children of the second arrangement supplanted those of the first. A union entered into in this less definite manner was often temporary, but it was official, and was concluded by means of the appropriate rites. The *Morgengabe*, or price of virginity, paid on the morning after the wedding night, was the public sign that the match was in order. The girl had been lent rather than given, but her relations had made the loan ceremonially, by contract, freely and in peace.

The story of Charlemagne himself shows how there were two ways of taking a wife. And Charlemagne was canonized—though admittedly much later. The emperor had begotten daughters but did not give them in marriage for fear of creating too many claimants to the succession. He kept them at home with him in his *Munt*, his power. But he did lend them in *Friedelehe*, thus providing himself with grandsons whose rights were as nothing compared with those of grandsons born of lawful marriages.

As for Charlemagne himself, he is known to have had four lawful wives—of whom one was immediately repudiated, and three predeceased him—and at least six temporary and private liaisons entered into while he was a widower, and not made public. He also had a partner, a *Friedelfrau* named Himiltrude, whom he had taken before his first full marriage. Pope Stephen II regarded this union as binding, and the son born of it was given the royal name of Pépin, designating him as a possible heir. But when Charlemagne divided up his possessions in 806, he did not count Pépin among his true sons and did not leave him his kingdom. Pépin rebelled but was vanquished and shut away in a monastery like some bastard born of an old man's fancy. Unfortunately for Pépin, the *Muntehen*, or lawful marriages, that followed Charlemagne's union with Himiltrude had produced sons.

This flexibility in the matrimonial bond proved useful over a long period. Written sources show concubinage of this kind to have been strongly established among the aristocracy of northwestern France in the tenth and eleventh centuries. Pehaps the influx of the Scandinavians promoted its revival; at any rate it was referred to as marriage "in the Danish manner."

Let us see what Raoul Glaber had to say about it later on, between 1040 and 1048, in Book IV of his *Histories*: "After their arrival in the Gauls, the Normans were almost always ruled over by princes born of illicit unions." This applies particularly to William the Conqueror, whose mother had married *more danico* Robert, count of the Normans. This was why William bore the nickname "the Bastard." His mother subsequently became the wife, probably the lawful wife, of a viscount. "But," Glaber continues, "this custom will not be thought too reprehensible if we remember the sons of the concubines of Jacob."

Glaber was a monk, with strict views on morals, but he did not feel bound to condemn this kind of union or to throw discredit on its offspring. He referred to the Old Testament, which certainly contained evidence of matrimonial practices very different from those recommended by the bishops; but this could cause problems. Panegyrists had to be careful when they compared the Carolingian king to Solomon or David, and anyone who ran afoul of the laws of the Church on sexual matters had no difficulty producing arguments out of the Bible to suit their cause.

Remembering, then, the sons of Jacob's concubines, Glaber noted that they "despite their birth inherited all their father's dignities, just like their other brothers, and were given the title of patriarch. Nor should it be forgotten that under the empire, Helen, mother of the Roman emperor, was also a concubine."

Nevertheless in the tenth and eleventh centuries the children of wives *more danico* were regarded as only second-class heirs, like the children of the *Friedelfrauen* in the Frankish period. William the Bastard had to fight hard to succeed his father, and if Philip I, as we have seen, struggled to have his marriage recognized as fully legal, it was largely because he was concerned with the succession to the throne.

The practice of concubinage lasted because it served family interests. It protected inheritances without, on the one hand, too openly thwarting the younger generation or, on the other, offending against the recognized secular system of values. This system prized masculine prowess; it encouraged its warriors and hunters to dream of daring exploits; it urged young men on to adventure. From such exploits they brought back women. Any of these chance unions might be regularized if the young man's father or uncle came to an arrangement with the girl's relatives, soothing away resentment and handing over the *Morgengabe*. Such arrangements helped to keep the peace. But the heads of families reserved the right to break the pact and replace it with a better one. They saw to it that no wives were introduced permanently into young men's beds unless the advantages they brought with them had been carefully weighed and found satisfactory. Only such women deserved the rank of wife, and to make room for them the concubines were, if necessary, dismissed.

The agreement setting up a concubinage was accompanied by rites, but those accompanying the pact for a lawful marriage were very different. For one thing they had to be arranged in advance, and for another they were much more lavish and public. The future wife had first to be ceremonially bestowed—the betrothal—and then ceremonially conducted to the marriage bed—the nuptials.

Not far from the marriage chamber a large crowd kept up a long and noisy party, having gathered together to certify the physical union, to rejoice at it, and through its own brimming pleasure to capture the mysterious gifts needed to make the marriage fruitful. For this was definitely a matter of flesh and blood. For the knights as for the priests, the purpose of marriage was procreation. The wife was led in procession to the house in order to produce legitimate heirs there. For that reason she was welcomed, absorbed into the household together with her expected offspring.

This is made clear in a passage from Book VIII of Dhuoda's *Manuel*. The author, a great lady and a contemporary of Charles the Bald, is teaching her son to pray and telling him for whom he is to sing the Psalms: "Pray," she says, "for your father's relations, who left him their possessions as a lawful heritage." She thus demonstrates the link between remembrance of ancestors and the handing down of the patrimony. "Pray for your father's relations" because your father received from them that which will make you rich and powerful in your turn. And Dhuoda goes on: "Who they were and what their names were you will find written down at the end of this little book." The dead people listed in Book X are the paternal grandfather and grandmother of the author's son, and his paternal uncles and aunts. No other forebears are included. Dhuoda tells her son nothing about her own ancestors.

The wife was sometimes so completely absorbed into the family of the one man who had the right to give her children that her own Christian name was changed. (At that time there was no family name or surname handed down from generation to generation.) Mathilde might thus become Blanche or Rose—a mark of her complete break with the past, her completed capture. Yet if she was to play her part in the house and fill it with legitimate children, her blood and her womb were necessary. And in her offspring that which came from her ancestors through her blood would mix with that which her husband inherited through his blood from his ancestors.

This conjunction was openly proclaimed in the choice of names for the children: boys and girls were named after forebears from both the father's and the mother's side. A family might appropriate a wife by changing her name, yet outsiders might still invade the clan in the form of the descendants named after them. This inevitable intrusion called for great caution, and long negotiations were necessary before families could decide to allow their blood to be mingled in the eventual nuptials.

Those responsible for the family "honor" on both sides were charged with conducting the preliminaries, which ended in a ceremony and in rites that, far from being boisterous and merry like those celebrating the *nuptiae* later on, were grave and solemn, taking place in an atmosphere of formal sobriety, solemn undertaking, and calm. The parents of the future husband came to the house of the future wife. Words were exchanged, engaging not only the man and woman to be united but even more the men who wielded power over them both—the *Munt*, as it was called in the Germanic tongue.

The spectators at this ceremony were fewer than for the wedding proper, but still too numerous for everyone to hear the words. But at least everyone could see the actions that went with them, actions signifying investiture and disinvestiture; they could see the objects passed from hand to hand to symbolize the transfer of possession.

The ceremony of agreement sometimes took place a long time before the consummation of the marriage, and such delay could involve risk. Some bold fellow might come and spirit away the girl, the *desponsata*. How are we to translate the word? Fiancée? Intended? These terms have lost most of their force now. But the ceremony of *desponsatio* really did tie the knot. The woman was now given.

The wife, once introduced into a house and family after so many precautions had been taken, nevertheless remained suspect, an adversary. Men saw marriage as a sort of combat, a fierce battle calling for constant vigilance. Although the overall contemporary picture of the cosmos put women in the same category as night, water, the moon, and all that is cold and blue, we can see, buried deep in the masculine psychology of the period, the feeling that women were more voracious and ardent than men. The husband was afraid he alone might not be equal to quenching her fires. Jonas of Orleans was sure of being understood when he warned husbands of the exhaustion in store for them if they did not use moderation. Moreover, a husband knew that the partner he confronted in the single combat of the marriage bed did not play fair. She feinted and dodged, and he was afraid of treachery, of being hit below the belt.

The moral attitude of the priests and that of the knights, old and young alike, was nowhere so similar as in this combination of contempt for and distrust of women as creatures both weak and dangerous. Every possible means was used to buttress this point of view. Scholars even made a childish attempt to press etymology into service. *Vir*, the Latin word for a male, was said to be related to *virtus*, or strength, rectitude, whereas *mulier*, a woman, was supposed to be connected with *mollitia*, softness, volatility, evasiveness. Contempt for and mistrust of women were good arguments for keeping them subjugated and restrained, as was urged in parts of Genesis and the Epistles, which churchmen never tired of reciting. Laymen applauded anything hinting that God's disapproval of fornication was stronger when applied to women than when referring to men, who were therefore allowed to punish them for it. And the bishops, while regarding it as their duty to watch over widows and repudiated wives as part of their general responsibility to protect the weak and "poor," left it to the men of the family to discipline their womenfolk in the same way as they corrected children, slaves, and animals.

This was a primordial and absolute right no one questioned, a right precluding any appeal to public justice. As we have seen, when a woman from Attigny made so bold as to lodge a complaint against her husband because of what went on in their home and perhaps in their bed, it created a scandal. The bishops were shocked, and referred the matter to the married men, who almost certainly referred it in their turn to the husband himself and his relations.

Family honor depended to a large extent on the behavior of the womenfolk. The great danger was that they might yield to the sin—the sin of the flesh—to which their constitution predisposed them. To guard themselves against dishonor, laymen deemed it necessary to exercise strict control over female sexuality. And, like the priests, they regarded marriage as a remedy against fornication—that is to say, fornication in the form they dreaded, fornication indulged in by women. A father had to marry off his daughters so as to guard himself against the dishonor they might otherwise bring on him. Charlemagne was scarcely cold in his grave before he was openly criticized for neglecting his daughters: instead of placing them under the authority of husbands by means of lawful marriages, he had left them to their innate perfidy. He was therefore responsible for conduct some said had tarnished the honor of the royal family.

It was a husband's duty to shield his wife from temptation. She was in danger because of her contacts with other men. In aristocratic households the master's wife welcomed the guests. Like the queen whose functions Hincmar described in the Carolingian palace, she supervised the supplies and looked after the goods of the household. She was responsible for storing and distributing dues and gifts. She directed a whole squad of male servants and had daily dealings with the chamberlain, their chief. What relations might she not entertain with this latter in the small, dark, secret room where the provisions, the jewels, the instruments and insignia of power were kept? The situation provided plenty of fodder for suspicion and gossip, such as was spread all over the Carolingian empire on the subject of Judith, wife of Charles the Bald, and Bernard, his chamberlain.

The danger was great. The worst danger of all was that a wife might be made pregnant by a man other than her husband, and children of a blood different from that of the master of the house might one day bear the name of his ancestors and succeed to their inheritance. The great and powerful of this world lent an understanding and attentive ear to what the priests had to say about the guilt of Eve.

All in all the evidence suggests that the leaders of the Carolingian Church were listened to seriously when they expounded their ideas on marriage before the heads of noble families—except when it came to their condemnation of what they called male adultery (i.e., repudiation) and of what they called incest. On these two points the two moralities— secular and ecclesiastical—could not be made to agree. The main pre- occupation of the aristocracy, the handing down of ancestral valor through the male line, made it essential for a man to be able to dismiss a wife who was slow to produce sons, and sometimes to change wives, when the chance of a more distinguished marriage presented itself. And when it came to the mingling of two bloods, this same concern was imposed on the choice of a partner: the man should take his wife from among his near relations, provided she did not come within the third degree of consanguinity.

The Christianization of marriage practices seems to have been effected easily enough in the lower strata of society, among people with few possessions and above all among those with none—the serfs, who did not even own their own bodies. Among the masses, about whom we know very little, the Church's version of marriage easily re- placed the secular forms of union, i.e., concubinage. Ninth-century inventories show peasants on large estates firmly paired off. The tighten- ing of the marriage bond served the interests of the masters: it helped to pin their dependents down on their tenures[15] and, by encouraging the lower orders to have children, increased the value of the lords' domains. At this level of society the Christianization of marriage strengthened production relationships. It only disturbed and threatened to weaken them when it came into conflict with the strategies of the nobility. That is why the clashes we see in the ninth century between the two morali- ties all take place at the top of the social pyramid, with the bishops and archbishops confronting the kings and the noblemen.

In the reign of Louis the Pious (a significant sobriquet), when the idea of an empire and the notion of the duties of a divinely appointed king were simultaneously taking shape, the Carolingian palace had opened its doors to the exhortations of the bishops. The palace had already been purified by the emperor himself, who had driven out his father's lady-friends and shut his sisters up in convents as punishment for what he considered immodest behavior. Eginhard, writing about the life of Charlemagne, skillfully inserted into his praises a trace of the disapproval it was then fashionable to express with regard to his hero's sex life. The *Visio Wettini* suggested that the great emperor had sinned in his lifetime and was now suffering *purgatio.* He could not enter Paradise until he had been cleansed of some secret offense, doubtless of a sexual nature. We know the distant origin of this suspicion: Charlemagne was supposed to have made love to his sister, and it was from their incestuous union that Roland, his nephew and his son, was born.

But obedience to the Church soon gave way to insubordination, and we can sense the confrontation stiffening in the time of Charles the Bald. Hincmar wrote his treatise *On Divorce* against the great princes, less "pious" than Louis, who were not at all averse to repudiating their wives: "A marriage that has been made legally cannot be unmade, except by spiritual separation decided on in common"—i.e., when both husband and wife decide to take religious vows—"or for physical fornication attested by public confession or open conviction. . . . These cases aside, a man must keep his wife *volens nolens,* even if she is *iracunda* [a shrew], *malis moribus* [shameless], *luxuriosa* or *gulosa* [lewd, or greedy for the pleasures of this world]. And if the husband puts away his wife for reasons of adultery, he may not marry again."

Thus the king of Lotharingia was forbidden to dismiss his barren legal wife in order to contract a lawful marriage with the concubine who had already borne him children. Through Pope John VIII, the Church began to treat sons of concubines the same as mere bastards born of a temporary encounter, depriving both categories alike of all rights.[16] This severity was new, and accompanied the rise of asceticism. The golden age of the episcopate—those years when the realism, discretion, and pragmatism of the great prelates had made possible a compromise between the doctrine of the Church and the practices of the nobility—was nearing its end.

In the aging Charles the Bald's palace at Compiègne, the great scholar Johannes Scotus Erigena meditated on the Greek texts that practically he alone could read. He dreamed of the imminent Second Coming of Christ and decided that in order to be ready to welcome the Light he must even now turn his back on the visible world and rid himself of its weight, i.e., of the flesh.

In his treatise *De divisione naturae* he pondered on Adam in the Garden of Eden, on man in his primal perfection, which sin destroyed but which was still remembered with longing, and toward the restoration of which every man must aspire with all his might. Scotus did not exclude the possibility that the bodies of Adam and Eve might have been united in Paradise, but he maintained that Adam could use his sexual organs, like all the others in his body, by mere willpower and without excitement or ardor. "In tranquillity of body and soul, without corrupting virginity, the husband was able, or rather may have been able, to render his wife's womb fruitful."[17]

Scotus thus imagined the human race being reproduced not *sine coitu*, without sexual conjunction, but *sine ardore*, without the heat of pleasure. In this Scotus was still close to Augustine. He ventured much further afield when he announced that "at the Resurrection, sex will be abolished and nature made one."[18] The rift in *natura* was what separated the sexes, and the end of the world would do away with dual sexuality, or more precisely with the female part of it. When the heavens opened in glory, femininity, that imperfection, that stain on the purity of creation, would be no more.

Scotus said this quite explicitly: "There will then be only man, as if he had never sinned." Behind this thought is the image of the androgyne of the first day of Creation. Did Eve, Adam's rib, really have an independent existence in Paradise? Was she really separated from Adam? Would she have been separated if there had been no sin? Was the Fall, for Scotus, simply the rift caused by the sexualization of the human race? And was his dream of reproduction as corporeal union without pleasure just a return to the original state of things, a fitting together again of what had been divided? But in this life such a reunification was impossible. It had to be waited and hoped for like the end of the physical world. Man must prepare for it by abstinence, by abandoning the vain quest for it hitherto pursued through the sexual act, with its grotesque postures and frenzies like those of the damned. Marriage was but an absurd mimicry of paradisal union. Once again it was condemned.

The condemnation of marriage emerged more clearly in the course of the tenth century, when the disintegration of the Carolingian order was accompanied by a rising tide of monasticism, which gradually submerged the whole Church hierarchy. What were the monks, the pure, but the "eunuchs" of whom Christ had spoken? They had cut themselves off from all sexuality. Eudes of Cluny, obsessed with defilement, never tired of saying that without sex the Devil would have less power over men. At the very end of the tenth century Abbon, abbot of Saint Benoît-sur-Loire, equated the social hierarchy with the ladder of spiritual perfection, each rung of which liberated the aspirant a further degree from sex. Good monks were not just chaste: they were virgin. They came first in the procession of mankind toward salvation, and those who followed ought to imitate them. As for the contemptible men and women who had decided to marry, they lagged so far behind at the end of the line, scarcely emerging from the darkness, that they were hardly to be distinguished from mere fornicators. Marriage, whether adulterous or otherwise, was evil. The words of Saint Jerome were echoed again: "Any man who loves his wife too much is an adulterer." If they wished to draw near to virtue, husbands and wives must separate. And many did so, caught up in the increasing current of repentance arising from the fear that the end of the world was at hand.

While generalized contempt for the world and rejection of the flesh were ideas disseminated by the reformed monasteries, a more specific longing to be cleansed of impurity probably explains why the prohibition of incest, to which mere lip service had been paid for the most part in the ninth century, was repeated with ever-increasing emphasis in the later Frankish councils. The Council of Trosly in 909 urged that families should make careful investigations to find out whether the future husband and wife were related. This preliminary *inquisitio* was to be carried out by a priest, who would therefore need to be present at the ceremony of betrothal. The Council of Ingelheim in 948 issued a similar order: families must clarify the remembered history of their ancestry. It was during this period that the procedures reflected in the correspondence of Yves of Chartres gradually came into use: the reconstruction of genealogies from people's memories and other sources; the calculation of degrees of consanguinity; and the attestation of such relationships by oath.

We can know little of the anguish and dread of those who saw the thousandth anniversary of the Passion approaching. But we do know that the penitential movement grew stronger at that time. Raoul Glaber, a useful witness because, like all his contemporaries, he considered spiritual factors to be the decisive ones, stressed the importance attributed to abstinence in the Peace of God movement.[19] At great open-air meetings where people gathered around holy relics and swore to abjure violence, the need to subdue all the instincts of flesh and blood was also proclaimed. The prelates who called for fasting and the laying down of arms called too for the restraining of sexual impulses. In Glaber's view the disorder of society came from the promptings of lust, which clearly affected the higher clergy as well as the nobility. If men wished to turn away divine wrath and renew the pact between themselves and God, they must be purified; they must practice renunciation. Now more than ever, marriage must be controlled. As a remedy against lust, marriage was for Abbon the lowest and most elementary degree of ascesis, or self-discipline, and must be treated by husbands and wives as an exercise in the same.

The early eleventh century is a good point at which to begin a study of the interaction between a set of moral values, their practical applications, and the evolving social structures contemporary with them. It was truly a critical moment; and the crisis in question was the genuine revolution that established, with much sound and fury, what we call the feudal system.

But this social upheaval, and all the turmoil that the peace councils and mass mortifications tried to exorcise, was masked during the first half of the eleventh century by what survived of Carolingian political and social structures. Once the shock of the Norman incursions and of the decline of the dynasty itself passed, there even seemed to be a sort of Carolingian renaissance, and that age of anxiety may have been experienced by those who lived through it as a sort of return to the monarchical order. That at least is the impression one gets from reading Raoul Glaber.

Glaber shows the Christendom of the year 1000 being led to salvation by two guides: King Robert of France and King Henry of Germany. The other kings barely figure: it is still the Frankish people who are the vanguard of history. Robert and Henry were kings of the same blood, cousins born of siblings. In age they were only a few months apart: in the year 1000, one was twenty-seven and the other twenty-eight. Together they worked to bring order to Christian society.

THE

CENTURY

CHAPTER III

MARRIAGE ACCORDING

TO BOURCHARD

enry was presented as a model Christian husband. He was venerated as a saint for the exemplary way he fulfilled that role. True, that was later on: the Cistercian pope Eugene III canonized him in 1146. A biography of him was written on that occasion, and its text reveals the idea of marriage held by certain clerics in the twelfth century rather than in the year 1000. The image that survives of Henry's wife, Cunégonde, is more recent still: her *Vita* and the bull that canonized her both date from 1200.[1] She was revered for her absolute conjugal chastity. Cunégonde, we are told, "dedicated her virginity to the King of Heaven and preserved it to the end with the consent of her chaste husband." The biography celebrates "those who castrate themselves for the kingdom of heaven's sake." Innocent III's bull relates that during the canonization proceedings, witnesses came forward and maintained "on the basis both of fame and of written record" that Cunégonde "had been joined in marriage to the emperor and saint Henry but had never been known by him carnally." The bull also records what Henry is supposed to have said to his wife's parents when he was on his deathbed: "I return her to you just as you entrusted her to me. She was a virgin when you gave her, she is a virgin when I give her back." The bull finally tells of a miracle: in order to clear herself of a suspicion of adultery, Cunégonde submitted to divine judgment in the form of ordeal by fire; but she walked on the red-hot irons barefoot and emerged unscathed.

This story of a *mariage blanc* cannot be traced further back than the end of the eleventh century. The legend, which is mentioned by Leo of Ostia in the chronicle of the Benedictine monastery at Monte Cassino, seems to have been invented by the promoters of ecclesiastical reform. It throws a useful light on what may have been the image of ideal marriage held at that time in rigorist circles. But no mention is made of this story by those who wrote while Henry and Cunégonde were still alive or shortly after their deaths. Neither Thietmar of Mersebourg nor Arnoud of Alberstadt make the slightest reference to it. As for Raoul Glaber, far from glorifying the couple's chastity, he deplores the sterility of their union. It was this circumstance that gave rise to the legend. The emperor Henry died childless, and the Germanic crown came down later to Henry IV and Henry V, both sworn enemies of the reforming popes. It was to get at these later monarchs that the Church celebrated the saintliness of him who had reigned in the year 1000.

The legend might merely have emphasized that Henry had refrained from putting away, or repudiating, a wife who was barren. Such obedience to the Church was beginning to be common in the middle of the twelfth century, but in the year 1000 it was still a sign of exceptional devotion. Henry had been brought up by churchmen at the cathedral of Hildesheim and was the friend of the great monastic reformers abbots Odilon of Cluny and Richard of Saint-Vannes. But as heir through his father to the duchy of Bavaria, Henry had to marry. He did not do so until he was twenty-three, and in his anxiety to avoid incest accepted a wife from a lower rank of the *nobilitas*. In 1002, when the bishops had to appoint a successor to Otto III, the fact that Henry, his first cousin, still had no children after eight years of marriage and refused to repudiate his wife, made him an ideal candidate for the electors, who hoped for another break in the line of succession. Once on the throne, Henry based his behavior on a mystical conception of kingship that found superb expression in the works of art he commissioned. They included sacred manuscripts, the golden altar at Bâle, and the cloak he wore on the most solemn occasions, embroidered with the constellations.

Henry, caught up in the millenarist movement, believed he was the emperor ruling over the end of the world, and in anticipation of this event he set about restoring order to the world and peace and purity to God's people. To do so he would have to be very pure himself, and this added to his reluctance to repudiate Cunégonde. He carried out his reforms in collaboration with the bishops, increasing their temporal power and allowing them regal prerogatives in their own territories. He chose them carefully, for their wisdom, from among the best clerics in his own chapel, recruiting those best fitted for the pastoral tasks of gathering the laity together and keeping them from wrongdoing. On the eve of the Last Judgment, politics and ethics were indistinguishable.

One of these bishops, Bourchard of Worms, is especially relevant to my investigation. He belonged to the highest ranks of the nobility, was extremely cultivated, and had been educated in the monastery of Lobbes in Lotharingia. This was Romanic country, and Bourchard's Latin shows the lasting effect of those early influences. He was not a monk but served God in the world, and when Henry II came to the throne he found Bourchard established in his own cathedral. Like the Carolingian prelates, Bourchard chose to grapple with the world and its carnal weaknesses rather than turn his back on it, and he also discouraged his canons from seeking refuge in the cloisters. He saw his duty as that of reforming Christian society through the word, through preaching and regular visitations during which he would both instruct and control his diocese. Between 1007 and 1012 he drew up the instrument of this pastoral vocation in the form of a collection of didactic texts known as the *Decretum*.[2] And here is the reason this Rhenish prelate interests me: the book he wrote in the quiet of his cathedral helps to pierce the darkness of the past and reveal a clearer view of its marriage practices.

Bourchard did not compile his book all on his own. He was helped by his neighbor the bishop of Spire, and his friend the bishop of Liège arranged for a monk at Lobbes to lend a hand. But at a time when episcopal sees were autonomous and Rome's predominance merely doctrinal, the book was nonetheless a very personal document. The bishop of Worms was forging an instrument for his own use, with no intention whatsoever of drawing up a code applicable to the Church as a whole.

When a prelate had to pronounce judgment, to punish, to hand out the penances that wiped away sin, he felt the need, if he was conscientious, to refer to precedent and consult the decisions of the ancients. He therefore needed within arm's reach an *auctoritativus*, or authoritative text, for each case. So he would search through the books around him, noting references, classifying them in what he judged to be the most convenient manner, and building up what is called a canonic collection, a selection of "canons," or precepts drawn from the Scriptures, the Fathers of the Church, and the decrees of the councils and the popes. Such manuals belonged to an old tradition, and though they were compiled with the specific needs of their author in mind, they could also be used by others.[3]

For several decades such collections had been improving, especially in the province where Bourchard had been a student. It became customary to cut up the long original texts and set out the extracts in question-and-answer form, with frequent references to relevant decisions handed down by the councils of the ninth and tenth centuries.

Bourchard of Worms arranged his collection in this way. Each case had a heading briefly setting out the reasons it had been chosen; this was followed by a selection of conflicting authorities, which enabled the bishop to hand out punishments with *discretio*, choosing when to be indulgent and when to be severe.[4] He was free to choose, since as yet there existed no general legislation.

Bourchard took ample advantage of his freedom, deciding between earlier authors as he felt inclined. Marc Bloch accuses him of going further: "The canonic collection compiled by the sainted bishop Bourchard of Worms between 1008 and 1012 is full of erroneous attributions and almost cynical alterations."[5] It is true that Bourchard often lent recent decisions the cloak of ancient authority, and here or there added or omitted words to clarify the text he quoted. But can he really be accused of cynicism? No one during that period professed a blind respect for the letter of a text; what mattered was its spirit, i.e., the spirit attributed to it. What mattered to Bourchard was practical efficiency, and by one adjustment here and another there he was merely putting the finishing touches to a tool he intended to use as skillfully as possible, in faith and charity.

Other people soon borrowed his *Decretum*. The manuscript was copied, and versions modified to fit local conditions found their way into all the episcopal libraries, where they remained in use until the middle of the twelfth century. Bourchard's *Decretum* was then superseded by Gratian's. But meanwhile the bishop of Worms's collection was immensely successful in the empire, Germany, Italy and Lotharingia, whence it reached northern France. There it was in common use: Yves of Chartres took most of his references from it. So Bourchard's *Decretum* provided a support for the thoughts and deeds of the Church leaders in the region with which we are concerned—in itself a good reason for examining it, and all the more closely because it devoted a good deal of space to marriage.

This is evident as early as Book I, section 94, where Bourchard was dealing with the network of informers he had set up in his diocese in preparation for his pastoral visits. In every parish seven men were chosen who would swear to denounce the parishioners' misdeeds to the bishop when he came. To help these panels with their *inquisitio*, Bourchard drew up a list of questions for them to put to themselves and to their neighbors.[6] Eighty-eight transgressions were set out in descending order of gravity, from murder down to such venial omissions as failing to serve consecrated bread. The first fourteen questions relate to murder, a major sin and one that—because of the network of feuds it gave rise to—seriously undermined the social order. But immediately after this category, in the second rank, came the twenty-three questions— more than a quarter of the total—dealing with marriage and fornication.

This part of the list also starts with the most serious sin, adultery (question 15) and ends (question 37) with a suspicion: has anyone encouraged adultery in his household by not keeping a careful enough watch over the women servants and female relations? This latter was a trivial act of negligence, easily excused by the fundamental obligations of hospitality. A decreasing scale of guilt emerges: guiltiest of all is a married man who takes the wife of another; next comes a man who keeps a concubine in his own house; then comes he who repudiates his wife and remarries; then he who merely repudiates his wife. Next, and of much less importance, comes mere fornication. This may occur in one of two degrees: the first where one or both of the partners is married, the second where neither is. Last in this part of the list, and very venial because it was so frequent an occurrence in large houses filled with chambermaids, is the dalliance indulged in by young men and single women.

Monogamy was clearly the primary concern. Prohibitions grew much more relaxed as soon as the marriage bond was no longer involved. Marriage is plainly seen here as a remedy against sexual desire, bringing order, discipline, and peace, and removing men and women from the sphere where unions are free, unregulated, disorderly.

The following questions deal with *abductio*, breaking the *desponsatio*, and incest. The latter is divided into two kinds and, because of the then current order of priorities, the spiritual kind comes first, i.e., marrying a woman who is one's godmother or god-daughter through either baptism or confirmation. Then comes the carnal kind. The next questions concern unnatural unions, and then, right at the bottom of the scale, prostitution.

If we take into account the other parts of the questionnaire—covering murder of husband or wife, abortion, infanticide, the machinations by which women try to gain their husband's love, or prevent them from begetting or themselves from conceiving children—we find that thirty out of the eighty-eight questions deal with sex. (The question on measures aiming at birth control or abortion are in the section on murder: toward the foot of the list, before the murder of a slave, or suicide, but after parricide, the murder of a priest, of one's own child, or of one's own husband or wife.)

Sex then, was at the heart of the notion of sin and defilement, after the shedding of blood but before "superstition." And at the heart of the mechanism of purification was marriage.

Bourchard's questionnaire had a moral purpose: it was meant to enlighten men's consciences and, by pointing out evil, awaken in them a healthy awareness of their sinful natures. But it had a disciplinary purpose too: helping to flush out evildoers so that they might be punished. The bishop would choose the appropriate punishment from among the prescriptions that formed the major part of the *Decretum*.

It was a monumental work, a sort of cathedral that had as its ground-plan the idea of progress toward salvation. Twenty sections mapped out the road from earth to heaven. The first five dealt with those whose duty it was to lead the way, to check and to correct, i.e., with the bishop and his auxiliaries, both priests and deacons. Then came the parish, the setting in which purification would be carried out. And this was followed by the instruments of purification: baptism and the Eucharist, the two sacraments administered by the clergy.

At the end of the road came the *Liber speculationum*, a grandiose meditation on death and the afterlife. This was immediately preceded by Book XIX, the longest of all, which in some manuscripts is entitled *Corrector* and in others *Medicus*. Here is to be found the key to the other world, the remedies that prepare men for a successful transition into it, which can cure of their last weaknesses those about to appear, no longer before the bishop, but before God. This list of medicines, unlike the earlier questionnaire, is not addressed directly to the sinners themselves: a sinner cannot cure himself. What Book XIX provides is a penitential, a graduated tariff of punishments to be used by those whose duty it is to mete them out.

In the turmoil of millenarism, this part of the *Decretum* may well have seemed the most useful part, even to its author. In his prologue to the text as a whole, Bourchard borrows from the introduction to an earlier penitential. Such lists of sins, together with the appropriate atonements, were common, for they made the priests' work easier. Too easy, in fact, for they made it unnecessary for the ministering clergy to think. In 813 the Council of Châlon had given a warning against such manuals, "full of errors and by dubious authors." But they were indispensable, given the forms penance took and the role it played in the Christianity of the year 1000.[7] To expiate his offense a sinner had to live a changed life for a certain period of time. He had to be "converted," to be transferred into a special section of society, and manifest that transfer by visible signs; he had to behave and dress and eat differently from everyone else. This withdrawal rid society of a diseased limb that might otherwise have contaminated the whole body. Penance contributed to social order and peace, and Bourchard, working to reform society, wanted to provide it with a powerful instrument of renewal. And so he brought his book to a close with what he intended as an effective penitential at last.

Between the prelude, dealing with the clergy and the sacraments, and this final section, the book consists of canonical texts on lay morality, which during this revival of the Carolingian spirit the bishops and the king were jointly charged with overhauling and correcting. Here the focus of the texts seems to proceed from public to private. The section begins with cases of violent breaches of the peace calling for ceremonial purification by the bishop. These are cases where blood (bloodshed and/or blood relationship) is involved. Books VI and VII of the *Decretum* deal primarily with homicide and incest. Further on the bishop is called on to intervene as the appointed protector of certain vulnerable social groups: first the professional penitents, the monks and nuns (Book VIII); then the women who are not "consecrated" (Book IX). Here some mention is made of marriage, but only, let it be noted, in relation to women as weak threads in the social fabric. Immediately after women, incantations and spells come, then fasting and intemperance (Books X–XIV), all of which are much less closely connected with public order. In the cases that follow (Books XV and XVI), the bishop acts only as aide and adviser to the temporal princes. Finally, most private and intimate of all and placed just before the penitential, come the texts against fornication. It is very remarkable that the parts of the book most concerned with marriage are so clearly separated from those concerned with sex. I think it proves that Bishop Bourchard, in the tradition of Hincmar and his Carolingian predecessors, saw marriage first and foremost as a social framework with which it was his duty, as a maintainer of public order, to concern himself.

The institution of marriage reappears in just the same light in the *Medicus* (see page 63). Here again we have a series of questions, but this inquisition, instead of being public and directed at the parish community as a whole, is internal and individual, a dialogue between confessor and penitent. The style is very laconic, on the order of "Did you do such-and-such? Well, you deserve so-and-so," with an occasional brief explanation thrown in to show the gravity of the misdeed.

To the general interrogation is added a supplement especially for women. Bourchard believes that their relation to sin calls for a closer inspection. Men and women are two different species. Women are weak and easily led, and need to be judged differently from men. The *Decretum* urges that their frailty be taken into account: "The Christian religion condemns in the same way adultery in either sex. But wives are reluctant to accuse their husbands of adultery, and cannot exact vengeance. Men, on the other hand, are in the habit of hauling their wives before the priest for the same cause."[8] The *Decretum* insists above all on the need to take account of female perfidy. A wife is naturally deceitful and should be kept, even as a matter of justice, under the strict control of her husband. "If after a year or six months your wife says that you have not yet possessed her, and if you say she is your wife, you must be believed because you are the woman's head."[9] So the rules cannot be the same for women as for men. That is why the *Medicus* subjects the female soul to special scrutiny; but since the "physician" or "corrector" is a man, this appendix to the penitential throws an interesting light on the idea men had of women at that time.

In their eyes a woman was frivolity personified, fickle, chattering in church, forgetting all about the dead for whose souls she was supposed to be praying. She bore all the responsibility for infanticide, for she alone was responsible for looking after the offspring: if a child died it was the mother who had killed it by real or sham negligence. One question asks: "Did you not leave your child too near the pot of boiling water?" Abortion, of course, was also the woman's affair. As was prostitution. Everyone knew women were always ready to sell their bodies or those of their daughters or nieces or other women. For they were lecherous and lustful. The questionnaire makes no mention of conjugal pleasure, though it contains many queries about the pleasures women may indulge in on their own or with other women or young children. These activities belonged to the women's quarters, the nursery, that strange but attractive world from which men were excluded and in which they imagined there took place perverse practices they were not allowed to enjoy.

The last part of the questionnaire is its most secret, for, as is the case with the collection of canonical texts, the penitential goes from the public to the private. In the interrogation common to both sexes the sins affecting the social order—homicide, theft, adultery, and incest—precede those usually committed between four walls—fornication outside marriage, magic, intemperance, sacrilege. And the severity of the punishment depends on whether or not the sin disturbs the public peace.

It is the tariff of penances itself that gives the clearest image of the set of values Bourchard had in mind. He undoubtedly kept as close as he could to ordinary morality, both for reasons of discretion and because he wished to be as effective as possible. The hierarchy of punishments corresponds to the hierarchy of offenses: the severity of the abstinence and the length of the purgation imposed on the sinner is proportionate to the measure of his guilt.

The long list of punishments in the *Medicus* may be divided into three categories. The first type prescribed fasting on bread and water—and of course the suspension of all sexual activity—for a number of consecutive days, calculated in multiples and sub-multiples of ten. The second type of punishment lasted much longer: the unit of calculation was a year. But it was less harsh, imposing abstinence only from meat eating and making love. It was also intermittent, concentrating on the *feriae legitimae*, or "lawful days," on which the Church summoned men to meditation. These included the three annual periods of fasting, and Wednesday, Friday, and Saturday of each week. Perhaps most importantly, this punishment was less obvious: as the devout imposed the same privations on themselves out of piety alone, the sinner could camouflage himself among the voluntary penitents. The third type of penance imposed for a period of seven years what the text, Latinizing a word from the Romance vernacular, called the *carina*, or quarantine, an additional fast on bread and water lasting for forty consecutive days.

Now let us see how offenses against matrimonial and sexual morality were distributed among these three categories.

With rare exceptions, it was offenses judged to be minor and very private that were to be redeemed by the first kind of abstinence—ten days on bread and water. This punishment applied to male masturbation when practiced in solitude (when two men were involved the penalty was tripled). It is worthy of note that the same penalty was awarded to a man who had fornicated with a *"femme vacante,"* a woman with no marital ties, or with his own maidservant. Great indulgence was shown toward men's sexual escapades if marriage was not involved: it made no difference to a man's punishment whether he masturbated or took advantage of a maid, as long as neither he nor she was married. But if his head was already in the noose of matrimony, then he had to behave himself. The same punishment—ten days' fasting—was handed out for any infringement of conjugal chastity.[10]

But what did that mean? Loving one's wife too ardently? Another passage sheds some light on the matter by inflicting ten days' punishment on a husband who had made love to his wife in a prohibited position, or when she was menstruating, or when she was pregnant. The penalty was doubled if the child had already quickened, and quadrupled into a *carina* if the offense occurred on a forbidden day. (The Church magnanimously halved the penalty if the offender was drunk.) In these cases the unit of mortification was still ten days, since the sin was committed in the privacy of the bedchamber and at night. But the "law of marriage" had been broken, and an over-zealous husband was seen as four times as guilty as a bachelor taking his pleasure where he found it.

For the bachelor had an excuse: he had no lawful wife to quench the flame of his ardor. Marriage, the remedy against lustfulness, kept men from sinning. Here, we see marriage on the verge of becoming a sacrament.

But marriage also called for self-discipline, and a husband who could not control himself deserved to be punished severely. The penalty was indeed harsh: four times ten days of penance—the same as for gouging a man's eye out or cutting off someone's hand or tongue.[11] The same, too, as imposed on concubines who, abandoned for a lawful wife, tried to cast spells on the virility of their former lover on his wedding day.[12] The parallels are startling.

At the other end of the scale, the longest punishment of all, forty days of penance each year for seven years, was the chastisement inflicted not only on bestiality but also on abduction and adultery. Seven years of fasting were handed out to a husband who made his wife available to other men, or to a man who had seized another's wife or a nun, the bride of Christ. If the culprit himself was married in such cases, the penance was doubled, not because the adultery was a twofold one for which the man alone was held responsible, but because he already had at his disposal the means of "appeasing his libido."[13] The same logic inflicted five days' fasting on a married man who fondled a woman's breasts; a bachelor got away with only two days.

The fact was, by abduction and adultery, male sexuality undermined the rules governing society. Abductors of women destroyed marriage contracts, committing a public crime that caused hatred between families, gave rise to reprisals, and defiled and divided the community. It was natural that such transgressors should have to perform—and for a long time—a penance making them conspicuous for what they were.

The same punishment was visited on a murderer, who likewise had committed a major breach of the peace. It is clear that the ecclesiastical code was based on that of royal justice: witness all the *Decretum*'s borrowings from the Carolingian capitularies in regard to this kind of misdeed. There were two aspects of marriage: one concerned with sexual and the other with social morality. But the second included the first. If the sex lives of husbands and wives were subject to special surveillance, it was because, by getting married, they had entered the regulated area of society.

The second and intermediate kind of penance applied to offenses committed in private, inside the home, but which were regarded as especially harmful: the sins committed by women were the main target here. The punishment for masturbation *started* with a unit of a year. If women were dealt with more severely than men for indulging in solitary and fruitless pleasure, it was because they were thereby trying to elude the twofold curse of Genesis, which doomed them to submit to men and to bear children in pain. The list culminates in infanticide (twelve years of penance), after ranging from abortion before the child has quickened, to negligence (suffocating the child in bed by unwittingly rolling over on it: three years), to prostitution (six years).

The same sort of punishment sometimes applied to men also—to sodomites, to those who fornicated with female relatives under the family roof, to those who resorted to the intervention of witches. Thus the male sex had to atone for shortcomings that made them weak and lacking in virility, which deprived them of their *virtus* and left them liable to fall under the power of women. None of the penances in this category has any direct connection with marriage.

There are certain features in the *Decretum* concerning manners and morality that are of particular note. First comes the fact that incest is treated as a separate issue. It has a section to itself, Book VII, which brings together the canons of all the Frankish councils prohibiting marriage between relatives falling within the seventh degree of consanguinity. As soon as it was publicly revealed that such a relationship existed between a husband and wife, both had to appear before the bishop and swear as follows: "From this day forward I will no more be united with this my kinsman or kinswoman: I will not have him or her either in marriage or by seduction; we shall not share our board, nor be under the same roof except in church or in a public place before witnesses."[14] These are the same words Philip I and Bertrade had to pronounce before they were freed of excommunication for incest.

This meant a complete rupture, after which both parties were free to marry again with the bishop's permission. Thus an incestuous marriage was regarded as null and void. It was not a marriage at all; it did not exist. It was as if the two fleshes had never become one, as if the blood relationship had prevented such a fusion. Incest belonged to a sector of morality apart from all others.

But sexual relations between kin did cause a defilement that had to be cleansed by penance. Copulation between relations—not marriage, because as we have seen that was impossible—is dealt with in Book XVII of the *Decretum*, on fornication. The texts chosen again come from the Carolingian councils, those of Verberie, Mayence, and Tribur. They forbid a man to know his wife's sister or daughter, his brother's wife, or the *sponsa*, or promised bride, of his son. These offenses reappear in the penitential, where punishments of the second type are imposed on them. The amount of attention the *Medicus*[15] devotes to this kind of domestic deviation suggests that home life in a noble household was a hotbed of sexual adventure. Outside the bedchamber of the master and mistress there was a private area full of females who were an easy prey: maidservants, female relatives, women still "vacant," or not yet disposed of (see page 67)—an open invitation to male licentiousness. In this small enclosed Paradise every man was an Adam: the young, the not so young, and first and foremost the head of the family, all were constantly exposed to temptation. One's sister-in-law might slip surreptitiously into one's bed; or one's mother-in-law; or one's future daughter-in-law, present in advance of the nuptials and easily the object of obsessive thoughts. The women were seen as perverse themselves, and likely to pervert the men. But we may regard them primarily as victims. Virginity appeared very vulnerable in such households. Was it valued very highly? Whenever there had been some dalliance between the sexes, always the man only was asked: "Did you corrupt a virgin? If you were going to marry her anyway and have merely offended against the nuptials, one year of abstinence. If you are not going to marry her, two years." That was all.

Bourchard wrote a handbook for judging offenses, not a treatise on morals. He was not preaching to the laity, and, except to graduate the severity of penances for husbands who had broken a few strict rules about dates and postures, he did not bring sex into his treatment of marriage. But between the lines we can detect something of the relationships between husbands and wives. We are given one hint when Bourchard speaks of the spells and incantations resorted to by women, always witches to a greater or lesser degree, weak creatures having to make use of devious methods. The object of such machinations was to manipulate love, to "change from hate to love or vice versa the *mens* of the man."[16] *Mens?* Did this really mean the mind, the feelings? No, it meant rather the drives, the passions, which lead to action.

Women were sometimes suspected of using these charms outside marriage. When an erstwhile lover contemplated lawful marriage with another, his former concubine might try out of jealousy to destroy his virility. But most of the offenders in this category were wives who, while ostensibly doing the cooking, made special dishes or potions designed to control their husbands' ardor. A wife might try to lessen her husband's virility in order to avoid unwanted pregnancies. Bourchard speaks of women anointing their bodies with honey for this purpose, then rolling in flour and using the mixture to make cakes for the over-amorous spouse.[17]

But more often such tricks were used for the opposite purpose. For, as everyone knew, women were insatiable. Then the moral reaction was stricter: after all, this was a world where men were haunted with anxiety about impotence, and often dabbled in magic themselves to enhance their sexual prowess. Only two years of abstinence were imposed on a wife for kneading bread with her bare buttocks, but five for putting menstrual blood in her husband's drink, and seven for making the potion with his own sperm.

In any event, marriage was seen essentially in terms of its social significance. Bourchard was anxious to cleanse it of sin, but his main preoccupation was order and peace. So he opens Book IX by distinguishing concubinage from lawful marriage. He insists on the public nature of the latter, and the penitential lays down a penance—the light and private one of a third of a year's abstinence—for anyone who has taken a wife without making a settlement on her or without going with her to church "to receive the priest's blessing as prescribed in the canons."[18] Bourchard wants marriage to be a public affair, openly displayed, but he skates quickly over the rite of benediction, as well as over the duty of the couple to remain chaste for the first three nights after the nuptials. But those were refinements of devotion, and in those days the Church did not dream of asking anyone to conform to them.

Nor does Bourchard make more than a fleeting reference to mutual consent. He puts the emphasis on the consent of the two families. And because "lawful marriages are ordained by divine precept,"[19] this agreement must be concluded in holiness, i.e., in the peace that comes from God. There must be no violence, no trickery. If a girl is taken from her family without previous arrangement—by abduction or seduction, or in other words if she is stolen—the couple must be parted once and for all. But on the subject of the *discidium*, or solemn and official rupture, as well as of remarriage and indissolubility, Bourchard was very flexible. He knew that too strict a line would interfere with social relationships. So the texts he quotes permit a prelate to dissolve many other unions besides those that are incestuous. The decision rests with him, after he has sensibly and meticulously weighed the defects of the marriage in question.

Of course, since women were usually the source of the trouble, the prelate first considers the behavior of the wife. Women were fornicators by nature, and if they were accused in his presence of adultery he had the authority of Christ for pronouncing a divorce. But above all women were deceivers, so the bishop had to take care not to be led up the garden path by wives claiming, for instance, that their husbands, probably too old, were unable to consummate their marriages. In such cases the bishop heard the husband's evidence first, and, if the husband denied the wife's charges, the wife had to stay married to him. The man was the one to be believed. But if the wife renewed her complaints a few months later, saying that she wanted a child, and if the husband's impotence was proved by "right judgment," i.e., by the judgment of God, the bishop was obliged to annul the marriage. But he must still be wary. Did the woman have an accomplice, a lover? Similarly, if a wife accused her husband of adultery, the bishop had to treat the man the same as he would treat a woman, breaking off a union that had been defiled. But when, in fact, did women ever come to the bishop for justice, asking to be rid of their husbands? The initiative always came from the men. But was it right to believe blindly the men's complaints and accusations? Might they not be motivated by desire for another woman? And did not many of them, in order to put the blame on their wives, actually throw them into another man's arms? Or, to get their marriages dissolved on grounds of incest, lure a sister-in-law or daughter-in-law into bed? Or say that someone had cast a spell on their virility, making them incapable of sleeping with their wives?

While the bishop had the power and sometimes the duty to dissolve the marriage bond, he was less at liberty when it came to allowing those he had parted to marry again while their former partner was still alive. Here he had to use his discretion. He had to remember that men were inclined toward polygamy; that they had power, physical strength, and money on their side; and, though they might be less cunning than women, they had more effective means at their disposal for obtaining a legal separation so as to satisfy their desires. The bishop put fewer obstacles in the way of remarriage for women, since it was not wise to leave them without a man to watch over and correct them. Married women were less dangerous than frustrated females living in other people's houses, provoking rape and adultery and breaking up peaceful marriages. Above all, was it right to stop a wife who had merely been the victim of her husband's misdeeds, and who had been legally divorced, from becoming available again for a profitable alliance? Only widows were suspect; a widow might have brought about her husband's death. Even if she were free of all suspicion of murder, she had only to contemplate another marriage and men would accuse her of already having illicit relations with her future consort. Should such remarriages be allowed? At the Council of Meaux the bishops had said yes; at the Council of Tribur they had said no. So now the prelate would have to decide for himself.

He needed to be much stricter in the case of men he had freed from their former wives. In his wisdom he had already severed a diseased limb, and the same wisdom must make him chary of allowing another union. Especially when, as was usually the case, the pretext for the divorce had been the wife's adultery. It was so easy to make accusations. People lived at close quarters to each other in noble households;

gossip was rife; there were always jealous observers prepared to say they had seen or heard something amiss. How could any man, even a bishop, fail to give credence to them, knowing as he did how consuming female ardor was? Had not the holy emperor Henry momentarily believed in the guilt of the no less holy Cunégonde, forcing her to submit to the ordeal by fire? But the bishop remembered the words of Saint Paul: He must do all he could to reconcile husbands and wives who had fallen out, seeking an occasion to bring them together again one day when their mutual resentment had abated. So there was to be no remarriage for husbands freed of adulterous wives, nor for those who had alleged that their wives had been abducted or that they themselves were impotent.

But were such men, then, not in danger of burning, being consumed by passion, since they would be deprived of the remedy for their lust? The danger was slight: a man left alone could easily resort for sexual solace to that inferior form of conjugality, concubinage. The difficulty then was that he would be deprived of true heirs. Here the bishop's precepts went counter not so much to carnal appetite as to matrimonial schemes designed to further family interests. But there were two cases in which the *Decretum* not only allowed but even favored a man's divorcing in order to remarry. First, if he could prove that the first wife had made an attempt on his life. Second, if he could prove that she was related to him.

In both these cases the blood taboo was involved. Bourchard was not concerned with continence, with limiting the sexual freedom of young men. For him the marriage contract linked families rather than individuals. It was this that made him pay so much attention to kinship impediments, though he knew very well how they might be exploited by men who had merely got tired of their wives. Bourchard's main preoccupation was peace: he saw marriage as the backbone of the social order. The *Decretum* is very Carolingian in spirit. Some might say it is Germanic. But the monastery at Lobbes, where Bourchard had studied and which supplied him with references and advice, was not in Germany, and his canonic collection would not have received the welcome it did from the prelates of northern France if the circumstances and problems it dealt with had been very different from their own.

CHAPTER IV
ROBERT THE PIOUS

King Robert of France was not canonized like his cousin Henry, but some of his contemporaries tried to pass him off as a kind of saint, as is shown by the appellation of "the Pious" that has come down to us. But above all it is shown by the work of a monk, Helgaud of Saint-Benoît-sur-Loire, who in the years following the king's death wrote a biography of him modeled on the lives of the saints.[1] The book, designed to aid churchmen both in their meditations and in their preaching, describes an exemplary existence. It insists on the king's virtues and how, because of them, he was able to heal the sick. His "most holy death" immediately opened to him the gates of heaven, where he then reigned unequaled in humility since the most holy King David. As Claude Carozzi has demonstrated, the panegyric is constructed around a central episode: the king's "conversion," when he decided to live the rest of his life as a penitent in order to atone for a sin—the same sin as that of David, against the ethics of marriage. The offense is referred to with discretion, but it lies at the center of the book and underlies its whole argument.

Helgaud has just been recording the king's edifying deeds and praising his terrestrial virtues—his sense of justice, his generosity, the clemency with which he performed his royal duties—when he pauses. "Malicious" critics had objected to such eulogies, saying, "No, these good works will not contribute to the king's salvation, for he did not shrink from the crime of illicit union, and went so far as to take to wife a woman who was not only a fellow godparent but also connected to him by blood." It should be noted that the biographer does not name this unlawful companion, and speaks of *copulatio* and not of marriage. What he is talking about is in fact incest. Helgaud replies to the accusers by asking who has not sinned? Who can claim to have a "chaste heart?" Look at David, that "most holy king." Helgaud develops the parallel, saying that David's "crime" was lust and abduction, while Robert's consisted in having "acted against the law of holy religion." Both monarchs committed a twofold sin: David was guilty of adultery and the murder of his rival, Robert of lying with a woman forbidden on grounds of both spiritual and physical kinship. But just as David had been healed and reconciled by Nathan, so Robert had been won back to virtue by the abbot of Saint-Benoît-sur-Loire. The king of France had admitted that his *copulatio* was shameful; he had confessed his guilt and parted from the woman whose contact defiled him. David and Robert both sinned, but "visited by God, they had done penance."

Like David, Robert confessed, fasted, prayed, and, without abandoning the position in which providence had placed him, lived like the monks who practiced mortification professionally. *Felix culpa*: it was a fortunate sin, for by reversing his conduct he was able to advance step by step toward beatitude. Helgaud prudently leaves it at that. But he does add an anecdote: Robert's father, Hugues Capet, on his way from his palace to attend vespers, saw a couple making love in a doorway and threw his cloak over them. The moral of this *exemplum*: praise to him who does not shout other people's misdeeds from the housetops. Such discretion was prescribed by the rule of Saint Benedict (44:6): "Tend your own wounds and those of others without revealing them or making them public."

Helgaud was a good witness, but his reserve leaves our curiosity unsatisfied. Another Benedictine, Raoul Glaber (see pages 42–43 and 53), is even more discreet, saying absolutely nothing about Robert's marital troubles. And this despite the fact that he had quite openly committed not only incest but also adultery and was just as guilty if not more so than his grandson Philip I: for though he took three lawful wives, when he married for the third time the first wife may not have been dead yet, and the second was certainly still alive and lurking in the background ready to leap back into the royal bed as soon as an opportunity presented itself.

In 988–989, just after his father ascended the throne, Robert, then aged sixteen and destined to succeed his father, was given a wife. Her name was Rozala, but in the family she now entered she was known as Suzanne. Three years later she was repudiated, but she survived until 1003. In 996–997, Robert married Berthe. He repudiated her sometime between 1001 and 1006. He then married Constance, who the following year bore him his first legitimate child. He thought of repudiating her too, but Constance, belying her name, was a violent and unmanageable virago who put up a stiff resistance.

This series of pacts and partings shows how marriage was practiced in one great household, that of the dukes of France who had just become kings. The first thing that emerges is that it was the father or head of the family who arranged people's marriages. When Robert, aged nineteen, dismissed the wife Hugues Capet had chosen for him, he may have been trying to show his independence. He was approaching manhood, and his friends may have been encouraging him to throw off the yoke of paternal authority. Much later, when Robert complained of his own sons' disobedience, Abbot William of Volpiano reminded him that he had been the same at their age. One thing is sure: before he went further and chose another lawful wife, this time making the choice himself, Robert waited until his father was on his deathbed. Robert was then twenty-five.

Another clear feature of his maneuvering was his preference for a wife of at least equal rank, someone belonging to the "order of kings." In 987, among the arguments advanced by the supporters of Hugues Capet against his rivals for the throne was the allegation that Charles of Lorraine had "taken to wife a woman from the order of vassals who was not his equal. How could the great duke [Hugues] have endured to see a woman born of his own vassals reigning over him as queen?"

The need for a wife of equal rank involved much searching, sometimes over long distances. For Robert's first wife Hugues Capet had cast his eye as far as Byzantium, where he had asked for the hand of the emperor's daughter. But he had had to fall back on Rozala. She would do, for her father was Béranger, king of Italy and a descendant of Charlemagne.

The blood of Berthe, the wife Robert chose for himself, was better still: she was the daughter of King Conrad of Burgundy, and daughter of King Louis IV d'Outre-Mer, the Carolingian king of western France. Constance's pedigree was not so dazzling: her father was only the count of Arles, though famous for having just driven the Saracens out of Provence, and her mother, Adelaide (or Blanche), was the sister of the count of Anjou.

Had Robert, like Charles of Lorraine, stooped to take a wife from among the vassal families? We know nothing of the ancestors of William of Arles; perhaps they too were descended from Charlemagne. At any rate, Constance's mother had been the wife of the last Carolingian king, Louis V, who certainly would not have welcomed into his bed any woman who was not of very high birth. Louis had dismissed her almost at once, and the count of Arles had married her, apparently without anyone mentioning adultery. And yet she had been "consecrated" as queen by the bishops, and the effect of such rites was indelible. Perhaps for that reason Constance was regarded as the daughter of a queen. By the thirteenth century, in the memory of Gervase of Tilbury, she had become daughter to Louis V, whom Gervase represents as giving both her and his kingdom to the son of Hugues Capet. Contemporary chroniclers probably did not credit Robert's third wife with Carolingian or royal origins. But nor did they do so in the case of Rozala, who really was of royal birth. It may be that by 1006 the desire for isogamy was less marked.

It clashed with the desire to avoid marriages between close relations. Hugues Capet had explained the difficulty to the eastern Emperor: "We cannot find a wife of equal rank because of the affinity between us and the neighboring kings." Henry I, Robert's son, had to go as far as Kiev for a wife. But considerations of rank came first. Robert and Constance may have been distant cousins; Robert and Rozala were certainly cousins six times removed, i.e., within the bounds of incest as defined by the bishops. Berthe, the most royal of Robert's three wives, was also the most closely related: she was his cousin only three times removed. We should note that the only degree of kinship that caused a marriage to be annulled in those days seems to have been that which applied in the case of Berthe, which was perfectly obvious. But for the son of the "usurper" Hugues Capet, it was worth defying the prohibition in order to marry the niece of Charles of Lorraine.

Of those three king's daughters, the first two had previously been married to counts: that was a usual kind of alliance, for dynastic politics required that an eldest son's wife should be chosen from a family more powerful than his own. Neither of the two girls was a virgin, then, when Robert married them off, but no time was wasted over that imperfection. Both of them were widows: Rozala the widow of Arnoul, count of Flanders; and Berthe the widow of Eudes, count of Blois. Both were seized upon in the early days of widowhood, and it was quite evident why they were chosen: through such marriages the Capetians hoped to gain a stronger hold if not on the crown then at least on the principality, the duchy of France. One part of it had been lost to wild Norman chieftains, as yet scarcely Christianized. The center, around Orleans and Paris, was under firm control. Elsewhere the counts of Flanders, Blois, and Anjou were building up individual power of their own. Capetian strategy was to make an alliance with one or the other of them when an opportunity occurred. Marriage was an excellent means to this end.

Hugues Capet had invested his hopes in Flanders. When Count Arnoul died, his son was still a child, and the idea of the 989 marriage was to make Robert, the heir to the kingdom, the boy's stepfather. But this presented difficulties. There was a danger that the transaction might involve the loss of the chateau of Montreuil, recently conquered and settled on Rozala as her dower. (It was later the dower of Philip I's first wife, also from Flanders; so we see certain parts of an inheritance being used in one generation after another to provide a dower for the wife of the head of the family.) Rozala, when she proved barren and thus useless, was repudiated "by divorce."[2] The separation was carried out in due form, except that the husband's family managed to hold on to Montreuil.

In 996, the Capetian's most urgent concern was to keep what he could of Touraine and resist the encroachments of the count of Anjou and the count of Blois. The first of these two was the more manageable, the second the more powerful and dangerous. Eudes, count of Blois, had been given the *comté* of Dreux in return for agreeing that his lord should be crowned in 987, and all the warriors bordering the area near Orleans were his vassals. Fortunately the houses of Anjou and Blois were at loggerheads.

At court the aged king inclined toward the count of Anjou, while his son and natural enemy favored the party of the count of Blois. When Eudes of Blois died in February 996, the count of Anjou seized Tours, and a few months later Robert, emboldened by the knowledge that his father was dying, seized Berthe, Eudes's widow. According to Richer, the historian, he was her "defender" to begin with, and in this capacity recaptured Tours. Then he married her, hoping to get control over the *comté* of Blois, as he had over the *comté* of Flanders, through the offspring of his new wife, in this case boys who had only just arrived at the age of majority.

The eldest son died almost immediately, while the second, Eudes II, soon became an arrogant nuisance, intriguing in the very heart of the royal household. The king was disappointed and decided to go back to the former friendship with Anjou. He did so by changing wives, a frequent method of reversing alliances. He dismissed Berthe and married Constance, first cousin to Fouque Nerra, count of Anjou.

But Eudes still had supporters at court, and did his best to destroy the new marriage. He almost succeeded, as we learn through the monk Odorannus of Sens.[3] Odorannus was a goldsmith as well as a chronicler, and very proud of his handiwork, which included the reliquary of Saint Savinien, made with gold and jewels donated by King Robert and Queen Constance in 1019. By this offering, explained Odorannus, the couple gave thanks to the saint for his former protection: Robert had gone to Rome, and Berthe, "the queen repudiated because of her close kinship, went with him, hoping, with the support of certain members of the king's court, that the whole kingdom would be restored to her by order of the pope." Constance in dismay turned to prayer and three days later was told that the king was coming back. And "from that time forth, Robert cherished his wife more than ever, placing all his royal rights in her power."

In 1022 the count of Blois and his friends launched a final attack; this was the episode of the heretics of Orleans,[4] excellent priests and friends of the queen. They were burned, but Constance survived.

All these intrigues show that lawful marriage, in a society widely given to concubinage, was first and foremost a political weapon. The wife was moved from square to square like a pawn. The stakes were high. They were honor, glory, and power.

I have not yet mentioned what was a major anxiety in all this: the need to perpetuate a lineage by the begetting of a legitimate son. This issue alone would suffice to explain Robert's behavior. Rozala had been fertile, but was apparently barren by the time she came to the young king. Richer says she was rejected because she was "too old." Berthe was not yet thirty and had proved her fertility. But five years after her marriage with Robert she still had not borne him a child, and this was deemed a good enough reason for dismissing her. Constance's advantage was her youth, and she immediately bore two sons. But once that was done Robert felt quite free, in 1008–1010, to repudiate her and take Berthe back. It was for this reason that he set out for Rome but, fortunately for Constance, Saint Savinien was watching over things.

So it was very easy to undo the bond of matrimony at the court of France, a province less backward than the Germania of Saint Henry. We historians, who see things from the outside only, are tempted to give three different motives for Robert's three marriages: Rozala was perhaps chosen because she was a king's daughter; Berthe because she was a trump card in the game being played in Touraine; Constance because it was urgently necessary to provide the crown with an heir. Of *ardor*, of the flame of desire, we have no right to speak. But whatever the explanations, it is remarkable that the precepts of the Church were so little regarded. What was the attitude of its leaders?

There is no evidence that they reacted very vigorously to the first repudiation or the first remarriage, even though the latter was adulterous and condemned as such by all the canons soon to be collected by Bourchard of Worms. The disapproving technical term, *superductio*, of which later chroniclers made lavish use in relation to Philip I, does not appear at all. The only trace of reserve is to be found in Richer's *History*; Richer was a monk from Reims who had no love for the Capetian usurpers. Making reference to Gerbert, his teacher, he writes that "the purest minds criticized as a sin" the king's repudiation of Rozala. But this was very cautious criticism, "without overt opposition." Richer later recalls that Gerbert may have tried to dissuade Berthe from marrying Robert. But that is all; there is no mention of bigamy. The marriage between Berthe and Robert was celebrated in due form by the archbishop of Tours, assisted by other prelates.[5] Even enemies of this marriage, like Helgaud, spoke only of the couple's kinship as being too close, within the prohibited degrees. Bishop Adalbéron of Laon, in a satirical poem, reprimands the count of Nevers for having, out of self-interest, advised in favor of this "incest."[6] That was the operative word. For those who wanted the marriage dissolved invoked not adultery but kinship.

This underlines the way ecclesiastical morality, as reflected in Bourchard's *Decretum*, stressed the sin of incest and separated it entirely from the problems raised by the Gospels' insistence on indissolubility. Thus, it was for "having against the apostolic prohibition married his cousin" that the king of France and "the bishops who consented to those incestuous nuptials" were ordered, by a council held in 997, to break off the union.[7] A year later, in Rome, another council, presided over by the Emperor Otto III, decided that Robert must leave his cousin Berthe, "whom he had married against the laws"; the assembly also imposed seven years of penance on both partners and threatened the king with anathema if he persisted in his sin. The bishops involved were suspended until they had done as they had been told by the council of 997.

Let us make no mistake: these were political measures. The papal court wanted the king of France to withdraw on two fronts. They wanted him to give the archdiocese of Reims back to the Carolingian bastard who had been deposed for treason; and also to stop supporting the bishop of Orleans against the monks of Saint-Benoît-sur-Loire, who wished to be freed from the bishop's control. The count of Anjou, whose interests had suffered a setback by the royal marriage, was also active on the sidelines, having conveniently gone on a pilgrimage to the tomb of Saint Peter.

Robert, shaken by all this, gave way on the question of Reims and the exemption of the monks of Saint-Benoît-sur-Loire; and the papal legate promised him "confirmation of his new marriage." To underline his preeminence over the bishops of northern France, the pope upheld the judgment, but not for long and not with conviction. The king kept his wife, and Archambaud remained archbishop of Tours. We should not be misled by Jean-Paul Laurens's painting, which shows King Robert and his wife abandoned by the bishops: he was drawing on an old legend, but in fact King Robert was never excommunicated. He did dismiss Berthe, but at least two, and probably as much as four or five years after the Council of Rome. And for other reasons.

Perhaps Helgaud was right, and the king was turning monk, thinking more about his soul and the enormity of his sins. Such things lie beyond our knowledge and can be neither confirmed nor denied. But at least this new divorce was based on valid grounds, the fact that the couple were cousins. Odorannus puts it quite plainly: Berthe was repudiated "by reason of kinship." Once their incestuous union was dissolved, both parties had a perfect right to remarry, and the most holy Robert did so. But when, in 1008 in Rome, he tried to get his third marriage annulled and his second reconfirmed, he was soon made to understand that the Curia would never countenance what would probably scandalize the most broadminded observer.

According to Helgaud, only a few disagreeable people ventured to doubt Robert's sanctity in the fourth decade of the eleventh century, and even they demurred only on the subject of his double incest. They said nothing about his "trigamy." What northern French bishop would have dared, if Rome had insisted, to excommunicate an anointed king? Their attitude became more rigorous after the middle of the century, when reform was starting to spread from the south and the legend of the chastity of the Emperor Henry II was being promulgated. It was then that disapproval arose among the precursors of Yves of Chartres and Pope Urban II.

The first critic whose comments have come down to us is the Italian ascetic Peter Damian. In a letter that must have been written between 1060 and 1072 to another rigorist, Abbot Didier of Monte Cassino, he recalls that Robert, grandfather of the then king of France, was punished for having married his kinswoman. The son of this illicit spouse had "a neck and head like a goose." Damian then describes the scene painted by Jean-Paul Laurens: the bishops excommunicating husband and wife, the pious folk terror-stricken, the king deserted by all save the two young servants who risked their lives to feed him but immediately threw everything he touched onto the fire. According to Damian, Robert was overcome by fear, and divorced his illegal wife in order to make a lawful marriage.[8]

This account, the source of which is unknown, was repeated in a fragmentary history of France written probably after 1110, by someone in the entourage of Louis VI. Louis was then quarreling with Bertrade of Montfort over her dower, as well as being engaged in putting down his half-brothers. So he permitted open criticism of the defects of his father, Philip I, who actually had been excommunicated for incest, and with justification. Nor did Louis mind if the criticism spilled over onto his great-grandfather. Better informed than Helgaud, the author of this more or less official account does not speak of consanguinity alone. He also confirms what Helgaud says, revealing that Robert was also godfather to Berthe's son. Robert, anathematized by the pope, persisted in his sin. *Amor*, perverse carnal passion, held him in thrall. "The woman was delivered of a monster; the king, terrified, was obliged to repudiate her; and so he and his kingdom were absolved."[9]

If this was a victory for heaven it was also a victory for the Church— a real one at the time this text was written, amounting as it did to the king of France's complete submission. To make the laity obey the orders of the Almighty and of the bishops, it was necessary, at the beginning of the twelfth century, to use the big stick, to exploit the dread lurking in the depths of everyone's mind of the teratological consequences of intermarriage.

The victory was celebrated long after the event. But it was an imaginary victory. Robert had not really been beaten.

CHAPTER V
PRINCES AND KNIGHTS

Robert was a king, placed above the common run of mortals by the coronation liturgy, which made him part of the *ordo regum* referred to by Adalbéron of Laon[1]—the only social category besides that of the servants of God to be seen then as an "order" organized, like the hosts of heaven, in accordance with a special ethic. Yet, in defiance of the Church, Robert, known as "the Pious," committed both incest and trigamy. So, in the first half of the eleventh century, we are not surprised to see other great personages who were *not* anointed kings pay as little attention as he did to the precepts of the Church.

Two examples. First, Galeran, count of Meulan. His behavior probably caused some surprise at the time, and he is dimly remembered in some of the vernacular writings with which courtiers amused themselves in the thirteenth century. Only his name survives in these works, but it is connected with the sort of anomalies to which marriage, in extreme cases, might give rise. As for his real behavior, all we know is that he dismissed his lawful wife. We do not know why, or if he took advantage of the grounds offered by too close a kinship or alleged adultery; nor do we know what he might have been hoping to gain from some new marriage. The wife he repudiated took refuge with a bishop, prelates being regarded as women's natural protectors. At that time many bishops in northern France were endeavoring to bring the peace of God to all the "poor" and all the defenseless victims of the soldiery.

When, in 1024, the bishop of Beauvais made the knights in his diocese swear that they would curb their violence, he made them specify: "I will not attack noblewomen, nor those men who travel with them in the absence of their husbands." (Women who did not belong to the nobility were already covered by the oath of peace guaranteeing safety from violence for all peasants and common folk.) The same promise was exacted on behalf of widows and nuns. In the absence of the man supposed to look after them—their *dominus*, or master—wives, together with their more meritorious sisters the nuns, and widows, were placed under the direct protection of God in the form of the leaders of the Church. Their claim to this help was all the stronger if they had been driven from their marriage bed. In such circumstances it was the duty of the bishops not only to take care of them but also, as Bourchard says in his *Decretum*, to exhort their husbands to take them back.

That was why Fulbert, bishop of Chartres, intervened in Galeran's case, and it is through him that we learn what happened. Replying to the archbishop of Rouen,[2] who had informed him of Galeran's "effrontery," Fulbert wrote that Galeran had been a thorn in his side for a long time. He kept telling him, Fulbert went on, that he could not marry again while his wife was still alive; so then Galeran claimed she had run away and asked Fulbert to give her back. If she refused he wanted the bishop to excommunicate her. Otherwise, he said, the clergy would be forcing him to commit fornication.

The wife did refuse to go back. She knew her husband, and preferred to go into a convent. Fulbert would neither force her to take the veil nor forbid her to do so. But whatever happened he was not going to make her go back to her husband, who hated her and would probably kill her. Galeran then urged Fulbert to let him take another wife, falsely alleging that the first one had deserted him. The bishop refused to authorize another marriage "so long as the *uxor* is neither dead nor a nun."

Fulbert's letter shows that the count of Meulan, after repudiating his wife, had already begun the procedures for marrying again, so that he was, spiritually at least and with a clear conscience, on the way to committing bigamy. Yet he wanted the new marriage to be approved by the episcopal authority. This was a universal wish at the time and in the upper levels of the society with which we are concerned, and Galeran backed up his request with a weighty argument: he had no wife; he was "burning"; he would sin.

Fulbert, an excellent jurist, seeing that it would be dangerous in this case to send the wife back to the husband, put forward another solution: she should take the veil. It was better than being murdered. And it was one of the functions of convents to take in wives who were having trouble with their husbands. Was there some correlation between the proliferation of convents for women in northern France in the eleventh century and the contemporary reinforcement of the scruples preventing nobles from purely and simply repudiating their wives?

My second example is more significant, and concerns the son of Fouque Nerra[3]: he was Geoffroi Martel, count of Anjou, who died in 1060. A fragment of the cartulary of the abbey of Ronceray[4] tells us the story in the style of a chronicle: the document, like many others of the period preserved in the ecclesiastical archives, records a dispute over a gift the donor or his beneficiaries did not want to hand over. The abbey claimed it had been given a vineyard near Saumur, but Geoffroi had taken it back and and granted it "to his wives, or rather concubines." That was the fatal word. The cartulary lists the women to whom the property was handed over: "First to Agnès, then to Grécie, then to Adèle, daughter of Count Eudes, then again to Grécie, and lastly to Adelaide, the German." *Primo . . . deinde . . . postea . . . postremo. . . .* The vocabulary is superb; it was a fine example of serial polygamy. We hear about it only by chance, because the piece of land in dispute was used as a marriage settlement. Like the chateau of Montreuil, which Hugues Capet used as a dower for his son's wife, the vineyard was not inherited but conquered. It had been captured by Fouque Nerra in 1026, at the same time as the chateau of Saumur, and he had settled it on his last lawful wife. She retained it when she was left a widow, and when she set out for Jerusalem in the hope of dying near the Holy Sepulchre she bequeathed it to her daughter Ermengarde, Geoffroi's sister, who was already a widow herself and who may have given it to the monks for the repose of her husband's soul.

The early history of this patch of vines throws a new light on the practice, said to be common to Indo-European societies,[5] of taking a marginal part of a patrimony—a part taken from acquisitions rather than from the main part of the inheritance—and giving it to the women of the family to be handed on from mother to daughter or aunt to niece.

But it so happened that Ermengarde's relations arranged for her to marry again, this time Robert, duke of Burgundy, one of the sons of Robert the Pious. Jean of Fécamp, a monk well known for his rigorist views, pronounced this second marriage illicit: the duke, "having repudiated his lawful wife, wallowed in an improper relationship defiled by cousinship."[6] The duke was in fact a relative four times removed of his new wife. This did not prevent the marriage from taking place, but Geoffroi Martel used it as a pretext for taking back that part of his dead mother's dower. He afterward arranged for each of his wives in turn to have it. Adelaide, the last of them, held on to it for two years after she had been left a widow, and then it was seized by the new count of Anjou, Ermengarde's eldest son (who became count because Geoffroi had no children).

Here we see another feature of such arrangements: the woman's lack of power over the *sponsalicium*, or *dos*, settled on her by her husband. It was rare for her to hold on to it for long if she was left a childless widow. If she was repudiated, her position was weaker still. Those who ruled the family, the men, had force on their side and were unwilling to let possessions that had once belonged to their male ancestors fall into other hands.

The text shows that Geoffroi Martel had, one after the other, four consorts whom the monks called "concubines" but who were really wives. The last of them was referred to as *uxor* in 1060 in the deeds of the chancellery of the *comté* of Anjou. The count, Geoffroi, was married first in 1032, when he was already twenty-six years old. His father, who died eight years later, chose for him Agnès, an heiress, widow of William the Great of Aquitaine. Agnès was a lady of high birth: daughter of the count of Burgundy, grand-daughter of a king of Italy, and a descendant of Charlemagne. At that period of their splendor the Angevin princes made marriages as brilliant as those of the Capetians, if not more so. Geoffroi dismissed Agnès in about 1050. It was not difficult. Everyone knew that she was already closely related to him by marriage when she became his wife. The monk who kept the register of deaths at the abbey of Saint-Serge noted in 1032: "The count took in incestuous marriage the countess Agnès, who had been the wife of Guillaume, his cousin" three times removed. And the author of the *Annals* of Saint-Aubin wrote: "Geoffroi took Agnès in incestuous marriage, and the town of Angers was burned down in a horrible conflagration," the prince's sin bringing down retribution on all his people. (For the year 1000 the same chronicle reports "the first burning of the town of Angers only a few days after the countess Elizabeth was burned." She had been put to death by her husband, Fouque Nerra, as the surest way of removing any obstacle in the way of his remarriage.)

Note, however, that Geoffroi lived quite comfortably for twenty years while committing the sin of incest. He began to feel defiled only when he decided to seek a new wife. Between 1049 and 1052 he married Grécie, another widow, a daughter belonging to the distinguished house of Langeais and previously married to the lord of Montreuil-Bellay. But by this connection Geoffroi, perhaps under pressure from King Henry I,[7] was moving a considerable step down the social ladder.

During the last eight years of his life, wives came and went: he dismissed Grécie, replacing her with Adèle, daughter of the count of Blois and his cousin four times removed—a relationship that would allow him to get rid of her whenever he felt like it. When Adèle was dismissed, Grécie was recalled, only to be replaced by Adelaide. This apparent fickleness was due to Geoffroi's paramount need to beget an heir. He was forty-five at the time of his first divorce, and in a hurry. He tried frantically, with one and another wife, but in vain: it was he who was sterile, though in those days men would never admit such a thing. On his deathbed he had to choose, for his successor, between the boys closest to him by blood, the sons of his sister Ermengarde. The elder received the "honor," the *comté* of Anjou; the younger got just one chateau, which he held in fief from his brother. This happened in 1060, and is one of the earliest examples in that area of what jurists call parage.[8]

In the first half of the eleventh century the princes or great nobles treated marriage in the same cavalier fashion as the king and seem to have paid even less attention than he did to the disapproval of the Church, or at least of some ecclesiastics. The great lords were freer than the kings, and they had just as imperative a duty to defend their own heritage. In my view their insouciant attitude toward the Church should be related to the changes then taking place in the aristocratic attitude to kinship. Following Karl Schmid and other pupils of Gerd Tellenbach,[9] I myself have written a good deal on that far-reaching phenomenon, the transition from one kind of family structure to another. At the end of the ninth century kinship was still perceived horizontally, so to speak, as a group including on one level, over two or three generations only, men and women who were blood relations, together with their respective consorts.

This pattern is reflected in Dhuoda's *Manuel* and in the *Libri memoriales*, registers that were used at funeral services and that grouped together in spiritual community, say, ten or so of the dead and a corresponding thirty or so of the living in a family cluster, linked together by the duty of prayer and the hope of salvation. But gradually, imperceptibly, this horizontal grouping was replaced by a vertical arrangement organized in terms of the *agnatio*, or male line only, so that the position and the rights of women dwindled, and as the line stretched back to cover more and more of the past, and thus of the dead, so it gradually reached toward a single ancestor. Through the years this ancestor grew more and more distant, until he was finally looked upon as the hero who originally founded the family.

The royal family had long exhibited such an image of itself, and in the first phase of feudalization, during the tenth century, that image was also adopted by the nobles who ruled over what were to become the great principalities. This new image was swiftly imitated throughout the aristocracy in the turmoil surrounding the year 1000, when the seigneurial system of exploitation was established,[10] isolating the nobility further than ever from the people.

Pierre Bonnassie,[11] deciphering the parchments in the archives at Catalonia—i.e., a region then part of the kingdom of France, though a long way from the one with which I am concerned—detects signs of trouble between 1030 and 1060. He sees youths expelled and forced to go far away, ostensibly on pilgrimage. Others took up arms against their fathers or uncles. Brothers slew one another, and contemporaries lamented that the younger generation were depraved and no longer had any respect for their elders.

In the house of the counts of Anjou I find the same sort of upheavals as those that shook, for example, the count of Barcelona's family.[12] Fouque Réchin challenged his elder brother's right to the *comté*, defeated, captured, and disinherited him, and never released him from the close confinement he had condemned him to in order to keep him out of the way. But can we be sure that such discord was new?

It is perhaps only more easily seen because record-keeping practices changed at that period. Dry and formal documents revealing almost nothing of the concrete details of life were succeeded both in Catalonia and in northern France by free and wordy narratives, spontaneous accounts of debates held in the presence of those who passed judgment. These chronicles, setting out their stories in more or less dramatic form, tended to dwell on the element of violence. Yet it seems, from various indications, that this violence took people by surprise.

Tension within families was growing at that time. This was perhaps partly the result of a rapid change in the rules traditionally governing the division of inheritances, and of the concentration of power in the hands of heads of families—the person a Cluniac document calls the *caput mansi* and Galbert of Bruges later refers to as the *caput generis*, the head of what was coming to be seen as a "race," or lineage.

The sons of such a figure felt frustrated and, as soon as they came of age, gave voice to their claims and grabbed by force what they could when they could. Equally bitter were the husbands of their sisters and aunts, who saw what they had hoped to inherit absorbed into the one estate. At the same time the man responsible for a family's honor would try to preserve its prestige by exercising stricter control over the marriages of the young men and women subject to his authority. He would hand over the women quite willingly but would allow only *some* of the men to contract lawful marriages, thus forcing most of the knights to remain bachelors, which only increased their resentment and unruliness. I regard these changes of attitude in the first half of the eleventh century as forming one of the major aspects of the "feudal revolution."

Within the fundamental transformation that in the course of a few decades turned the ruling class into small rival dynasties rooted in their estates and clinging to the memory of their male ancestors, marriage seems to have played a crucial role, as it did in the consequent competition for and distribution of seigneurial power. The kings and great feudal princes tightened the bonds of vassalic friendship by using marriage as a means of making alliances and of providing their most faithful followers with wives. But, above all, marriage was a way of striking out on one's own: some knights, by taking or stealing a wife or receiving one at the hands of their lord, managed to escape from another man's house and found one of their own. Contemporary documents tell us little about this phenomenon, but it is reflected a century and a half later in the way the descendants of these fortunate bridegrooms remembered their founding fathers: they would imagine their most distant ancestor as a young man, an adventurer, a knight-errant who, after a long quest like that of Sir Gawain or Sir Lancelot, settled down and established himself through marriage.

Such memories may have been distorted, and I shall treat the question at more length when I come to examine the records in which they are preserved.[13] But in the course of the transformation of which we are speaking, relations between married couples also changed, and here contemporary texts are more explicit. Certain of the documents preserved in archives and cartularies afford us a glimpse of how the marriage contract gradually took on a different form.

When a Church estate acquired a new piece of property, it sometimes happened that the monk or canon in charge of managing the estate preserved, in the file recording the transaction, a document (provided by the donor or vendor) that had been drawn up earlier, on the occasion of a marriage, or more precisely at the time of the *desponsatio*, or first stage of the marriage procedure. Indeed, in regions where the tradition of juridical writing had not been entirely lost, it was a symbolic requirement that a parchment containing the terms of the marriage agreement should pass from hand to hand in the presence of the assembled families and friends.

Such documents are very rare in the provinces with which I am dealing, so I must stray beyond them a little and turn back to an exceptionally rich source of information belonging to the period around the year 1000. I refer to the cartularies of the abbey of Cluny, the cartulary of the cathedral of Mâcon, and other records belonging to more humble religious establishments in that neighborhood. These documents contain occasional fragments, surviving by chance, of what universal custom then required be written down.

However small the village concerned, whatever rung the participants occupied on the ladder of fortune, and even if they came from among the peasants and smaller landowners, whenever a man and woman were married there had to be a contract defining their respective rights over the property involved. I do not lose sight of the fact that the customs reflected in the sources mentioned above may not have been exactly the same as those prevailing in the Ile-de-France and Picardy. Nor do I forget that we must not expect too much from this kind of document: the notaries who recorded them used a formal language that conceals the underlying reality and tells us almost nothing about marital relationships except those that had to do with landed property.

Among the deeds in question some, but very few, deal with what came to be called the dowry, the gift parents made to their daughter, or rather to her and her husband, when she married: "To you, my dear son-in-law and his wife, I and my wife give. . . ."[14] (The original Latin is often very rough.) The son-in-law is mentioned first in accordance with the hierarchical order: the man is the "head" of the woman (see page 25).

The year 1000 also provides us with another vestige: I call it "vestige" because the document itself has not survived. But it is referred to in a later transaction. This time the wife is the prime mover, but she does not act alone ("I and my husband [*dominus*]"). Together they present Cluny with two country estates. But the two farms come from the wife's mother, who "when marrying off her daughter gave them as a dowry (*in dotem*)."[15] In this case it was the mother alone who bestowed the dowry; the father was probably dead. Note that the property had come down from the mother's own forebears: an aunt of the benefactress had earlier donated these lands to God and the monks of Cluny. Sister, mother, daughter—here again we see part of a family fortune left at the disposal of the women for their marriages and funeral benefactions [charitable gifts, usually property or money given to the Church in exchange for Masses to be said for the salvation of the donors' or others' souls].

A third and final reference dates from the second half of the eleventh century. A knight shares with his brothers the heritage left by his father, all, that is, but a very small portion that the father had given to "his sisters and daughters," probably on the occasion of their marriage.[16]

It cannot be said that a young woman absolutely had to bring a dowry with her when she married. Her new husband, on the other hand, certainly was obliged to make a settlement in her favor. In the Mâconnais it had to be done by a *carta*, or deed of gift. This could be very brief. Here are three such documents, all drawn up in the year 975–976 by country priests in the area around Cluny: "To my gentle and most gracious *sponsa*"—she was not called *uxor* until after the nuptials—"I Dominique, your *sponsus*, seeing that by the will of God and by the counsel [*concilium*] of your relatives and mine I have espoused you [*sponsavi*], and if God wills shall enter with you into lawful community, give you by way of dowry the half of my portion. . . ."[17] Dominique came from a family of small landowners, so he was giving his bride half his share in a farm he owned jointly with his brothers; she thus became part-owner of the joint possession.

The second deed says: "For the love and goodwill I bear you, and for the good services you have rendered me and in other matters have promised me, because of all that I give you. . . ."

Finally, the third document, referring to the civil law (the old Roman law formerly adapted for the use of the Burgundians), says: "Seeing that for the love of God, of my parents, and of my friends, I have married you in accordance with the Gombette law,[18] for my part I give the entire half of all that I own to you, my *sponsa*, and endow you [*doto*] before our nuptial day, and after that day you shall do with it whatever you please."

Though such peasant contracts took various forms, they all emerged from the same background; every scribe repeated the same formula, whether from memory or by copying it out of some handbook. What the documents all reveal is, firstly, the distinction that was made between betrothal and nuptials. The property agreement precedes the physical union, but the wife does not assume possession until after the night the husband possesses her. After that she is complete mistress of her portion, which is equal to that retained by her husband. She enters a family that accepts her as a full coproprietor of the estate. One *sponsus* explicitly says: "I give you a share in my fraternal heritage, which will come to me from my father and mother."[19]

It should also be noted that the husband is represented as acting alone. He always refers to himself as "I," without qualification. There is also an obligatory reference to love and "goodwill." Nevertheless, the formulas adhered to make it clear that feeling and individual decision are subordinate, on the one hand, to the will of God and, on the other, to the "counsel," in other words the decision, of the two families.

Written records become more grandiose when it is the rich and powerful who are being married. Let us look at the document recording the *sponsalicium*[20] of Oury, master of the chateau of Bâgé in Bresse, who together with the lord of Beaujeu was the most powerful of the count of Mâcon's vassals. The document was drawn up in 994 in the city of Mâcon, written down in extremely good Latin by a canon of the cathedral there, and signed by the count and countess. Its long and stately preamble sets forth the ecclesiastical theory of what constitutes a good marriage, recalling "ancient custom" and "the law of the Old and New Testaments," which contained "the confirmation of the Holy Ghost, teaching us through Moses about marriage between man and woman." Genesis 2:24 is quoted: "Therefore shall a man leave his father and mother, and shall cleave unto his wife; and they shall be one flesh." Also, as Matt. 19:6 declares: "What therefore God hath joined together, let not man put asunder." Lastly there is a reference to the marriage at Cana: "Our Lord who became a man and who made men was pleased to be present at the wedding in order to confirm the sanctity of the full authority of marriage."

It seems that Oury himself read aloud this part of the text, actually speaking the words from the Scriptures. So we see how, because of the need to have such a transaction recorded in writing and the inevitability of using priests to set it down, the morality of the Church was able to infiltrate the minds of the laity, pervading such hitherto secular acts as the exchange by which a girl was bestowed on a man in return for an offering on his part.

"For that I, Oury," he continues, "respecting this authority, guided by the counsel and exhortation of my friends and aided by heavenly piety, defer to the general custom concerning marital association: out of love, and according to ancient usage, I give you, my most dear and loving *sponsa*, by the authority of this *sponsalicium* . . ." and he goes on to list, not a share in a jointly owned estate, but a series of separately named properties making up a large domain. These have been taken from the overall fortune of Oury's family and are now, with the agreement of his brother (the parents being dead), given to his bride in perpetual gift "to have, sell, give away, and to do with what you will according to your free will."

This emphatic declaration uses the same words as those the village priests transcribed in cruder language, on scraps of parchment, when mere nonentities got married.

✵ But marriage formalities changed during the half-century that spanned the year 1000. The last deeds recording *sponsalicia* to be copied out in the cartularies of our area date from the 1030s.[21] They fell out of use because legal procedures were changing; it was no longer necessary to produce written evidence before tribunals, since those who had to pass judgment now relied on oral testimony or on proofs of the judgment of God.[22] Thus, archivists no longer troubled to preserve such documents. But it was still customary for the husband to make a formal gift to the wife at the time of their betrothal: the archives of Notre-Dame de Beaujeu contained a document dated 1087 in which a man recalls that he married a wife "under the dotal system, giving her a third of his rights over a farm."[23]

Another probable reason why monks and canons gave up keeping records of such contracts was that after about 1030–1040 a husband's power over the whole of a couple's property became so complete that the wife's prerogatives were purely fictitious, and there was no point in mentioning them.

This seems to have been the general trend. What had been an equal association between husband and wife gradually changed into a miniature monarchy in which the man ruled as king. This male predominance was reinforced by the tendency for family relations to be defined more and more in terms of vertical lineage (see pages 92–93). The splitting up of family fortunes was undesirable; the number of claimants to them needed to be limited—and that number could be halved simply by excluding women from the succession. So, as we can see from these various indicators, women's power over hereditary property was gradually retracted.

First, the share granted to the wife in the deed of *sponsalicium* became smaller. It was a half at the end of the tenth century; it might still be a half in 1008.[24] But in documents drawn up between 1005 and 1008,[25] the husband is already parting with only a third of his land, adding to it a little present in the form of a small field or vineyard. After 1030 even this disappeared. Of more far-reaching consequence still were clauses restricting a wife's right to dispose freely of her part of the property. These clauses appear in documents dating from 1004, 1005, and 1006. The gift now lasted only for the wife's lifetime: when she died, it is expressly stated, the property settled on her at the time of her marriage was to pass to the couple's heirs.

We see Oury of Bâgé, whom we have met before, increasing with the same love and goodwill the gift he had made ten years earlier to the same most dear and loving consort. Probably his brother had died, Oury had inherited his property, and it was his duty to restore the balance between himself and his wife. But now he takes care to stipulate that after her death "these things shall come back to the children who have been or shall be born to us."[26]

The wording used in the villages was even more restrictive: "If we have heirs the dower will go to them; if we do not, we two shall have the usufruct as long as we live, and after you die it will go to my relations."[27] (Note that even during her lifetime the wife does not own the property—she only shares the usufruct of it with her husband.)

This kind of arrangement became firmly established, together with another that was less strict: "After my death, one-third will revert to my relatives; with the rest you will do as you wish."[28] We must remember that such documents were drawn up by priests, who took care to keep something back from the man's relatives in the hope that it would be used to pay for masses for his soul.

At this point the wife's rights were, however, still real. If she survived her husband, she enjoyed legal use of the property settled on her at her marriage until she died. Bernard, a knight setting off for Jerusalem between 1031 and 1045, divested himself of all his worldly goods. He gave to the abbey of Cluny the third he had inherited from his father of the property he owned jointly with his two brothers. He also gave the abbey "a third of what his mother owned for her lifetime, and which would go to the monks after her death."[29] In 1037 another Bernard gave away all he possessed, with the consent of his brother, his wife, and all his friends. Cluny received half the inheritance, while Bernard's brother kept the other half. As for his wife's *dotalitium*, Bernard could dispose of it freely, and he gave that too to the monastery, stipulating only that his wife should retain a life interest in it.[30]

A last vestige of the dwindling rights of wives is observable during the reign of King Robert: "To my dear son, I your mother, out of love and goodwill"—the same formula as a husband used in dowering his wife—"give you that which I hold in *dotalitium* from my husband and from my father."[31] In this marriage the wife's settlement had been made up of property from her own family as well as from her husband's. The donatrix is here ceding bare ownership, retaining the usufruct for her own lifetime. The significance is clear: the husband had just died, and it was necessary for the widow to reaffirm her rights against the claims of her son.

Another extract from the Cluny archives reflects a similar situation. Round about 1080, a woman, with the approval of her three sons, gave the abbey a large estate. "This *villa*," says the record, "she had as a gift from her husband and her son, when the husband shared his honor among his sons."[32]

Just as a marriage settlement could protect a woman against the dangers of widowhood, so it might also be a guarantee against those of repudiation. In the document quoted above (page 99), Notre-Dame de Beaujeu was given the *sponsalicium* the woman had retained all her life, although her marriage had been dissolved on grounds of consanguinity. Not all husbands were as high-handed as Geoffroi Martel with the land they had once bestowed on their bride.

The stipulations laid down in this sort of deed came into effect when the marriage ended and the wife was left alone. Up till then her rights were swallowed up in those possessed and exercised by her husband. This happened more and more as relations of kinship were reduced to those of lineage and people thought increasingly of the family group as that formed through descent along the male line. A deed of gift dated 1025 reflects this attitude: "In the course of time the legitimate sons born of my seed by my lawful wife will succeed in turn by just and legal line of generation."[33] The "sons" and not the "children" were the sole true heirs; daughters, like bastards, were excluded. Here we observe (1) the privilege of the male and (2) the importance of lawful marriage.

As a result, the authority of the husband—the "master," the "lord," who bore the same title as God the Father—increased. He managed not only the part of his own family heritage that he had settled on his wife, but also the property that might have come to her from her family. It was all at his disposal. Admittedly he needed her consent, but it was he who spoke and acted. In 1005 a knight gave away "all the possessions his wife's father had in a certain place and that he himself held [tene-bat] on behalf of his wife."[34] At the end of the same century a wife gave Saint-Vincent de Mâcon the dowry she had received when she was married, but the gift was given "by the hand" of Bernard, her husband.[35] All the rights involved in a marriage came to be concentrated in the ever more grasping hands of the man.

The gradual take-over by the husband of the whole of a couple's property, together with arrangements designed to reduce the size of the dower and to ensure its reversion to the male line, were aimed at protecting landed property from a particular danger: that the woman of alien blood who had been introduced into the family might misuse the part of the heritage that had been handed over to her. But the strengthening of the husband's power only increased another danger: anyone who gave a sister, daughter, or niece in marriage was afraid the outsider who now had power over her might lay hands on her family's heritage.

The documents I have been examining do in fact speak of the rights of sons-in-law, but only late in the day, after the middle of the century. Round about 1050 a knight called Achard, lying on his deathbed in his house near Cluny, dictated his last wishes. He listed the lands he was offering to God for the salvation of his soul and asked his relatives to give their approval. In other words, he asked them to renounce their own rights and to share both in his gift and in the spiritual advantages it was expected to bring. His sons were the first who came to see him for this purpose, followed by a cousin, then another close relative, and lastly Achard's son-in-law and his wife, Achard's daughter. The son-in-law was the last man in the procession, but in accordance with the natural hierarchy he came before his wife.[36]

At about this time the sons-in-law of dead benefactors start to loom larger and more menacing among the growing number of men whose releases religious establishments had to purchase at ever higher prices if they wanted to enjoy in peace the donations of the pious.

The answer to such threats to the family fortune was to reduce the right of a married daughter to the inheritance, limiting her claim to property that had once formed her mother's dowry and now formed her own. This meant that only a marginal part of the family estate was in danger of being sacrificed. Nevertheless, when the head of a family died leaving only daughters, the husband of the eldest might appropriate the whole inheritance, supplanting the uncles and cousins and taking the place of his father-in-law. This happened in three instances in the Mâconnais region at the end of the eleventh century.[37]

One of the short chronicles included in the Cluniac cartularies shows how a husband might make use of his wife's rights in such circumstances.[38] The viscount of Mâcon, traveling back exhausted from Jerusalem, died in Lyons, not far from his home. He was a "young man," a bachelor, and left an enormous fortune. The count of Mâcon, "having seized the viscount's sister in marriage, claimed the whole *honneur* for himself." It was for this he had stooped to marrying a woman descended from a vassal. But here he came up against the monks of Cluny, to whom the dead man had donated nearly all his possessions. This obstacle proved too much for the count, who dismissed his now unprofitable wife, alleging "proven reasons," i.e., consanguinity. The woman was then passed on "to a certain knight," one of the count's vassals. By giving the lady as a reward to one of his young followers, the count was cutting his losses and securing the knight's gratitude. For the woman still had claims on the property, and she and her new husband sold them to the monks at a very stiff price. Had it not been for them, she would have brought all her ancestors' fortune to her new marriage, for she had no surviving brother.

If a wife did still have a brother when the head of her family died, it is quite clear what happened: the rights of the brother to the property given to her on her marriage took precedence over the rights of the husband. Take the case of one son-in-law called Roland le Bressan,[39] an appellation that reflects his reputation as an adventurer. It so happened that he had married a widow, the daughter of the lord of Berzé, owner of a chateau. Before her remarriage the lady made a large benefaction to the monks of Cluny, keeping for herself only a life interest in the property concerned, which had come to her from her father on the occasion of her former marriage. She died in 1100, and to take possession of her donation the monastery had to do a lot of hard bargaining with the men who were either still in control of the land in question or all too eager to seize it. In other words, with their benefactress's husband and brother. Finally they both agreed to renounce their rights[40] and promised to have the gift approved by the *infantes* of the dead woman when they were old enough to act on their own behalf. But such a concession had its price. Hugues of Berzé, the brother, was given two hundred *sous* and a palfrey, a handsome compensation that shows a brother retained considerable power over the part of a family fortune his sister had received as a dowry. To the husband, Cluny gave much more: he got three thousand *sous*.

What the administrators of the abbey were really buying out was not the husband's own rights but those of the children his wife had borne him. For, says the text, Roland gave the 36,000 pieces of silver to his brother-in-law "to buy lands in the name of the said children." The money had been given to him but had only passed through his hands, for it no more belonged to him than did the consent he had given. His children had been speaking through him. The lands in question had never been his, and his wife's brother, his sons' maternal uncle, retained a right of inspection over them. It was also this brother's duty to look after his nephews' interests and, as chief guardian of the family fortune, to reinvest in land the compensation granted to them while they were still minors.

On the basis of these customary though still variable usages, of which we can catch only a few glimpses, a whole strategy of marriage was built up. The head of a family did his best to marry off all its available young women. By thus distributing the blood of his ancestors, he was making alliances that would be reinforced in the next generation by the special relationships ensuing between the sons of these marriages and their mother's brothers. I return to northern France for an example. Hilduin of Ramerupt had through his wife inherited the *comté* of Roucy, and to strengthen his hold on it had married his widowed mother-in-law to his own brother. He arranged the marriages and remarriages of his seven daughters, and three generations later we can trace some hundred and twenty of his descendants.[41] On the other hand, prudence required that someone in his position should allow only one son to take a lawful wife, unless for one of the others he could find a brotherless young woman, hence an heiress. Two of Hilduin's sons married: one was able to go and live with his wife's family, while the other inherited, apparently intact, the "honor," or major part, of Hilduin's family fortune.

As for surplus males unable to enter a religious community through the influence of some uncle who was a prior or a canon,[42] they just waited and hoped to be given a wife as a present one day, as had been the case for the count of Mâcon's vassal; or else they set off for distant parts to make their fortune. Early eleventh-century records for the Mâconnais region show many such young men leaving for Jerusalem in search of wealth as well as salvation.

These records are plentiful enough for us to be able to trace the growth of whole knightly families in the neighborhood of the abbey of Cluny in the eleventh century, and so to gauge the effectiveness of the policy described above, designed to control the menfolk's marriages. Just after the year 1100, this policy put a speedy end to the proliferation of heirs, which for decades had been splitting up the huge estates built up during the Carolingian era; it also set a limit to the number of aristocratic families. Around 1100 there were thirty-four of them, about the same number as there were parishes in this very small area of France, the only one where such a survey could be adequately carried out. Only three of these families had been formed, two generations earlier, as a direct result of the fruitful marriage of a younger son. In all the rest, despite the birth of many children, strict discipline had prevented the growth of any minor branches around the main trunk. Take

Bernard Gros, lord of the chateau of Uxelles at the beginning of the eleventh century. He had six sons. Two became monks. Three were knights and remained unmarried. Only one had a legitimate son, who by 1090 was sole owner of the fortress and all the rights appertaining to it.[43]

One of the results of this pruning of the family tree was that women were more than ever subjugated by men, and by the same token men were secretly more frightened than ever of their wives. They dreaded the women might take some insidious revenge by way of adultery or murder. Contemporary chronicles are full of princes who were supposed to have been poisoned by their wives, and of allusions to "female intrigues," "pernicious wiles," and spells of all kinds cooked up in the women's quarters. We can imagine a knight of the eleventh century lying trembling and suspicious in his bed every night, beside an Eve whose insatiable desire he may not be able to satisfy, who is certainly deceiving him, and who may be plotting to smother him under the bed covers while he sleeps.

CHAPTER VI
THE HERETICS

I am struck by the coincidence that in the twenties of the eleventh century, at the same time as the matrimonial practices of the knights were changing as noted in Chapter 5, we also see the rise of movements denounced by the leaders of the Church as heretical.[1]

Here were two parallel tremors contributing to the general quaking of the kingdom of France. The upsurge of heresy was certainly not unconnected to the "terrors of the year 1000," the great wave of religious dread that gathered in anticipation of the millenary of Christ's passion. The call to repentance and purification was heard on all sides, and on all sides brotherhoods dedicated to renunciation were being formed, some of them rather dubious. But, at the same time, heresy was undeniably one of the forms adopted by resistance to the introduction of "feudalism," i.e., to a new distribution of power.

Heresy brought together many of those who felt oppressed: the better-off peasants, excluded from knighthood and liable to seigneurial exactions[2]; townsfolk awaking from their torpor; and of course women, now under stricter restraint and thwarted by men in the exercise of their rights. Was there some connection between the deterioration in the position of women and the proliferation of deviant religious sects?

Like all ideologies of protest, this heresy, persecuted and finally destroyed or forced underground, left few traces behind it, and those that do survive are all indirect. Heterodoxy is detected through its suppression, and by way of the sarcasms and condemnations it evokes. It seems to have erupted everywhere, but the information available to us speaks of three points where it broke out in the north of France: Champagne, where a heresiarch preached near Vertus; Orleans, where repression fell on the leaders of a distinguished group of liturgists and religious scholars at the cathedral of Sainte-Croix and in the chapel royal; and Arras, where, after the guiding spirits fled, there remained some of their "unlettered," or lay, disciples, not all or even most of them necessarily poor.

These various sects saw themselves as little bands of the chosen, whose members, like monks and nuns, had converted, changed their way of life, and "transferred themselves out of the world and its wickedness and into a community of the holy." Turning away together from the world, aspiring to things spiritual, and eschewing evil and the things of the flesh, their program was not very different from that of the monasteries. Except that the heretics refused to be part of the Church. This refusal was the main ground of accusation against them, and is the theme that emerges most clearly from the questionnaires used to unmask heterodoxy. The heretics would not accept piety as an institution, nor would they agree that priests were necessary as mediators between man and God. They regarded the clergy as superfluous, and wanted to destroy the Church.

The Church struck back, scattering the heretics and burning some of them at the stake. But in terms of the conduct displayed by the two sides and of their search for salvation and angelic purity, the distance between the orthodox rigorists and the heretics—and those from Orleans came from among the "best" of the clergy—seems to have been very small. For both sides the great evil was sex, and both loathed marriage just as Johannes Scotus Erigena[3] had done (see pages 50 and 114). But the heretics condemned it much more radically.

According to Jean de Ripoll, the heretics of Orleans "denigrated nuptials." Abbot Gozlin de Saint-Benoît-sur-Loire, suspected of sympathizing with the heretics, had to swear that he "did not forbid nuptials," i.e., physical union as distinct from spiritual (which was achieved through the *sponsalicium*). "Mad" Leutard in Champagne, whose body, according to Raoul Glaber, was invaded by a swarm of bees, "drove away his wife, claiming he was repudiating her because of the teachings of the Gospel."

They all pondered the Gospels, and in particular on Matt. 19:10–12, where the disciples suggest to Christ that, in view of the difficulties arising out of women's proneness to adultery, "It is not good to marry." Christ replies, "All men cannot receive this saying, save they to whom it is given," and goes on with the passage about eunuchs, ending with "[those] which have made themselves eunuchs for the kingdom of heaven's sake." But were not those who could "receive this saying" the "chosen," the few who had quit the world and its wickedness, the members of the persecuted sects? In Luke 20:34–35, Jesus is reported to have said: "The children of this world marry, and are given in marriage: But they which shall be accounted worthy to obtain that world, and the resurrection from the dead, neither marry, nor are given in marriage." The heretics interpreted this as meaning that marriage prevented one from rising up toward the light. As they were preparing for the return of Christ, their ambition was to abolish sex altogether. So they allowed women to join them, treating them as equals and claiming that everyone in their communities lived together as brothers and sisters, in perfect purity and in the *caritas* that reigned among the angels in heaven.

It was probably this claim that shocked the rest of the world most. It went completely counter to the fundamental structure of society. One of the reasons heresy failed was that it was seen by its contemporaries, and represented to them by its enemies, as a kind of feminist movement. In his account of the Orleans trial, the monk Paul de Saint-Père of Chartres takes care to include among the condemned a woman, a *monacha*. Raoul Glaber insinuates that the "poison" of false doctrine was brought to Orleans by a woman. It was an easy way of discrediting the sects.

Was not woman a natural troublemaker and poisoner, an instrument of Satan?

Above all, the detractors of heresy branded as hypocrisy the heretics' claim to reject sex while living in mixed communities. How, sneered the critics, could laymen, without the special grace that clerics acquired through the rites of ordination, live in close proximity with women without indulging in fornication? They must be lying, they must be imposters, wallowing in debauchery. Hidden from view in the dark forests propitious to female magic, they were reveling in communal sex. Anyone who tried to dissuade laymen from marriage was inciting them to fornication and incest: all the sources agree on this subject. Raoul Glaber declared that, for the heretics of Orleans, "debauchery was not a sin." Paul of Chartres repeated the gossip of the cloisters, according to which each heretic, after their meetings, took the woman who happened to be nearest to him, even if it was his mother or sister. Later the heretics ritually burned the children born of their unnatural unions, it was said, and used their ashes as charms.

But to return to reality, what happened was that at the very moment when marriage started to be more strictly controlled for the protection of ancestral fortunes, there arose a radical protest against marriage itself. In this context as in that of actual heresy, we must distinguish two different levels among the participants. One was the level of the learned, those who were in the limelight: this category included the clerics of Orleans, who marched to the stake with complete self-assurance, as though to a triumph. The other level, if not exactly "popular," of the common folk, was "unlettered," lay, and much less sure of itself: in Arras, faced with the bishop's inquisition, frightened men and women meekly and silently abjured. But we must not, as orthodox propaganda tended to do, confuse the two categories and assume that they shared the same attitude toward the institution of marriage.

A small group of *"parfaits,"* or "perfect ones," insisted on continence if not virginity for everyone, so that all could become like the angels; but these enthusiasts were soaring far above the majority of their supporters, who had no intention whatsoever of withdrawing from the world and re-

nouncing its pleasures. For them heretical protest was just a way of resist-
ing the Church's interference in marriage procedures.

As the new pattern of social relationships forced the ruling class to
control more strictly the way it perpetuated itself, the morality preached
by the Church became increasingly irksome. André de Fleury, referring
to the sect at Orleans, says not only, as does Jean de Ripoll, that they
"denigrated marriage" but more precisely that they proclaimed that
"marriages do not need blessing; let every man take any woman he likes,
whoever she is." This corrects rather than confirms the gossip repeated
by the monk Paul of Chartres, setting out the principle, misunderstood
or deliberately distorted, on which such tales were based.

The heretics' rejection of marriage was a refusal to accept the sacralization of sexual intercourse: according to their beliefs, priests should
have nothing to do with the ceremonies that took place in the vicinity of
the marriage bed. The heretics' attitude was quite consistent: they condemned at one and the same time priestly privilege, ritualism, and the
flesh. Marriage was carnal, and it was sacrilege to try to sanctify it. It
belonged to the world and its wickedness, and had nothing to do with
the *parfaits*: it was not their business to regulate it since, whether or not
it involved incest or adultery, it was a defilement. So anyone who persisted in getting married might choose "any woman he liked"; whoever
she was, he was sinning. All the priests' investigations about degrees of
consanguinity and incest were beside the point. The heretics, maintaining that it was incongruous to pronounce a blessing on physical unions,
categorically opposed the development of a marriage liturgy.

In this they had the sympathy of all who were worried by any distinction's being drawn between lawful marriage and concubinage that would
relegate the latter, together with incest and bigamy, to the category
of the illicit. This probably explains why the heretics' protest received
support not only from priests living in concubinage who refused to be
forced into celibacy, but also from members of the nobility who wanted
to be able to choose their bedfellows freely and dismiss them equally
freely when they felt like a change.

So I take up Francesco Chiovaro's question: was not heresy most virulent in those regions where the priests first started to intervene in the marriage ritual, and at the time when their intrusion began? For the present purpose I am considering heresy not in terms of the fundamentalist theory at the heart of it, but with regard to the widespread repercussions of its preaching. And I am singling out one social aspect of the heretics' teaching: their unwillingness to let the priests lay down the law about marriage. Nor could heads of great families just hand over this authority to the Church, for on it depended the perpetuation of aristocratic power.

Among those who took up the heretics' challenge was Gérard, bishop of Cambrai-Arras. The little book he ordered to be written after the trial of 1024 contains the arguments he used to try to win over heretics and, together with the supporting scriptural references, forms a kind of exposé of orthodox doctrine. The passage dealing with marriage[4] throws valuable light on the attitudes of the enlightened members of the episcopacy.

Gérard's object is to defend the Church as an institution, to assert the value of the sacraments, and to justify the clergy's right to regulate relations between God and the faithful. He therefore argues the necessity of distinguishing among the "orders" [*discretio ordinis*], saying that by God's will men are divided up into a hierarchy of categories according to their function. Men devoted to the service of God on earth are at the top of the hierarchy, just below the hosts of angels. It is therefore incumbent on them to attain as nearly as possible a state of angelic purity; and it is upon their purity that their pre-eminence depends.

The bishop of Cambrai's argument was echoed by his colleague Adalbéron of Laon in a poem he wrote between 1028 and 1031 and dedicated to King Robert.[5] This gives us a more detailed view of the system. Members of the "order of the Church" are subject to "divine law." This "holy law sets them apart from all earthly defilement" and exhorts them to "purify their spirits and bodies." God "subjects mankind to them" if they are chaste; in order that they may remain so they are forbidden to marry. But the prohibition applies only to them. How could it apply to everyone, since the human race must survive until the Last Day? The function of both "nobles" and "serfs" is to beget children. Adalbéron mocks the Cluniacs, who preach monastic chastity to the aristocracy. However, the reproductive function must be carried out in the best possible manner; i.e., it must be done according to the rules, every man mating within his own "order," the functional group in which God has placed him. There must be no misalliances. Moreover, the sexual act must take place within the framework of lawful marriage. Far from being prohibited, marriage is actually prescribed for the laity: virtuous marriage, of course, lived out in accordance with Christian principle and under the supervision of the priests.

Gérard of Cambrai says the same thing when he sets about refuting the heretics' doctrine on marriage. In their view "married people could in no way be counted among the faithful"; husbands and wives were ejected from the sect, expelled into outer darkness. In marriage, there was no salvation. How was Gérard to answer that? He saw that he had to be careful and steer between two extremes: he must neither put everyone off marriage, nor urge everyone toward it. "Because men of the Church and men of the world belong to different orders, it is right that different kinds of behavior should be required of them." Gérard's attitude on marriage rests on his image of society as a compartmentalized hierarchy, as opposed to the heretics' egalitarian ideal.

He divides moral law into two halves. (Of course, he is talking about men only. He deliberately excludes women because of the paramount *distinctio* separating the sexes, a difference so fundamental and so obvious that he does not bother to mention it.) Ecclesiastical man, he says, having left the world and taken the "side of God," cannot submit himself to the marriage bed without damaging the *cingulum*, or belt, which is the badge of his profession. (The allusion to the sexual act is clear.) By doing so he would lose his special freedom and no longer be subject to that "divine law" which, as Adalbéron also says, liberates him from earthly "servitude."

As for "secular" man, "neither the Gospels nor the Epistles forbid him lawful marriage." He must submit to only one condition: "Matri-

monial *voluptas*, or pleasure, must always be controlled [*subjecta*]."
There are times for physical union, times when one may know one's
spouse, and others when one must stay away from her. "God is not
pleased by marriages that incite men to sensuality and pleasure as if
they were beasts, and lead them to give themselves up to lust as might
horses or mules." But "anyone who uses marriage so that, in the fear of
God, its intent is the love of children rather than the satisfaction of the
flesh cannot, merely for the sin of marriage [*culpa conjugii*], be excluded from the community of the faithful."

Gérard goes on to say that marriage comes under the "law of human
custom." He was a practiced rhetorician, well aware of the distinction
between *lex* and *consuetudo* established by Cicero in *De inventione* and
affirmed more recently by Abbon of Saint-Benoît-sur-Loire in his canonic
collection. When Gérard linked the two expressions "law" and "custom," he did so deliberately. He wanted to underline the difference
between divine and human law, and to disparage the latter by equating
it with mere custom. He was talking to the heretics, trying to counter
their arguments, and he knew their intellectuals were sensitive about the
word *lex*. He admits that divine "law" does exclude marriage, forbidding it to clerics who have chosen "the side of God." Marriage belongs
to another, inferior and less firmly based, set of rules, i.e., to custom. This
was a clever argument, but it was fraught with problems, for it suggested that marriage, because it was carnal, had nothing to do with the
holy; that it was not a sacrament; that it was not an institution of the
Church.

Both Gérard and Adalbéron refer to various patristic authorities,
including Gregory the Great and Augustine, but also Denys and Scotus
Erigena, whose books were within reach in their cathedral libraries and
who reinforced their loathing of the flesh. Their own repugnance was
scarcely less than that of their heretical opponents. In this respect
Gérard was very close to those he was preaching to: their "masters"
read the same texts as he did. For Gérard, marriage was essentially
impure, part of the "world and its wickedness," the lot of those lesser
men who remained bound to material things. Marriage would be perfectly acceptable if all physical joy were banished from it, but that was

impossible. Pleasure could only be "controlled," governed. So marriage was always a "sin," which was why all laymen, even kings, were subordinate to the priests, who were pure.

Although Gérard of Cambrai took this view, I do not believe he should be regarded as belonging to the pre-Augustinian tradition. In my opinion he belongs rather to the line of bishops who were his own predecessors: Jonas of Orleans, Hincmar of Reims. Like them, he appeals to Saint Augustine, declaring that "love of children" justifies marriage. Like them, he takes care to conclude by saying that "the law of human custom" is reinforced and "confirmed" by divine "authority." It may not be actually promulgated by God, but He backs it up. Gérard here cites the New Testament—Matthew and the Epistles of Peter and Paul. He does so first of all to stress the need for the wife to submit to her husband—to point out that God ordained female inferiority, that key to all social organization. He then goes on to use these sources in support of the indissolubility of marriage. Above all, "the unbelieving husband is sanctified by the wife, and the unbelieving wife is sanctified by the husband" (1 Cor. 8:14). So marital union does some good: it provides for an exchange of services, and thus promotes the circulation of grace.

And that was precisely why the teachings of the heretics were pernicious. "If the conjugal bond was inevitably a cause of perdition for man," Christ, "come to repair what was corrupt, would have uttered neither warning nor precept as regards this sin [culpa]." Marriage was inevitably a sin—Gérard is a Manichaean here—but it was a sin that could be "repaired": a man could free himself of it, as of the other forms of corruption with which Christ concerned himself. Gérard follows directly in the steps of Jonas of Orleans when he says that sexual intercourse within marriage is among the venial sins.

Like the bishop of Laon, the bishop of Cambrai, a superb model of "discretion," fell back on Carolingian structures to confront the upheavals besetting northern Gaul in his own day. Influenced by the millenary anguish of his contemporaries, he preached a matrimonial morality that laid stress on the penitential—the need to observe periods of abstinence, the duty of eschewing pleasure. But he avoided preaching extreme asceticism, believing God did not require man to act like an angel. Following the example of Hincmar, he assigned all that concerned marriage to the realm of the "world," i.e., of the laity.

Gérard was not nearly so concerned about lay marriage as he was about clerical celibacy. The Latin discourse expanded in the *Libellus* was not addressed to the unlettered inhabitants of Cambrai but to the priests. For, at the beginning of the eleventh century, amid the great turmoil from which new powers were emerging, the prelates' great preoccupation was to try to save the monopoly, privileges, and immunities of the servants of God. Their policy was based on the general belief that the men charged with sacrifice, the mediators who interceded with the unseen powers, must keep well away from women. If the clerics were to claim that the spiritual was superior to the temporal, if they were to preserve the hierarchy that subordinated the laity to the clergy, they had to establish a sexual distinction between men, with some of them consigned to perpetual chastity.

Like the *Decretum* of Bourchard of Worms; like the debates in which Emperor Henry II and the king of France discussed with the pope how to restore the world to order; so Gérard of Cambrai's declarations helped to pave the way for Church reform and the struggle against the Nicolaitans, which was essentially the fight against married priests. Millenary ideology and the penance that went with it attracted many laymen to the cloister, to join the monks and canons whom their bishops had recalled to order. And many heads of great families agreed with those who advocated clerical celibacy: they feared competition from clerical dynasties and were glad to see obstacles put in the way of their continuation. Above all, having gone to the trouble to stow away so many young men in cathedral chapters so as to limit the expansion of their families, they did not now want them allowed to beget legitimate children.

But it was a hard struggle. The battle was already raging in 1031 in northern France when the Council of Bourges excluded the sons of priests from religious orders, forbade young women to be given in marriage to priests or deacons or the sons of either, and barred anyone from marrying the daughter of a priest's or deacon's "wife."[6] Thirty years later the bishops meeting at Lisieux were still telling canons that they must dismiss their female companions; but they were so discouraged that they let country priests keep theirs.

They were obliged to keep returning to the charge, battling in vain against obstinate resistance. Very little survives of the writings of such churchmen as took the other side of the argument, for in the end they lost. But certain fragments do show the arguments they used.

Continence, they said, was a gift of grace. It could not be imposed; people could not be forced to be pure. What was needed was another, less institutional kind of distinction, taking into account individual temperaments. Advocates of this policy called for charity: Saint Paul had spoken of marriage as a remedy for lust; why should it be denied to priests? They cited the story of Lot and his daughters, showing by this example that anyone proud enough to think he can dispense with marriage is in great danger of falling into fornication. They admitted that continence was best; but there was some good in marriage. They too appealed to Carolingian tradition, maintaining that for everyone the distinction between good and evil corresponded to that between marriage and fornication. It was untrue that for the servants of God the dividing line lay between marriage and continence.

But when they asked that all men, whether priests or laymen, should be treated the same; when they denied the social distinction between the realm of divine law and that of human law on which the reform movement was based; then they were exposing themselves to the accusation of heresy. It was an acute controversy, and the common people often sided with the priests who refused to break with their female companions. But protest seems to have gradually died out in the last decade of the eleventh century, and in the end the "Gregorians"[7] won.

The main casualty of this long struggle was concubinage, the half-measure between the two extremes. The bitterness of the battle had led Gérard of Cambrai to advocate the simplest solution: the *viri ecclesiastici* should have no female partner at all, lawful or otherwise, while the *viri seculares*, who needed a female partner, must have a lawful wife. No physical union was allowed outside the *connubium legitimum*, solemnly entered into by both religious and secular rites.

At the Council of Rome in 1069, the canon issued by the Council of Toledo in 398 insisting on monogamy—but leaving the choice between marriage and concubinage open—was quoted once more. After that, however, it is never mentioned again in official documents. From then on the leaders of the Church, while expelling marriage from its own fold, began to aim at trapping the whole of the laity in a net in which each mesh was a duly consecrated marriage. There were to be no more free unions, no more couples living on the fringe. Bachelors must become part of a "house," a "family" governed by a lawfully married head.[8] Both the clerical and the aristocratic models of marriage were thereby altered.

As we have already seen, the changes that took place in aristocratic society during the eleventh century—the use of family fortunes as a base for ambition, the strengthening of lineage patterns, the increase in the powers of fathers and husbands—all these, largely because of the frustrations such changes gave rise to, were not unconnected to the upsurge of heresy. But this trend also clearly accorded with the aims of those who wished to reform the Church, suiting their designs when it required the young men of a family to be governed by the eldest, and the women to pass straight from virginity to lawful motherhood, and from the strict domination of a father to that of a husband, future father of their children. The value of marriage went up simultaneously within the moral system of the aristocracy and within that preached by the prelates.

But, when it came to other aspects of the two moralities, the differences became sharper. The advocates of reform were primarily concerned with making marriage less carnal. To get the better of the heretics' preaching, the bishops had had to adopt one of their adversaries' arguments. Above all, the monks, despisers par excellence of the world of the flesh, had placed themselves in the vanguard of the fight, proclaiming more loudly than anyone that marriage could and should be chaste, and desire banished from the couple's bed.

On the symbolical level they were trying to minimize the part played by the nuptials in the ritual of matrimony and to emphasize, by contrast, the part of the procedure that had to do with the union of souls. So they stressed the betrothal, with its according of wills, its mutual consent, its instituting of the "charity" that was the core of the marital relationship. Once children had been conceived—in the course of a few brief descents into hell—man and wife were urged to live in a state of spiritual fraternity very similar to that advocated by the heretics.

To these demands for chastity were added the Church's bid for control over marriage contracts. As marriage became more and more a matter of ethics, with emphasis gradually shifting to its spiritual aspect, it fell increasingly under the influence of the priests. When the priests forbade clandestine unions, they received the support of the heads of families. But these same family heads objected when the clerics started to interrogate would-be bridegrooms. Had the man dismissed a concubine or a previous wife? Was he related to the girl he wanted to marry? This kind of inquisition and the difficulties it tended to bring to light were a hindrance to family arrangements. Yet, as the reform went on, ecclesiastical authority grew more and more pervasive, until finally it broke with Carolingian tradition and went so far as to set itself up as sole arbiter in the matter of marriage.[9]

The first traces of this exorbitant claim can be seen in northern France around 1080.

"Feudalization," or "seigneurialization," had gradually paved the way for Church leaders to assume such legal powers. In the course of the eleventh century, the bishops and abbots had appropriated seigneurial prerogatives: staving off their lay rivals—lawyers, counts, lords of chateaux—they had come to exercise regalian justice over some of their subjects and to impose punishment for certain public crimes. These included abduction and adultery. Once the habit of meting out punishment for these infractions of the marriage law was established, the clergy then felt able to take the further step of transferring such cases into what Gérard of Cambrai called "the side of God." Thus, through mere judicial practice, "divine law" gradually encroached upon the "law of human custom."

But it was chiefly the difficulties they encountered in their conflict with married priests that caused the bishops to extend their jurisdiction. It was of paramount importance that the opposition should be made social outcasts, lawbreakers. They therefore had to be tried. There is no doubt that the first people to be brought before an exclusively ecclesiastical court on matrimonial charges were recalcitrant canons who declined to part with their wives.

I have already referred to the bitterness of the struggle against Nicolaitism, which caused the Church as a whole to close ranks under the leadership of the pope. This necessary concentration of *auctoritas* gradually limited the *discretio pastoralis*, the power of each prelate to regulate penalties in his own diocese. Penitentials fell into disuse; experts toiled in libraries to unify the different codes and draw up a general rule. Not a rule that was flexible, as "custom" had been, but a "law" as fixed as "divine law." It relegated marriage to the very edge of what was considered lawful, a narrow precipice between the high ground of salvation and the chasm of irremediable perdition. But marriage did just manage to remain on the right side of the dividing line; the new law did not thrust marriage over into the realm of sin as the heretics of the 1020s had done, and as the irrepressible deviant sects were again doing. Instead, it tended to sacralize the institution of marriage more and more, so as to justify the Church's right to control its practice, and so as to bring it within the jurisdiction of canon lawyers.

Thus, in the last decades of the eleventh century, began the age of the jurists in northern France. It was the time of Pope Urban II and of Yves of Chartres, his devoted agent, both of whom decided to condemn the king of France as the obstinate Nicolaitans had been condemned: to cut him off from the community of the faithful because his marital behavior did not conform to the law.

The parallel development of family structures and ecclesiastical doctrine explains why Philip I was treated more severely than his grandfather Robert had been. But in throwing light on why he was excommunicated, it also tells us why he persisted in his offense.

AROUND

LEVEN

HUNDRED

CHAPTER VII
THE LIVES OF THE SAINTS,
MALE AND FEMALE

We are now back where we started, at the time when clashes between heads of great families and reforming prelates were becoming more common and more serious. The resounding condemnation of King Philip I was the most striking sign, but far from the only one, of the worsening situation. I shall confine myself to one other example: the case of another prince, the count of Poitiers, William IX of Aquitaine, the writer of songs. He had sided with his lord the king, and ordered the bishops to be cudgeled out of his capital when they came to repeat the anathema against Philip.

The fact was that William was in just the same position as his sovereign: he had twice got rid of one wife in order to marry another. After being lawfully separated from his first spouse on grounds of kinship, he soon replaced his second with a "superducta," or supernumerary consort, who was herself married. The prelates excommunicated him, as they had Philip, for incest.

This period of tension repays close examination. Our sources of information are still ecclesiastical, but the world now exerted greater pressure on clerical authors. Whether they hated the world and pretended to flee it, or plunged into it in an effort to save it, they were all beginning to talk more, and more realistically, about the concrete facts of life.

The reforming prelates attacked the highest nobles head on. They accused them of the worst possible crimes, hoping that by branding them as limbs of Satan they would prevent the common people from following their example. And to counterbalance this they praised the heroes of their cause, magnifying their virtues and perpetuating the memory of their deeds. To encourage people to imitate these heroes, they ranked them among the saints, those tutelary beings already among the heavenly hosts, to whom every pious sinner could turn for help and intercession. When pilgrims went to visit their tombs, they were regaled with detailed accounts of their lives.

The first versions of such histories were usually compiled to support the canonization of the saint in question, to persuade the bishop of the diocese or the archbishop of the province to proceed to the solemn elevation of the relics. Written in Latin in a monastery, just like the biography of King Robert, such histories were read and reread in the privacy of the religious communities. They also served as sources of anecdotes for more discursive accounts in sermons preached to unlettered congregations, though, because such discourses do not survive, we can only guess their gist from the original texts.

But these latter do lift a corner of the veil, giving us a glimpse of the Church's pastoral policy and in particular of some aspects of its propaganda about lay marriage. They strike us at first as unattractive, cluttered as they are with platitude and extravagance, and constructed according to the rigid formulae of a long tradition. But if we take them for what they are, some of the most polished weapons in an ideological struggle, they show us how the facts were manipulated to serve a cause and indoctrinate an audience. I have chosen four such works of edification from the region with which we are concerned, all written at the height of the crisis, between 1084 and 1138.

The first is quite different from the rest, more extremist, and comes from a distant source, the abbey of Saint-Claude in the Jura, one of the most ascetic of religious houses. It preaches a fundamental contempt for the world and speaks of marriage as a kind of fall from grace. It is a biography of Saint Simon.[1]

His father, Raoul, was a descendant of Charlemagne and had acquired a number of *comtés*. When he was already count of Vexin and count of Crépy, he got hold of the *comté* of Bar-sur-Aube by marrying the heiress, a widow. The contract had been signed and she was already his *sponsa*, but before the nuptials the knights of the chateau of Joigny handed her over to another nobleman. Raoul hastened back, seized both Joigny and the bride, and shut her up in La Ferté-sur-Aube long enough to make sure she was not pregnant. Then, in his absence, a local squire captured her, but she was rescued and tucked up at last in the count of Crépy's bed, where she eventually bore him two daughters and two sons.

In 1060 Raoul dismissed his wife—either this one or another he had taken since. King Henry I had just died, and now Raoul, by marrying his widow, Anne of Kiev, moved closer to the throne. This was dangerous: Philip I was still only a child. The wife Raoul had repudiated complained to the pope: "Despoiled of everything by her husband, she had been dismissed on a false charge of fornication." Raoul was excommunicated, still not for adultery but for incest: "Contrary to the law, he had lain with the wife of the dead king, who was his cousin." These vicissitudes, known to us through Clarius of Sens and through other texts used by Chifflet and Mabillon, illustrate the use that was made of marriage in this social class before the launching of the Gregorian offensive.

When Raoul was dead, his elder son killed in battle, and his two daughters married, the *"honneur"* of the family passed to Simon, who defended it against all comers, including King Philip. Simon, said to have been tempted by his father's sin of *cupiditas*, and admonished by Gregory VII, by the abbot of Cluny, and by the legate Hugues of Die, for a long time followed monastic practices in secret. In the end he joined the hermits of Saint-Claude and died in Rome around 1080–1082.

Simon's morbid aversion to worldly pleasures distracted him from the family duties with which he found himself encumbered on his brother's early death. He begot no sons. He obstinately refused to marry. Yet when peace was made with the king, he was offered a wife, the most noble and of course most beautiful daughter of the count of La Marche.

Simon pretended to agree to the arrangement, traveling to the Auvergne, going through the ritual of the *desponsatio*, and returning in great pomp for the nuptials. When he arrived the *sponsa* took him in her arms; he offered no resistance, but took care there should be no ardor in the embrace, at least on his side. After he had been conducted to the wedding chamber and everyone thought he was taking his pleasure, he in fact spent the night preaching his wife a sermon. According to his biographer, he outdid Saint Alexis, who was concerned merely with his wife's salvation; for Simon "converted" his lady, persuading her to "renounce lust, continue chaste, and take a vow of virginity." Before dawn he dispatched her to the convent of La Chaise-Dieu and took himself off as quickly as he could, only just escaping the wrath of her father.

No sooner was Simon back in the Ile-de-France than he was summoned to Normandy by William the Conqueror, to whose household his father had sent him to be educated when he was a boy. "Having long experience of your loyalty and affection," said William, "I wish to add a further gift to the fostering you have already received at my hands. I have refused my daughter to suitors of renown, and I bestow her on you, choosing and adopting you as son of my inheritance."

Thus, princes were competing for this young man, still not twenty-five years old but the possessor of vast powers: they wanted him as a son-in-law so that his sons could be their sons' nephews and thereby linked by a bond of special affection to their own family.

Simon, "regarding this favor as diabolical," offered William humble thanks: "Great were the kindnesses with which you surrounded my childhood . . . but we are up against a serious obstacle; my lady the queen, your wife, is connected to me by birth." It was true, though the relationship was a distant one: they were cousins six times removed. William suggested he would make inquiries among the older inhabitants of the region and talk to the bishops and abbots. Suitable gifts of alms could surely remove the impediment. But Simon, count of Crépy, indoctrinated by the Gregorians, answered that the dispensation must come from the pope. He left at once to fetch it, but on the way to Rome he became a monk.

Simon was a shameless liar. The count of La Marche and his daughter; his companions-in-arms who knew nothing of the hair shirt he wore beneath his armor; William, duke of Normandy—he took them all in. This apologia for heroic chastity is also an apologia for saintly cunning. With its farfetched tales of asceticism it belongs to the extravagant fringe of the reform movement, and is very distant from my other three examples.

These belong to a pastoral policy on the part of the Church that was effective because it was moderate and based on social reality. All three were written on the western borders of the principality of Flanders, between Boulogne and Bruges. They set forth, for the instruction of laymen destined to marry, the forms of conjugality that enlightened prelates judged to be sound and salutary.

The hero of one of them is the "most noble" Arnoul, a scion of the Flemish house of Pamele-Audenarde. An angel had appeared to his mother when she was carrying him and told her to name her child Christopher: he would be a bearer of Christ and become a priest. But the head of the family took charge of him, had him baptized with his own name, and as he was a well set-up youth decided that he was to be ceremonially invested with arms "according to the rites of chivalry." He was to be the family's champion. Arnoul performed the duties of a champion valiantly, smiting the enemy and winning fame and glory. "He was offered most illustrious marriages," but refused them. Finally he escaped, though he too had to lie, dressing up for the purpose and telling his mother he was setting off for the French king's court, when in reality he went to the monastery of Saint-Médard de Soissons, where he discarded his "soldier's shield" for a better service, the service of God.

Arnoul, like Simon, rejected the married state for himself. But at least he did not attempt to keep other people from it. Instead, he tried to help them to be virtuous within their marriages.

The account of his life demonstrates the moral attitude of the Church in both its aspects. Marriage (1) is dangerous, so those aspiring to perfection eschew it. This was the stance both of the out-and-out ascetics and of the heretics. But marriage (2) does suit ordinary men, and God accords it his blessing because it ensures the reproduction of society and the preservation of social hierarchies. This was the ethic of the Carolingians.

Arnoul, tonsured but clinging to his military habits, created some disturbance in the cloister and was removed to a cell outside. In his seclusion he remained silent for forty-two months, and then began talking nonstop through the small window of his cell.[2] He uttered exhortations and advice, addressed particularly to the Flemings and Brabantines (Flemish and Belgians), and his reputation grew. As a recognized defender of lineal *"honneur"* and the family virtues, he acted as mentor in the sort of difficulties that especially preoccupied the aristocracy at that time, i.e., questions of kinship. He helped to make marriages successful, or in other words prolific. As we have already seen, it was through Arnoul's intercession that providence at last gave Philip I's queen, Berthe, a son. Arnoul himself chose for the child the royal name of Louis.

Another wife also had recourse to his powers.[3] Her husband, one of Saint Arnoul's former companions-in-arms, had fallen into bad ways, and heaven had punished him for it: all his children had died, one after the other, and now he was seriously ill, at the point of death. His nephews were only waiting for his demise to eject his wife and seize her dower—an example of the danger that always hung over a widow without children. But Arnoul took the threatened lady under his protection, and the ailing knight was brought on a litter "before his window." Arnoul exhorted him to mend his ways, and in particular to pay the bishop his tithes. To the wife the saint promised a great happiness "because she had tended her husband faithfully during his illness." The morality governing virtuous marriages rewarded wives who served their lords and masters well. Three months later the knight, restored to health, begot a son and heir, much to the annoyance of his kinsmen, and the virtuous mother "lived long enough to see her child lawfully married and the begetter of sons of his own."

Arnoul, with a reputation for talents like this, became the hope of the great families. Not only did he intercede to make marriages prolific—a point on which ecclesiastical and lay morality most nearly converged—but he also helped parents prevent their children from making misalliances, another level on which the two points of view agreed.

Guy of Châtillon-sur-Marne had betrothed his daughter to a knight,[4] a good match and his own equal in fortune as well as in birth. Unfortunately the girl preferred another, inferior in advantages, and swore she would kill herself if deprived of "the embraces she desired." The parents consulted the recluse, and Arnoul, faithfully interpreting episcopal policy, began by recalling the principle of common consent. We seem to hear an echo of Yves of Chartres himself—who was arguing in support of the same principle at the very time that the abbot of Oudenbourg was preparing to write Saint Arnoul's life story. "Canonic authority," says Arnoul, "forbids that a girl should ever be married to a man she does not want. I therefore enjoin you to give the maid to the man she loves, so as not to force her into unseemliness." But wait, he goes on, and you will see your daughter "begging for the very *sponsus* from whom she now longs to get away." Just do as she wishes for the time being, he told the parents, and your *"honneur"* will not suffer.

The parents followed Arnoul's advice and were not sorry for it. We must not suppose Arnoul was relying on what the text refers to as "girlish inconstancy," expecting the young wife to commit adultery with her parents' favored suitor and abandon the first marriage for a second. That was impossible, for the first marriage was indissoluble. But Arnoul had a miracle up his sleeve.

The man the girl loved was a "youth," one of the gallants whom parents of high rank dreaded to see hanging around their daughters. But he had a reputation as a knight, and after his marriage tried to add to his fame by continuing to risk his life. It was not long before he lost it, and the difficult daughter was left a widow. Heaven had chosen this roundabout way of ensuring that she should "return to the love of the husband her parents had chosen for her from the beginning and, joined to the second husband, bear with a quiet heart the loss of the first."

Thus, love was reconciled with virtuous marriage. God, touched by his pious servant's prayer and the pious parents' hopes, permitted family politics and episcopal instructions to fit in neatly with each other.

My two remaining examples are particularly instructive. They tell the stories of two women, one unhappily married and the other the mother of many children. Their biographies were intended to put forward a female model of marriage, but at the same time they also reveal what marriage was actually like for noblewomen at that time. Both by what they say and what they leave out, by the way they either embellish or denigrate the real facts, they show how Church leaders tried, discreetly and within certain bounds, to correct matrimonial practices among the laity.

The first of these two histories, or at least the original version of it, was written in 1084, when the bishop of Noyon-Tournai, aided by the count of Flanders, was trying to bring some order into the marshy areas on the shores of the North Sea, a wild country gradually being won from the stagnant waters.[5]

In the parish of Ghistelle, near Oudenbourg (where the bishop had charged Saint Arnoul with establishing a Benedictine community), a cult had spontaneously grown up around a certain burial place. The sick came and drank water from a nearby pond in the hope of being cured. All around the grave the mud had turned into stones, which when the faithful took them back home turned into gems. The woman buried there was venerated and prayed to as a martyr: she was said to have been murdered by her husband's henchmen.

This upsurge of popular religiosity had to be controlled and directed into proper channels, so it was decided that the relics should be solemnly elevated and the woman proclaimed a saint. By way of preparation for the ceremonies, Drogon, a monk from a neighboring abbey who was an expert in hagiography, was charged with recording the legend and turning it into a work of edification. A few years later his text was revised and made more effective by another monk.[6]

The name of the woman whose beneficent powers were radiating around Ghistelle was Godelive, a Germanic name. The second of her biographers considered it necessary to translate the name, for devotion was beginning to spread in areas where the Romanic tongue was spoken. The new name was Cara Deo, beloved of God, a very suitable name for a saint. Too suitable, perhaps. Yet she was not a myth. Contemporary records bear traces of her father, a knight who was a vassal of Count Eustache of Boulogne. So Godelive too was born of "famous parents," though in one of the lower strata of the aristocracy, as was her husband Bertolf. He was one of the count's officers in the Bruges area and was described as "powerful" and "of distinguished race according to the flesh." So the couple were well matched in rank. But the marriage was not a successful one, and this *Life* of Saint Godelive (see note 5) describes its defects in order to show what a marriage really ought to be. First it should be arranged by the two families concerned, and they ought to begin by considering the moral qualities of the man and woman involved.

In Godelive's case her father and mother did indeed make the fateful choice. Their daughter was suitably meek; she was pretty, too, though dark, with black hair and brows. Drogon hastens to add that this only made her skin look the whiter, "which is delightful and pleasing in women and a credit in many." So she was surrounded by a swarm of suitors professing "love." But her parents "chose Bertolf because of his *dos*": he was the richest of the candidates. But to marry for money was to ask for trouble. There was also another flaw: Bertolf had done nothing to attract or woo the girl herself. (She did not, however, have to be consulted; he spoke directly to her parents.) But—and here was the snag—he acted entirely on his own, being a younger son who had left home to seek his fortune. Yet he too had a mother and father, and he ought at least to have asked their opinion. He was later reproached for this, and the rebuke was a weighty one. A fundamental principle, accepted unconditionally by heads of kinship networks, was that a good marriage was the business not of individuals but of families.

A second precept was that a husband had charge over his wife and must stay with her. Now it so happened that Bertolf came to hate his wife, and this happened immediately, when, in accordance with custom, he was taking her from her parents' house in the Boulonnais to his own place at Ghistelle, near the coast of Flanders, where he lived with his mother. Bertolf's mother was separated from his father, so in this "little house" the matrimonial bed was vacant. It was a longish journey for the bridal couple, and they had to sleep on the way. In the course of the trip the devil made the husband change his mind, and his aversion was only strengthened by his mother's attitude when the travelers arrived: she made fun of the bride's looks and of her black hair.

Bertolf's family were at fault in not giving his wife a better welcome, but, as Drogon said, "all mothers-in-law hate their daughters-in-law. They long for their sons to get married, but when they do they soon grow jealous of them and their wives." (Here is one of the reasons why this biography is so interesting. Its concrete references to ordinary, everyday life and its quotations of popular sayings make it more informative than a straightforward chronicle.) So Bertolf would have nothing to do with his wife. He began by refusing to take part in the nuptial ceremony, which in accordance with custom took place in his own house. During the three days that the ceremony lasted his place was taken by his mother. That a woman should play this role was scandalous: both moral and sexual order was violated.

Then Godelive was left alone in the conjugal home. *Desolata*, she spent all day at her loom and all night at her prayers. "With the aid of these two shields"—work and prayer—"she warded off the shafts of the daydreams with which young people are commonly afflicted." It was Godelive's second biographer who invented this description. His job was to make the previous version more convincing, and with this in mind he sought to show that Godelive, though abandoned to her own devices, did not fall into bad ways. For it was generally believed that women, and especially young women, succumbed to sin, i.e., lust, as soon as they had no man to keep an eye on them. In the case of a married woman such surveillance was the duty of the husband. He should be there in times of both good and bad fortune, and since "by right" he was bound to be a support to his wife, he should live with her "patiently" until death. They were two in one flesh, or rather "through marital union they formed but one body."

The flesh, the body. . . . As far as I can see, those who originally supported Godelive's canonization never thought of regarding her as a virgin martyr, though by the time the Bollandists—Belgian Jesuits—

published the second version of the *Vita* it was chiefly as a virgin that she was venerated in Ghistelle. But in the eleventh century she was looked upon as a wife, a woman in the fullest sense of the word, and it was as such that in the two texts I am now examining she was put forward as an example of conjugal virtue.

For the Church's third principle was that once a marriage was consummated by the *copulatio conjugii*, it was indissoluble.

Bertolf deserted Godelive. He wanted to get rid of her. But according to her biographers the idea of simply repudiating her never crossed his or his father's mind. Instead, the family plotted against her and treated her so harshly that she began to break down. They put her on bread and water, and, worn out by all these "insults," she fled. But that was a sin. It was only to be expected, but Drogon makes no allowances. The monk of Oudenbourg, touching up the first version of the biography, admits that by running away Godelive broke the "law of the Gospel," which forbids anyone to separate those whom God has joined. A wife had no right to leave the marital home. Godelive did leave, barefoot and hungry, but accompanied by a manservant (only immodest women traveled without an escort). She appealed for justice to her father, the man bound to defend her rights if her husband failed to do so. Her father, without much enthusiasm, complained to the count of Flanders, the unsatisfactory husband's lord.

At this point both versions of the *Life* insert a passage claiming that the Church alone had jurisdiction over marriage. As far as I know these two documents are the earliest ones to make such a claim in this region. Drogon neatly gives the argument to the count, who says he is not competent to judge such matters. They concern "Christendom," and it is up to the bishop to lead those who "stray from the holy order" back into the strait and narrow path. "I am but an auxiliary," he says, meaning he represents only the secular arm.

It was for the bishop to admonish, and for the count, if necessary, to constrain. This was a Gregorian division of labor, with *auctoritas*, or authority, on the one hand and *potestas*, or power, on the other, and the spiritual given preeminence over the temporal.

The bishop of Noyon-Tournai decided it was his duty to reconcile husband and wife. There was no presumption of adultery, no question raised as to the husband's impotence, no doubt cast on the consummation of the marriage. Godelive was not so lucky as the count of Meulan's wife (see page 87). For since then canon law had become more rigid, now requiring that she be brought back under Bertolf's roof.

Bertolf swore an oath not to mistreat her anymore, but he kept her shut up alone, without any contact with men. People were shocked at this privation and pitied her for being without "bodily pleasures." But she affected to despise such things. At this point in the story, which is full of echoes of Marian liturgy, we catch a glimpse of the ideology of *contemptus mundi*, contempt of the world. But it is no more than a glimpse. For the saint, accepting her privations, was already on the road to martyrdom: Bertolf had made up his mind to do away with her, to have her killed one night by a couple of his serfs.

So he reappeared one evening, a smile on his lips, and made his astonished spouse sit on a cushion near him, in just the classical arrangement for amorous conversation. Then he took her in his arms and kissed and embraced her. She, though not responding, offered no resistance. She was prepared to perform her marital duties if they were demanded of her. "You are not used to my presence," Bertolf whispered, "or to being delighted with sweet words, or to the shared joys of the flesh"—this last being a necessary element in a virtuous marriage—". . . I mean to put a true end to our spiritual divorce, to treat you as my beloved wife, and, gradually leaving hate behind, to make our souls and bodies one again . . . [for in you] I have found a woman who undertakes to join us together through her constant love, making us love one another forever, more than any husband and wife on earth before."

This was a eulogy not only of spiritual but also of physical love, and the corollary was that, if a magic potion was necessary, it must be used. Bertolf's speech was also an encomium on feminine submission, and after some hesitation Godelive gave in. "I am the servant of the Lord, and trust in Him. If it can be done without crime," she would go with the servants he would send to take her to the sorceress. They strangled her on the way.

The hagiographer marvels at such virtue. First Godelive turned to

God, fearing to separate herself from Him by dealing in magic. But then she agreed to do so, deciding in favor of marriage "so as not to be separated from the Lord who joins together husbands and wives." Here is the principal and astonishing lesson of this pious work. Marriages are made by God Himself. They are therefore holy. But this sanctification includes the flesh, together with the love that is referred to throughout, a love that in no way violates the necessary hierarchy by which an obedient wife is subject to her husband. The couple not only speak of love, they also make it. And though in 1084 the bishop of Noyon showed himself to be bolder than many of his colleagues would dare to be for a long while; though he was both clear-sighted and aware of the need to adjust his teaching to reality; yet he does not seem to have wanted this tale of an unhappy marriage to be used as an excuse for regarding true marriage as anything but a complete and loving union of body and soul.

Our other female champion of the matrimonial virtues is very different from Godelive. She is Ide, countess of Boulogne, a very great lady whose married life was a great success. The Church authorities were urged to canonize Ide not by the people but by her grand-daughter and heiress, the wife of Etienne of Blois.[7] In 1130, when Etienne thought his chances of becoming king of England were improving, his wife began to campaign for having the second of her grandmothers recognized as a saint, the first, Margaret of Scotland, already enjoying that status. So the monks of Vasconvillier, the guardians of Ide's grave, were asked to write the story of her life.[8]

There was nothing unusual about Ide's life except that she was Godefroi of Bouillon's[9] mother, so the biographer had to make motherhood the main theme of his panegyric. His reluctance is already visible in the prologue, where he tries to explain away the position in which he finds himself. The saints, he says, help mankind to resist the assaults of the Devil; so providence has placed them in all ranks of society. Even in the inferior stratum made up of women. There are women among the saints; married women, even. But of course they must be mothers. In such cases they are "entered in the book of life by reason of their merits and the merits of their sons." Then comes a eulogy on virtuous marriage: it is a cure for lust; when lived "according to the law," it is blessed with fruitfulness; it must be chaste. "True, virginity is good, but it has been shown that chastity after childbirth is great."

Once having set up these principles as a safeguard, a Benedictine might risk demonstrating how a married woman could be a saint. He does so discreetly, in the Cluniac manner, with an acute sense of social timing. Like the bishop of Noyon, but tending in the opposite direction, he adapts the teaching of the Gospels and of Saint Augustine to the secular values prized among the higher aristocracy.

In his account of Ide's exemplary married life the words *genus*, *gignere*, and *generositas* constantly recur. They all have a physical connotation, insisting on the notion of blood, that is, aristocratic blood and noble birth. "By the mercy of God," Ide was a link in a genealogical chain. In 1057, when she was sixteen or seventeen, she was judiciously given in marriage by her father, the mighty duke of Lothier. He had taken counsel, and mindful of the fame that allowed "the valiant to join together," accepted the offer put forward in due form by the envoys of Count Eustache II of Boulogne, a "hero" of "most noble race" and "of the blood of Charlemagne."

Ide, married to Eustache "in accordance with the usage of the catholic Church," led a married life typical of all good Christian wives. This entailed first of all obedience: her piety increased "by agreement with her husband and by his will." How could a wife be pious against her husband's wishes? She was also discreet in the management of her home. And she was chaste. She conceived children "according to the apostolic precept," i.e., "by using her husband as though she had no husband," eschewing pleasure. No mention is made of any daughters, but of her three sons the second was Godefroi de Bouillon and the third Baudouin, king of Jerusalem.

As a girl Ide had been told of the glory that would spring from her womb. In a dream she saw the sun descend from the sky and rest for a moment in her bosom. The biographer takes care to dispel any suspicion of adolescent eroticism. Ide was asleep, he says, but her mind was turned "toward higher things." So the dream, far from inciting her to lewdness, was a portent of holy motherhood. Ide decided to suckle her sons herself, a practice apparently uncommon among the aristocracy at the time: she wanted to prevent her boys from being contaminated and "led into wicked ways" by another woman's milk. In this work of edification a generous body obedient to the husband's authority is the source of all the good for which the female saint is revered.

After Ide's husband, Eustache, died in about 1070, she remained a widow, "rejoicing in the nobility of her sons," "enriched by the love of heaven," and "united to the eternal bridegroom by a life of charity and celibacy." Women must always have some man to guide them; so, having passed from her father's authority to that of her husband, she now came under that of her eldest son, who had succeeded his father as Eustache III.

Ide went on producing offspring, no longer through the flesh now but through her wealth, or more precisely through her money. For she had handed over her hereditary possessions to the men of her family in exchange for cash. She used these funds (the ultimate source of which was still her father's *genus*—and acting of course with the "counsel" and "advice" of Count Eustache) to bring forth spiritual sons, rebuilding and restoring churches throughout the Boulonnais region and founding three monasteries. They were all for men only; none but her male progeniture mattered.

In this way Ide gradually came to belong to another family. The abbot of Cluny adopted her "as a daughter." But, though she left her son's house, she did not become a nun. Still under a man's direction—that of the abbot of La Capelle-Sainte-Marie—she lived near the monastery with her female attendants, taking part in the services, but "in moderation." Her main activity, however, was as a foster-mother, comforting and caring for the poor and the monks, "serving" men as women always should. The miracles she performed bore further witness to her maternal powers.

One morning a little girl who was dumb took refuge under her cloak. This was analogous to another pregnancy, and the child, born again in spirit, began to speak. Her first word was "mother." But later she sinned and had a child out of wedlock. Twice this happened; twice she went dumb again; twice Ide cured her, cleansing her of her impurity.

This made-to-order panegyric was addressed to the men who were the heads of aristocratic families. It instructed them on chastity and "the ways of the catholic Church"—but discreetly. Nevertheless, in order that at least part of the message should get across, the text laid great stress on the need for wives to submit to their husbands, and on the genetic function of the female body. It did not trouble to mention love. Instead, it celebrated parturition and the established order, praising a sanctity related solely to the former.

The Cluniacs were well aware of the main value ascribed to women in the seats of the mighty, and of what the heads of noble familes expected to be told.

CHAPTER VIII
GUIBERT OF NOGENT

I now come to two documents of exceptional interest, written at the same time as the lives of the saints examined in chapter VII, and by authors from the same region of Beauvaisis.

One is very inward-looking, the work of a monk living in a small abbey near Laon. Its author, Guibert, was a Benedictine who had withdrawn from the world and was haunted in his anxious seclusion by an image of marriage largely inspired by fantasy.

The second document, on the other hand, looks outward onto the world of reality both intellectually and socially, being concerned with learning and with urban life. We are back again, in fact, to the writings of Yves, bishop of Chartres, who was wholeheartedly engaged in direct action. Gradually, through a consideration of precise and concrete problems, Yves built up a pastoral policy and theory of marriage that became the established view of the Church's rigorist scholars.

In 1115, eleven years after Philip I's reconciliation with the Church, Guibert, the sixty-year-old abbot of Nogent-sous-Coucy, wrote his *Memoirs*.[1] They make up an extraordinary book, blending autobiography in the manner of Saint Augustine with straightforward chronicle. History is seen in terms of one then-recent scandalous event: the outbreak of communal riots in the nearby town of Laon in the year 1112. It may well have been these disturbances that actually brought the monk to write his book—to emerge from his meditations to consider the urban world, with its financiers, its rapacious knights, and all the secular impurities that should normally be shunned by the devout. Guibert depicted that world in all its wickedness in order to persuade those to whom his book would be read to aspire more ardently than ever to that unsullied world, that promised Paradise, prefigured symbolically here below in the monasteries and the Holy Land.

Seven years earlier Guibert had written another book, *The Action of God as Revealed Through the Franks*, celebrating the great eastward migration designed to bridle military violence and redeem the soldiery from its sins. By setting out for Jerusalem, knights could escape the corruption of the world just as others could by shutting themselves up in a cloister. When Guibert embarked on his *Memoirs* his object was to provide "examples" to help his brother monks in their striving for perfection, though at the same time he hoped to find an audience outside the walls of the abbey. But the book was based on the single postulate that the world was loathsome, and in making use of his evidence we should bear in mind that his systematic pessimism is bound to have distorted his view.[2]

And yet by its very excesses the book paints an instructive picture of matrimonial behavior among the knightly classes in the second half of the eleventh century. Guibert speaks at length about his childhood, and thus about his father and mother.[3] His father, like Godelive's, belonged to the lesser stratum of the aristocracy. He was one of the knights attached to the chateau of Clermont-en-Beauvaisis, and had been married in 1040, when the reform movement within the Church was just beginning. His father-in-law was a man of power and importance, the protector of the monastery of Saint-Germer-de-Fly (of which Anselm of Canterbury was once prior) and a rung above his son-in-law in the aristocratic hierarchy. This was common enough: the wife of Eustache of Boulogne had been of higher rank than he, and Bertolf's case was probably similar. Guibert's mother was not an heiress, so she came to live in her husband's house. Guibert speaks of his father as a "youth" at the time of his marriage, but this tells us nothing about his age. The bride was just twelve, the limit below which both secular custom and canon law forbade girls to be married. It was not surprising, therefore, that the marriage was not consummated at once. Yet there was an immediate outcry, with people alleging that the sort of magic described by Bourchard of Worms in his *Medicus* was to blame. But the culprit casting the spell, instead of being, as usual, some rejected concubine, was said to be "a little old woman," the groom's jealous stepmother, who had wanted him to marry one of her own nieces. Guibert had no doubt that witchcraft had been at work, saying that "among the ignorant," meaning the laity, such magic was common practice. In fact, the habit of marrying girls off at such a tender age often resulted in similar mishaps.

An incomplete marriage was useless to a family because it produced no heirs. Similarly, since it did not extinguish lust, it did not fulfil the function required of it by many churchmen. Could it be regarded as a real marriage? It is not certain, at this period, that the marriage had actually been consecrated. Did the *desponsatio* alone constitute so close a tie that it could not simply be undone? It is worth noting that those concerned in this case shrank from merely breaking the whole thing off without more ado. Due ceremony was observed. The husband as well as the wife was advised to enter religious orders: was not a monastery the proper place for a man who was impotent? Many churchmen thought the couple should part in this way, by common consent. But the husband refused.

After three years had gone by another solution was tried. The canonical texts brought together by Bourchard of Worms allowed a man unable to have sexual intercourse with his wife to divorce her. But his inability had to be proved. "Evil advisers"[4] urged the young man in this case to try another partner and, "as is the way of young men," he boldly did so. He took a concubine, though this could hardly be regarded as bigamy; after all, was he really married? Moreover, the partner chosen for the experiment was of low birth and had no standing as an actual wife. Concubinage still flourished, then, at a lower level than that of lawful marriage. The result was conclusive: a child was born. But it soon died, as did many infants, accidentally or otherwise, legitimate or illegitimate, though the death rate was higher among the illegitimate. In any event, the marriage could not now be dissolved on grounds of the husband's impotence.

So the family set to work on the wife. First they mistreated her in the hope that she would run away and thus break the marriage up on grounds of desertion. The girl was subjected to, and survived, humiliations similar to those Godelive had been unable to withstand. The parallel between the two stories is striking: Guibert wanted his mother too to be regarded as a holy woman [although he never took official steps to that end], and emphasized both her beauty and her fortitude. She bore all the hardships heaped upon her.

One more ground for divorce remained: fornication on the part of the wife. Attempts were made to force the girl into infidelity, or at least to persuade the parents to break off the *desponsatio* themselves in order to arrange a better match. A "very rich man" was lured into the house. But still the girl resisted. God, comments her son, gave her a piety stronger than her "nature" and her "youth." Grace saved her from "burning." Her heart—meaning her blood—remained under control. Guibert saw his mother as an anti-Eve, the strong and virtuous woman of the Scriptures, the wise virgin, chaste and cold as charity.

At last, seven years after the nuptial ceremony (though we must remember that seven was a symbolical number; if it is correct, the wife would then have been getting on for twenty), her husband "knew" her. The spell on his virility had been broken by another "little old woman," using countermagic of the kind that Godelive's husband had pretended to have recourse to. Neither Guibert of Nogent nor the monk of

Bergues-Saint-Winock telling the story of the saint condemns this use of sorcery. It was pleasing to God as long as it was white magic, promoting lawful unions. At all events, when this solution was reached, the wife, meek as Godelive, "submitted herself to her conjugal duties," passive as a good wife should be, unflinchingly lending herself to her husband for him to release his excess energies.

A marriage was blessed when it was fruitful, and this one was eminently so. Girls are not mentioned, but apart from them there were four sons (one also a monk at Nogent, like Guibert). Guibert was the last-born, and his mother nearly died bringing him into the world. He complacently describes her further ordeal, a labor lasting more than a day.[5] The pains began on Good Friday, in sympathy with the sufferings of Christ. Because the mother looked as if she were dying, those about her wanted to have a Mass said, but the liturgy prescribed for the day before Easter did not allow this. So the child about to be born was offered up at the altar to the Virgin Mary: if the baby was a boy he would go into the Church; if it was of the "inferior" sex, *deterior*, the girl would remain a virgin. The child was born, the mother revived; it was a boy.

Guibert was eight months old when his father died. He calls this death providential: if his father had lived he would probably have gone back on his vow and made him into a knight.

The family now began to consider how to get rid of the widow.[6] She was no longer of use: she had produced enough sons—too many, even. She still had her dower, though, and her influence over her sons. Her family were approached: Would they not like to take her back? She was still young, and could be used to make other marriages. Holding her own against those who would get rid of her, the lady took Christ as her protector: it was difficult to drive her away from the foot of the cross. So she stayed, but was still in the clutches of her husband's relatives.

Her brother-in-law's son, now head of the family, considered it his duty to treat her as he treated his own sisters, daughters, and nieces, and to provide her with a husband. And power was so distributed within the family that she could not oppose his decision. But at least, she insisted, the man should be of higher rank than herself. They could not deny her this; she was of better birth than they, and that strengthened her position. But, as we have seen, hypergamy, or social superiority in the wife, was the rule in aristocratic marriages. This disparity exacerbated men's fear of women, provoking them to project the notion of defilement onto their wives as a way, according to Mary Douglas,[7] of exorcizing the danger the women embodied.

In the present instance the condition laid down by the lady was an insurmountable obstacle to her remarriage. It was impossible to reverse the usual balance and still find a suitable husband. So Guibert's mother, through her obstinacy, managed not to break "the union of her body with that of her husband by the substitution of another flesh." Unlike the heretics, the official Church did not condemn remarriage. But rigorists like Guibert considered, with Saint Jerome, that widowhood, though inferior to virginity, was much more meritorious than the married state. And Guibert's mother, like Saint Ide, chose to impose on herself the special obligations required of that *ordo.*

The first of these duties was, by certain pious practices, to relieve the sufferings of the souls of the departed. Guibert gives a striking example. He relates how his mother saw her dead husband appear in corporeal form, like the risen Christ. Like Christ, the spirit forbade his body to be touched. He had a wound in his side, and nearby lay a wailing infant. The wound in the side, by Adam's rib, meant that the husband had broken the marriage pact. Guibert believed that his father had sinned by taking a concubine after the *desponsatio.* Guibert thus shared the view of Yves of Chartres, who at the same time Guibert was writing his *Memoirs* was endeavoring to establish the ruling that, even if the nuptials had not yet taken place, nor the couple's bodies been united, a husband and wife were indissolubly married if they had given their mutual consent to the union and exchanged vows. It had come, then, to be accepted that concubinage was no different from fornication. So Guibert found his father guilty of fornication and bigamy.

As for the child in the vision, it was of course the bastard who had died unbaptized and was therefore now in torment. Guibert's mother asked the apparition what she should do. Works of charity, answered the dead man, who then revealed the name of his illicit partner, a woman still alive and living in the house: new evidence of how sexual exuberance might be indulged in under the culprit's own roof. Guibert's saintly mother, to aid the dead child's redemption, adopted a newborn infant, thus taking the sin upon herself. As a penance she undertook to endure its crying—another indication that ladies of the aristocracy did not usually take care of their infants themselves.

As a widow, Guibert's mother was also bound to fast, to attend the offices of the Church, and to be generous in the giving of alms. She in fact gave away most of the income from her dower, at the expense of her husband's relatives. But finally, after twelve years, she left.[8]

Imagine her position. She was now in her thirties, surrounded by men but entrenched in her chastity. She had gradually fallen into the power of the priests, in particular of the priest who lived in her house and taught her sons. He was also her spiritual director, and interpreted her dreams. One morning, to the great surprise of her children, friends, and relations, she said she had dreamed of remarriage. There could be no doubt about it: the new husband was Christ, and it was to Him she wished to be united.

Women in her position lived their frustrated lives hemmed in by clerics great and small, all trying to gain power over them. But sometimes the priests were challenged. In this case one of their opponents ran through the house crying out that "the priests have nailed a cross on this woman's back!" Guibert says he was possessed.

Be that as it may, Guibert's mother left, accompanied by her confessor, and went to live at the gates of the monastery of Saint-Germer. She cut off her hair, made herself look older, dressed like a nun. She had crossed the Rubicon; her youngest son followed her and entered the monastery.

Guibert was exceptionally intelligent and sensitive. I see him as typical of all the late-born sons of couples like his parents. What we are able to glimpse of his childhood shows him rejected—because of the lack of a father and his mother's adoption of the illegitimate child to redeem her husband's sin. Moreover, Guibert was destined for the Church, for he came from a military environment where all attention was concentrated on his eldest brother, a knight, and on his cousin, the head of the family, whom Guibert hated.[9]

His isolation and resentment made him cling to his mother and regard her with morbid reverence.[10] She was beautiful, modest, and above all chaste. She at least, amid the brutishness and violence of the knightly race around her, despised the flesh and shut her ears to obscene stories. Guibert clung to her apron strings: the first time he was separated from her was when he was made abbot of Nogent; he was then over fifty. A similar bond joined him to the Virgin Mary, to whom he had been dedicated even before he was born (see page 143). For him she was the lady par excellence, the mother who was inaccessible and— unlike his earthly one—undefiled.

At Saint-Germer, when he was twenty, Guibert wrote a treatise on virginity, refuting Eusebius of Caesarea and proving that Saint Paul was never married. Guibert is an excellent example of the frustration of younger sons. Some became soldiers and worked off their complexes in adventure, abduction, or—a milder form of the latter—the ritual of courtly love. Others became priests or monks, devoted themselves to the Virgin, and campaigned to eliminate the physical and pleasurable elements from marriage.

Like all the "youths" forced to remain celibate by the system of kinship networks, Guibert bore a grudge against the *"seniores"* lucky enough to have wives. He condemned them in the person of his father, berated him just as the young Catalans whom Pierre Bonnassie (see page 93) came across in eleventh-century archives did their fathers, hauling them before judges and charging them with heresy, drunkenness, and lust.

The grudge was linked to two obsessions. The first was a hatred of bloodshed and violence, i.e., of masculine force. In Guibert's *Treatise on Relics* this takes the form of disgust for the sordid physical remains that were venerated as sacred tokens. The second obsession was a hatred of sex, reflected in the *Memoirs* by stories about castration—all the tales of Laonnais lords mutilating prisoners taken in battle and hanging them up by their testicles.

Guibert remembered one story related to him by the abbot of Cluny's nephew, and liked it so much he included it in his book. It concerned a young husband guilty of loving his wife too well[11]—"not like a husband, which would be normal, but like a usurer, which is not." He equates an immoderate love of money with an immoderate love of sexual pleasure. The young man, going on pilgrimage to Compostella, had taken his wife's girdle, or belt, with him, and the Devil appeared to him in the form of Saint James and ordered him to castrate himself. He did so, then cut his throat.

The idea of emasculation was linked to horror of women, a fear that was reinforced within religious houses by the tales told by inmates who had taken the habit late, and were not virgins, to others like Guibert, who had no direct experience of such things. One such witness to the voraciousness of women was the elderly Beauvaisis nobleman who took refuge in Saint-Germer, half-dead with exhaustion: "His wife performed more energetically than he in matters of the marriage bed."[12] Whether it was a question of widowers marrying young girls as their second wives, or youths marrying younger girls still as their first, men were terrified of women. In the old days, says Guibert, at least they had been modest.[13] But how could they be modest now, dressed provocatively, surrounded by would-be seducers, tempted by bad example?

Guibert's view of the outside world was distorted not only by his didactic purpose but also by attitudes arising out of his childhood experience—in other words, out of the marriage practices of his class and time.

What happened in the city of Laon in 1112 showed how sadly the world was going to rack and ruin. Guibert demonstrates how the abscess that burst in the riots had been forming in the course of a long drawn-out conflict.[14] The protagonists were Thomas of Marle, a lustful and sexually perverse lord, and Sybilla, his stepmother, equally lewd and perverse, the new wife, *superinducta*, of his father, the lord of Coucy. It was a duel between Mars and Venus, blood and sex, and behind it lay the sins of the flesh. Sybille was a Messalina,[15] and to marry her the lord of Coucy had repudiated his wife, Thomas's mother, herself guilty of fornication. Thomas himself was probably a bastard. Thus, the final explosion—social warfare, with the common people daring to rebel against their natural masters, and in their fury actually plotting against them—had its origins in lust. Guibert had no doubts on this score, as we see by the way he frequently relates the riots to the marriage.

Reading Guibert, we at first get the impression that attitudes changed extremely slowly. This is a useful lesson to historians, who are always inclined to overestimate the immediate influence of innovation. The sort of behavior described in the *Memoirs* scarcely differs from that glimpsed more briefly in the records dating from around the year 1000. The same heresy as that denounced by Gérard of Cambrai eighty years earlier was still present, just as deep-rooted and all the more entrenched because of its support among the peasantry. To counter this heresy and its condemnation of marriage, Guibert takes up the words of Adhémar de Chabannes and of Paul, the monk from Saint-Père of Chartres[16]: to reject marriage is to give free rein to all the impulses of lust. The sect to which the heretics belong was an association of equals, a commune as repugnant as the municipal commune that caused the riots, but sexual instead of civic. And again we hear the same old story of how, at night, men and women secretly mingle, and when the torches are put out indulge in orgies. The offspring of such excesses are burned, and their ashes mixed in dough to make the heretical Eucharist. But now there was something new: the pretense of chastity conceals homosexuality. "Men go with men, women with women, for they deem it impious for the man to enter the woman." How could it be otherwise? The only couples who can escape temptation are those who, like Simon of Crépy and his *sponsa*, retire into separate cloisters.

If heresy survived, so did Nicolaitism. Guibert's relatives wanted to take him away from Saint-Germer so that he could make a career for himself in the secular Church [in parishes, not within a religious order, or rule]. This was around 1075, when, according to the *Memoirs*, the movement against married priests was gaining force in northern France, or north of the Alps as the text puts it. Certain noble families backed the campaign, hoping the purge would make it easier to place some of their sons in good clerical posts.

The head of Guibert's family managed to have a married canon dismissed, and prepared to install his young kinsman in the post thus vacated. But the canon fought back and, having influential connections, was able not only to get the whole of Guibert's family excommunicated for simony but also to keep both his job and his wife. So resistance to the Gregorian reform was both powerful and effective, and was still making itself felt when Guibert finished his *Memoirs*. A council held in Soissons in 1121 had to wage a hard struggle to maintain clerical celibacy. There were strong arguments against it. A life of Saint Norbert, founder of Prémontré, quite close to Nogent, related how in 1125 a little boy of five, unconsciously siding with those who regarded clerics as men like any others, had a vision of the child Jesus being borne in the arms of a married priest.[17]

In the early twelfth century, habit also weighed as heavily as ever on matrimonial practices. In particular, concubinage still survived among the aristocracy. As already mentioned, Guibert had no liking for the head of his family. "He [the family head] refused," he said, "to be ruled by the law of the laity"; i.e., he would not obey the Gregorian rule and contract a lawful marriage. This was his "debauchery," and Guibert refers to the consort of this provost (or steward of the king's rights in the city of Laon), the mother of the provost's children, as his "concubine."[18] This word as used by churchmen applied to any wife who was unlawful, whether because of bigamy or of incest. It is what Guibert called Sybille of Coucy.[19] But did not the term also express the disapproval felt by Guibert and the leaders of the Church for any couple whose nuptials had not been celebrated according to the prescribed rituals? Wasn't the "debauched" cousin simply rejecting the ceremony the priests were trying to impose?

We know that at about this time, in 1116, the monk Henry of Lausanne, who was to be condemned for heresy in Toulouse in 1119, was preaching in Le Mans not against marriage itself but, as the "spiritualists" in Orleans had done in 1022, against the sacralization of marriage. "Consent in itself constitutes a marriage," Henry proclaimed, agreeing on this point with orthodox opinion, "whoever the person"—he believed questions of birth and kinship were not the Church's business—"and without need for celebration, publication, or institution on the part of the Church."

However much the rigorists denounced them as incitements to free love and hence to fornication, such pronouncements were based on a contempt for the flesh they themselves shared. It was unseemly to mix sacred matters with the rites preceding procreation, the union of the sexes being unavoidably repugnant. To declare that marriage should be entered into quite freely was a threat to family politics, and monk Henry had to flee. But his preaching also went counter to the clergy's desire to involve itself in marriage ceremonies. They were already making attempts at it in this region at the beginning of the eleventh century, as is shown by the reactions of the canons of Orleans in 1022. Had they achieved their ends a hundred years later?

Outside the royal and a few princely families, it does seem that the marriage ritual remained secular for a very long time. This is certainly true of the nuptial festivities, the banquet, and the procession leading the couple to their house and wedding chamber. But what about the betrothal, the *traditio* or ceding of the bride by the leaders of her family? The Cluniac records of *sponsalicia* mention God and love as early as the year 1000, but they speak chiefly of the dowry.

In the church at Civaux there is a capital that may date from late eleventh century.[20] It is the only embellished capital in the nave and addresses a silent admonition to the laity. One side of it depicts sirens trying to lure men out of a small boat: the men are sailing on the perilous sea of sin; the danger comes from women. To secure himself against this, the laymen must marry. The other side of the capital depicts marriage. It shows a husband and wife hand in hand. But they are looking away from each other, as if to convey that in the act of procreation chaste couples turn away as far as possible from the unclean deed. However that may be, only two, not three, people are involved. There is no family head present; they have taken one another of their own free will. But there is no priest either, though later Christian iconography never tired of asserting the necessity of his presence.

Another capital, this one carved at Vézelay in about 1100, depicts the temptation of Saint Benedict. A man leads a woman by the hand toward another man. The word *diabolus* is written twice, once above the man who is giving away the woman and once above the woman herself: lust is the daughter of the Devil. The giver in marriage here is the father, not the priest.

In those days an image was the best medium for spreading a message as widely as possible. But in the difficult task of tracing the evolution of marriage rites, we do not get much help from images. Images concerning marriage are rare; and, since all the art that survives is religious, this rarity indicates that marriage was not regarded as sacred. Such images as do survive are difficult to interpret. More convincing evidence is provided by liturgical and other texts, though even this testimony remains conjectural, as the books cannot be dated with certainty and we are not sure exactly how they were used. We may find a certain written formula in a pontifical; but where, when, and about whom was it actually uttered? A road marked by this kind of milestone is bound to be hard to follow.[21]

The custom of involving a cleric in the successive ceremonies of *desponsatio* and *nuptiae* seems to have come via Normandy and to have spread toward Cambrai-Arras and Laon. A manual written at Evreux in the eleventh century contains the prayers said by a priest officiating in the house of the bridal couple. He blesses everything—the wedding presents, the ring, the bedroom before the couple enter it, the marriage bed. But is all this anything more than a series of exorcisms to ward off evil, precautions taken at the moment of most danger, when the couple are about to be united, at nightfall? A later pontifical dating from the second half of the eleventh century and used in the diocese of Cambrai-Arras shows that part of the ceremony had by now been transferred to the church. "After the woman has been wedded (*desponsata*) by the man, and legally dowered, let her enter the church with her husband." There, before Mass, they knelt and received a blessing.

So the ritual practices introduced two centuries earlier for the marriage of queens subsequently became more widespread. The ecclesiastical authorities had succeeded in establishing that in the midst of the rites of passage, between the ceding of the woman, the promise, the verbal engagement on the one hand, and on the other her introduction into the nuptial chamber, she should be presented at the altar, and that a blessing should be bestowed on the couple already formed but not yet physically united. Just that and no more. A Soissons missal of the eleventh century does mention a blessing of the ring before the Mass, and a blessing of the wedding chamber after it.

There thus seems to have been a very gradual application of the recommendations of the synod, held in Rouen in 1012, prescribing that before the wedding meal "the husband and wife, fasting, should be blessed in church by the priest, fasting." The sanctification ratified a previous investigation: "Before according the couple the blessing of the Church, the priest should verify that there is no incest or bigamy involved." But not until the twelfth century do we find a set liturgical procedure in the surviving Church manuals. These are mostly Norman, though one of English origin was used in Laon between 1125 and 1135. By this time the *desponsatio* no longer took place in the bride's own home. The rings were blessed, the deed of settlement read, the common consent called for, all at the church door—and all by the priest. The priest was now present, a special witness, though still a passive one. He did not perform any acts of primary importance, he was not positively involved. "Then let him come who is to give away the bride"—the main protagonist, the head of the family, the girl's father, brother, or uncle—"and let him take her by the right hand"—like the Devil on the column at Vézelay—"and let him give her to the man as his lawful wife, with her hand covered if she is a maid, with her hand uncovered if she is a widow." The husband slipped the ring on and off three successive fingers of the wife's right hand—in the name of the Father, the Son, and the Holy Ghost—then placed it on her left hand. He next made the pledge, "With this ring I thee wed, with this gold I thee honor, and with this dowry I thee endow." According to the Laon manual, the wife then had to prostrate herself at her husband's feet. Then everyone went into the church and the couple were blessed, under a veil except in cases of remarriage. After Mass, at nightfall, when the couple went to their marriage bed, the priest was to go and bless the wedding chamber and then, once again, the couple: "God of Abraham, Isaac, and Jacob, bless these young people and sow in their hearts the seed of eternal life."

The ceremonies thus constituted a sacralization of marriage, though still a discreet one. The priest had not yet replaced the father at the crucial moment of the joining of hands and the giving away of the bride. The earliest record of this decisive change comes from Reims in the second half of the thirteenth century. When the abbot of Nogent was writing his *Memoirs*, the battle was apparently far from won. Hildebert of Lavardin, bishop of Le Mans, declared that the benediction "united in marriage"; this was in answer to the preaching of monk Henry. But we should note that Hildebert regarded a benediction as a special favor, and the stress he lays on it suggests that he had to overcome stiff opposition. For the laity, marriage remained a secular matter. They thought it a good thing for the priest to come and say some prayers over the marriage bed, as he did in the fields to bring rain, and over swords and hounds to make them effective. But otherwise laymen preferred to keep the clergy at a distance.

Among the knights whom Guibert of Nogent castigated, marriage was really a matter of business, a way of preserving or increasing the family "honor." In this cause no holds were barred, including abduction, repudiation, or incest. As I read Guibert's *Memoirs* I try to see the "mighty" of those parts through his eyes. Among them were Jean, count of Soissons; Enguerrand, lord of Coucy; and Enguerrand's son, Thomas, known as Thomas of Marle, because while awaiting the death of his father he lived on the estate he had inherited from his mother. Both Enguerrand and Thomas seem to have been very rapacious, seizing by force the rich girls whom Dominique Barthélemy has dubbed *"filles à châteaux."*[22]

Enguerrand and Thomas, who had to defend their principality against formidable rivals, were obliged to make useful marriages. But this was not easy, and sometimes involved violence. According to Guibert, Enguerrand abducted two women in quick succession. In about 1045 he had taken Ade of Marle from her husband, the count of Beaumont. Then he got rid of her and took Sybille, wife of the count of Namur.[23] The count of Namur, who was fighting in the service of Emperor Henry IV, had left his wife in a chateau in the Ardennes. Enguerrand went there and had no difficulty in seducing Sybille. Guibert depicts her as consumed with desire: Geoffroi of Namur, he says, though younger than Enguerrand, had been unable to satisfy her.

Guibert the abbot was blind to the political maneuvering that was going on—all he saw was the *libido* involved. Abduction and adultery were here compounded by incest. Like Philip I and William of Aquitaine, Enguerrand was not related to the woman in question; but he was related to her first husband. And like the king and the duke before him, Enguerrand was excommunicated. But the bishop was his cousin, and he was spared the anathema.

The *Memoirs* acknowledge that Thomas used marriage to acquire property. Left a widower by his first wife, daughter of the count of Hainaut, around 1107 he abducted one of her cousins, who was already married. But he dismissed her because she bore him no children.

Repudiation presented no problem: wives were always either found to be too closely related to their husbands or guilty of adultery. Ade of Marles was accused of adultery. Jean of Soissons,[24] to get rid of his wife, asked one of his friends to slip into her bed one night after the lights were out. She drove out the interloper with the aid of her maids. Was this mere gossip? A letter written by Yves of Chartres confirms that Jean brought a case against his wife accusing her of infidelity, claiming proof through the ordeal by fire.

Was Guibert too harsh, too pessimistic? What we know about the behavior of King Philip does not conflict with what Guibert says about the lesser lords who were his own neighbors. Fouque Réchin, count of Anjou, was even more given to polygamy. In 1060 his uncle Geoffroi Martel had married him to the daughter of one of his followers. She died, and Fouque then became the son-in-law of the lord of Bourbon. He broke this marriage off on grounds of kinship, and took to wife Orengarde of Châtelaillon. But by 1081 he had tired of her and had her shut up in the monastery of Beaumont-les-Tours. Next, to set the seal on a reconciliation with William the Conqueror, Fouque promised to marry one of his daughters, then tried to back out, but the legates had their eye on him and he was forced to annul the *desponsatio* in due form: in the abbey of Saint-Aubin d'Angers, genealogical tables going back seven generations were drawn up, and it was shown that the *sponsa* was Fouque's kinswoman.[25] Another family tree drawn up in the same monastery suggests that Fouque was also separated, this time after the nuptials but again on grounds of kinship, from a daughter of the count of Brienne.[26] Before 1090 he was negotiating with Robert Courtehouse for the hand of Bertrade of Montfort. Bertrade, as we know, left Fouque, and the chronicles relate that she took the initiative because she did not want to be "sent away like a whore," as her predecessors had been.

Fouque, as we have already noted, went too far.[27] But similar machinations can be seen everywhere. Henry I of England was vehemently opposed to a marriage between his nephew William Cliton and the count of Anjou's daughter, and the pope eventually annulled the match on grounds of kinship, Henry having won him over, according to Orderic Vital, "by an enormous load of gold, silver, and other spices."[28] Corruption and violence; the use of the ban on incest to get round the ban on repudiation, or to denigrate already undesirable connections; prelates sometimes difficult and sometimes docile, but always serving their own purposes—there is enough evidence of all these to show that Guibert was not exaggerating.

We might think, perhaps, that he was imagining things when he dealt with sexual practices in neighboring chateaux. Apart from that aspect of his behavior, Enguerrand of Coucy might have been considered highly praiseworthy: noble, generous, courteous, highly respectful of the clergy. Unfortunately he was also lascivious and an inveterate womanizer. His son, Thomas, kept a handful of "prostitutes" under his own roof, and the same words recur again and again: *meretrices, pellices*. And did not William of Malmesbury, a prey to the same obsessions as Guibert, imagine the duke of Aquitaine founding an "abbey" at Niort especially for his concubines?

Jean of Soissons was led astray by bad company.[29] He lived surrounded by heretics, Jews, and of course whores. What he really enjoyed was raping nuns. He neglected his young and pretty wife for an old woman he used to visit in the house of a Jew. But he was punished: he fell ill. The priest inspected his urine and made him promise to control himself; in this the priest was backed up by the doctors, who were churchmen too and believed that spiritual uncleanness, especially in the form of lust, was manifested in the bodily humors. The count listened to these exhortations to chastity. But one Easter night at matins, while his chaplain was expounding the mystery of the Resurrection, Jean kept sneering and saying, "Fairy tales! Hot air!" "Why do you come then?" asked the preacher. "Because of the pretty girls who come here to sleep [*coexcubare*] with me," was the answer.

This exchange makes one wonder about the prevalence of unbelievers or rather the influence of heresy, an influence perhaps more widespread than is commonly thought. The same inveterate sinner, Jean of Soissons, on his very deathbed, when called on by the priest to repent of his worst sin, love of the female body, retorted: "I have been told by wiser people than you that women should be common property, and that the sin you speak of is of no consequence." The words Guibert attributes to him are those that had been attributed to the heretics of Orleans a hundred years before.

When Guibert, depicting the wicked world he hated in the darkest possible hues, maintained that there was an inextricable connection between heresy and depravity, are we to suppose he had lost touch with reality? Or were the ascetic rigors some of the *parfaits* imposed on themselves seen as a kind of license for all the rest to leave purification to the minority and indulge their own passions freely? We have seen that the author of the *Memoirs* was not exaggerating unduly when he showed women being passed back and forth from one marriage to another by the knights of the Laonnais. Was he being any more fanciful when he wrote about the uses the knights put their women to? As has earlier been noted, historians cannot measure the role of desire.

What are we to think, then, of the desires of the women? The lady Sybille of Coucy had never controlled hers. The nobleman who protected the abbey of Saint-Jean de Laon boasted of having shared her bed before her first marriage.[30] Everyone said she was pregnant when the count of Namur married her; but it is of note that this was considered shocking.[31] Sybille deserted the count of Namur because he could not satisfy her.[32] When she was old and fat she married her daughter to a young man she herself had fallen in love with, so that he could come and live near her. She then persuaded her son-in-law and lover to be her elderly husband's ally against her stepson. This is an example of excessive and malign wifely influence, reversing the natural order and creating disorder, riot, and degeneracy, which eventually infected the city of Laon itself and the whole region. Sybille owed her power to her wealth and her noble birth. But in Guibert's eyes she owed it chiefly to her physical charms.

While some women admittedly managed to use their physical attributes to get the upper hand of their husbands and be mistress in their own house, we must not forget the victims—all those women who were ill-treated or repudiated. If they took refuge with the bishops, the latter, who were strong advocates of reconciliation, would often send them back again to their sufferings. Communities sworn to abstinence offered a surer asylum. And so, on the borders of Brittany, a number of noblewomen who had had enough of marriage became followers of Robert of Arbrissel, their timid little group roaming the woods, scarcely distinguishable from the heretical communities where women lived side by side with the leader's male disciples. At night the men slept on one side, the women on the other, and the leader in between, presiding over an exercise in self-control that had spread to France from Britain. But a community in which men slept near women in order to defy the lusts of the flesh—this was regarded as madness, a scandal, and Robert soon had to give it up. Fontevraud, the monastery he founded instead, was mixed, but the male and female inhabitants were separated by stone walls.

What was the position of women? Did any of them exercise real power? It is a question we cannot answer. We cannot even ask it without taking into account not only the social and physical factors involved (the husband's customary inferiority in rank, and the extent to which he was governed by sexual appetite) but also the ambiguity of the game played by the churchmen—ambiguous because their position was equivocal too.

The story of Abelard belongs to this period. The authenticity of his correspondence with Heloise is now regarded as doubtful, and the letters, if not entirely apocryphal, were at least tampered with: but in addition to presenting an edifying sermon on conversion, they reflect the attitude toward marriage of certain members of the ecclesiastical intelligentsia. Like Saint Jerome, these scholars condemned marriage because it stood in the way of philosophy. But they were still attracted to women, and Abelard was torn by this attraction, unable to choose between prostitutes, who repelled him, middle-class women, whom he despised, and noblewomen, who could not be had without a great waste of time. He fell back on the niece of his host the canon. It was easy to seduce her in the intimacy of the home. He offered to make the union official, but kept it secret, private, without any blessing or nuptial ceremony. In the end his only choice was between this clandestine state of affairs and castration, either physical or spiritual.

How many Abelards were there among the clergy, themselves tempted and torn, insisting that laymen must contract indissoluble ties but at the same time envying them and jealously trying to impose on them the chastity they themselves were forced to observe?

The number of convents for women multiplied in northern France at the end of the eleventh and the beginning of the twelfth centuries. Such refuges were becoming more and more necessary. The strict control families exercised over their young men's marriages, together with Church reforms separating priests from their wives and leaving the women homeless, created surplus females needing to be rounded up and given shelter. But might not even larger numbers of unhappily married women have been tempted to leave the conjugal roof for these religious havens? The prelates foresaw the danger.

Let us go back to Ermengarde, who was given in marriage by her father, Fouque Réchin, to William of Aquitaine. After William had repudiated her she was married to the count of Nantes. She tried to leave him for Fontevraud, asking that the marriage be annulled. But the bishops refused, and Robert of Arbrissel had to send her back to her husband, exhorting her to be obedient, to accept her lot in life, her "order" as a wife and mother.[33] She was to be patient and resigned, he said, and follow a little rule specially designed for her. It provided for much giving of alms, but neither too much prayer nor too much mortification, so that her body should remain healthy. What she was supposed to do was endure even under pain of death, even were she to be burned alive, as the wife of her great-grandfather Fouque Nerra had been burned for alleged adultery. But Ermengarde, the daughter of a prince, astounded the bishops at the Council of Reims in 1119 by appearing before them, a widow at last, to accuse her first husband of bigamy. But then had not she herself, they might have replied, in both her marriages, shown herself to be difficult and disobedient?

The intrusion of churchmen into conjugal matters caused resentment on the part of the husbands. William of Aquitaine, supposed author of the earliest Occitan poems and the first exponent of courtly love, in the tenth song of the Jeanroy edition of his works makes fun of women who fall under the sway of priests and monks and "frustrate the love of knights." They commit mortal sin, he says, and should be burned at the stake, like wives who commit adultery. He then introduces the metaphor of the firebrand, with its obvious erotic connotation. True, the poem is supposed to be comic, to make men laugh among themselves. I interpret it not as a precursor of the chivalric debates between priest and knight that were to be popular a hundred years later, but as an angry expression of the animosity husbands felt against spiritual directors who challenged their power and encouraged their wives to be frigid. This is the only direct echo that has survived of such feelings. At the point we have now reached, the beginning of the twelfth century, the voices of the servants of God drown out all other sounds.

We have heard what the monk had to say. Now let us turn to the bishop.

CHAPTER IX
YVES OF CHARTRES

The writings of Yves of Chartres[1] are not so spicy as those we have just been considering, but they do teach us a lot about marriage in the knightly classes, for his object was to correct behavior he regarded as reprehensible, and in castigating it he gives us a picture of it. His view of the world was perhaps just as severe as that of the abbot of Nogent, though he himself was not a monk. But he had lived for long periods in monastic communities and had been a fellow student of Saint Anselm at the abby of Le Bec. In 1078, when he was thirty-eight and already middle-aged, the bishop of Beauvais made him head of the model monastery of Saint-Quentin, a fraternity observing the very strict rule of Saint Augustine.[2] This experience left Yves an ardent supporter of the reform, as he demonstrated in the affair of Philip I.

This case gave him an opportunity to speak out and formulate clearly the principles of the reform, which required above all that laymen, especially the most powerful among them, should submit to the authority of the Church and allow it to supervise their morals, especially their sexual morals. It was by this means, through marriage, that the aristocracy could be kept under control. All matrimonial problems had to be submitted to and resolved by the Church alone, with all judgments based on a uniform set of laws.

Yves of Chartres was canonized for the diligence with which he had worked to establish these standards. He devoted all his efforts to the task from 1093 to 1096, at the height of the conflict between King Philip I and those who wanted to separate him from Bertrade. Working from two preliminary collections, the bishop produced the *Panormia*, a clear and rigorous synthesis. It consisted of eight sections—as compared with the seventeen of Bourchard's *Decretum*—each of which was divided into subsections individually titled. Taken as a whole it enables us to measure the progress of rationality in the eleventh century. The small world of the leading churchmen was waiting for just such an instrument.

Yves's classification of canonical texts was more discriminating than that of his predecessors. He made no attempt to conceal inconsistencies: he even added to the contradictions by introducing extracts from the Roman laws currently being exhumed by the enthusiastic jurists of Bologna. His intention was to leave judges free to choose among the texts available, according to the circumstances with which they had to deal. "If others have written in a different sense," he answered the bishop of Meaux,[3] "I understand it as follows: wishing out of mercy to anticipate certain people's weakness, they have chosen to soften canon law. Between the two opinions I find no difference save that between justice and mercy. And whenever, in a particular case, these two confront one another, they are subject to the appraisal and decision of the rectors (i.e., the bishops). It is for them to take into account the salvation of souls and, mindful of the quality of the people concerned and of the expediency of time and place, to apply canon law sometimes strictly and sometimes with indulgence."

But since the days of Bourchard of Worms the "discretion" allowed priests had changed in character. It was no longer a matter of discrimination and the mind, but of moderation and the heart. Yves of Chartres started from the postulate that, while it was permissible to interpret merely disciplinary precepts in a spirit of charity, when the law expressed the divine will itself there was no room for compromise. When he speaks of marriage he relies on two unshakeable assumptions: that it is indissoluble and that it is essentially spiritual. Thence are derived a prelate's two main duties: to stress the importance of the reciprocal engagement involved and to restrain the impulses of the flesh, condemning without fear or favor anything to do with violence, fornication, or incest.

Yves of Chartres aims at freeing these injunctions of all the less crucial regulations that may obscure them and bringing them forward into the clear light of day. Unlike the bishop of Worms, he did not compile a penitential: his work was not addressed to spiritual mentors who hear confessions of all kinds, but specifically to the men wielding the jurisdiction over marriage to which the church claimed sole right. That is why his collection of canon laws, as it passes from those concerning priests to those concerning the laity, has at its center two major sections containing the key passages of the whole book: one "dealing with nuptials and marriage" and the other "dealing with divorce."

Those called upon to make judgments are directed toward four main points. First, the deeds and words by which a marriage is made. Yves intended to promote acceptance of the ritual requiring the presence of a priest at the ceremonies. He therefore assembled texts relating to the public nature of the celebrations and to the need for the pronouncing of a blessing.[4] But he insists from the outset on the primary importance of the accord between husband and wife, the *desponsatio*[5]: neither party must be passive when the bride's father places her hand in that of the groom. And, since they are coming together deliberately, they must have reached the age of reason: seven. Furthermore, the principle is formulated that the nuptials are of secondary importance; that the couple themselves are united before their bodies become one. So the pact of *desponsatio* is itself indissoluble.[6]

This leads to the second point: the need to disembody marriage as far as possible. Wedding celebrations should be modest, without too much merriment and without any unseemly dancing. Quotations from Saint Augustine recall that the sole object of the union of the sexes is procreation.[7] Citations from Saint Jerome recommend chastity: "To make love voluptuously and immoderately in marriage is adulterous." And what is meant by *illicitus concubitus*, misuse of one's wife? What is meant is the use of parts of the body not intended for procreation.[8] But, as everyone knew, it was the wife who was the instigator of lewdness in a marriage, so she must be strictly held in check. Passage after passage from Ambrose and Augustine are adduced,[9] placing the woman under the *dominium* of her husband. "If there is discord between husband and wife, let the husband subdue the wife and let her submit to him. A submissive wife means peace in the home." And, "Since Adam was led into temptation by Eve, and not Eve by Adam, it is just that man should assume government over woman." "The man must command [*imperare*], the woman obey [*obtemperare*]." "The natural order is for the woman to serve the man." "Let her be subject to the man as he is to Christ." Let her be veiled "because she is not the glory or image of God."

Conversely, a man should not take too much trouble with his hair. Yves had already condemned "immodest fashions" in one of his sermons.[10] "By divine ordinance man has primacy over woman," and an inordinate abundance of hair, which would veil him too, would be a sign that he had abdicated his supremacy. The way men and women dressed, and the way they treated their bodies, should reflect the fundamental differences upon which the social order is based, i.e., the subordination of female to male.

The third point concerns the law of monogamy, thus raising the question of concubinage. The best way of absorbing this kind of union into the system was to equate it with lawful marriage: if the man treated his concubine as if she were a wife, then their union was indissoluble.[11] It was no longer permissible for a man to dismiss a concubine in order to marry. Marriage "in the Danish manner" is categorically condemned. Moreover, many texts are quoted to support the ban on remarriage after divorce.[12] Divorce may be granted for "carnal reasons," i.e., fornication or incest; but the separation achieved is only physical—the spiritual bond remains.

Book VII of the *Panormia* is significantly headed, "Concerning the undoing of a carnal union by reason of carnal fornication." The flesh is contemptible; the body can therefore be moved to and fro like an object. But—and this is the fourth point—only the Church has the right to do so. The Church may separate couples on grounds of adultery[18] and also on grounds of "spiritual fornication," as when one of the partners betrays God by being a heretic. But a priest may not grant a separation except as a last resort, after doing all he can to reconcile the union. On the other hand, when incest, the second of the carnal causes of separation, is involved, the priest is obliged to break off the union. No "reconciliation" is possible: no one can change his own blood. One of the preliminary texts from which Yves worked contains a text on the divorce between Robert the Pious and Berthe, which was probably used in the attempt to get Philip away from Bertrade. It declares a marriage automatically annulled as soon as consanguinity has been proven.

It is understandable that in those days the prelates fighting against bigamy, as committed by the king of France and the duke of Aquitaine, should have laid great stress on incest. But how were they to reconcile the Church's absolute ban on bigamy—which is not mentioned in the Gospels or in all the rest of the Scriptures: Leviticus is much less severe —with the principle of absolute indissolubility enunciated by Jesus? Yves managed to get round this contradiction. Concentrating his research on the law of monogamy, he brought together the canonical texts previously assembled by the bishop of Worms, and gave them a fresh treatment. He was as cavalier as Bourchard himself had been, if not more so, omitting from the decrees he was quoting any phrases that might seem to authorize remarriage after divorce. An authority quoted by Bourchard allowed "a man whom his wife has tried to kill," and who therefore has the right to dismiss her, to "take another wife if he wishes." When Yves repeats the quotation he leaves out the last part.[14] Similarly, on the subject of exiles kept too long away from home, Bourchard quotes an authority who says, "Let them take other wives if they cannot be continent." This has disappeared from the *Panormia*: Yves refers to the passage in one of his letters but quotes only part of it.

In his day this was an acute problem. Many knights from northern France went far afield in search of adventure, and we know from Orderic Vital that at the time of the conquest of England the forlorn ladies of Normandy threatened, "We shall take another man." But what was the Church to say now to Crusaders who returned to find that their wives had committed adultery? What should the bishops do? Allow them a divorce? When the archbishop of Sens asked the question of Yves, he got the following answer[15]: the knights should agree to be reconciled with their wives, remembering "the frailty of the female vessel, showing indulgence toward the weaker sex, and asking themselves whether they had never sinned." Failing that, they should remain chaste until their erring wives died, for otherwise they would be committing adultery. It was in this connection that Yves "edited" the quotation from Saint Augustine.

So much for our brief survey of the legal norms set out by Yves of Chartres: they have been the subject of various learned studies and are easily available. What we are interested in here is the light they shed on the sort of behavior they were intended to correct. Even more useful is Yves of Chartres's correspondence, which acts as a complement to the collection of canon laws, for they explain to those using the norms how to apply them, and thus tell the historian how theory stood up to practice.

Collections of letters were very popular about that time, and the epistles they contained were highly polished compositions written in accordance with set rules. Some were written for pleasure, but most were intended to be useful and to instruct. Some time after 1114, when people were applying to him from all sides for his opinion, the now elderly bishop of Chartres set to work on what he had preserved of his correspondence, making some cuts but more additions. He wanted to produce a useful work of reference, and he succeeded. It was consulted far and wide, and copies were especially numerous in the west of France. It was reproduced in Laon too. In some manuscripts it is given a place among the theoretical writings on marriage. Yves's correspondence does indeed treat at length of matrimonial questions.

Some of the letters—letters of guidance addressed to laymen—exalt the virtues of the married state. There is a short missive to King Louis VI[16] when he was on the point of marrying a niece of the countess of Flanders, "a nubile maid of noble condition and good character," and thus perfectly suitable. But Louis hesitated and was being urged to make up his mind. Yves of Chartres added his voice to the chorus. Human society was made up of three "conditions": "those who are married, those who are chaste, and the leaders of the Church. . . . Anyone who before the eternal Judge is not found in one of these 'professions' will be excluded from the heritage of eternity." A man had to belong to one of the prescribed categories: hovering on the fringe was no longer allowed. Louis was a king, so there was no doubt about it: his duty was to beget children. "If he had no successor the kingdom would be divided against itself." So he must take a wife—a lawful wife, naturally. He must stop sitting on the fence and occupy the place assigned to him—in "the order of married life." There were three reasons for him to make haste: he needed to lay waste the hopes of those who coveted the crown, to "repress the illicit impulses of the flesh," and to silence those who mocked him. Why were they laughing at Louis? Did they presume he was impotent? A homosexual?

There is a similar letter to the count of Troyes. The count was thinking of going to Jerusalem, of changing from one *ordo* to another and entering into the service of God. But he must take heed: Satan often disguised himself as an angel of light. "He persuades some to neglect their marital duty toward their wives; he tries, under the appearance of chastity, to incite them to illicit lechery and their wives to adultery." You have a wife, says the letter, and you cannot leave her without her consent. "If, without your wife's consent, you served chastity, even if you did so for God, you would not be serving your marriage, and the sacrifice would not be yours but hers."

Yves's correspondence examines all the difficult cases upon which senior churchmen might be called to pronounce judgment, and the analysis of such problems is presented in question-and-answer form. It strikes one that some of these dialogues may have been imaginary: certain eventualities could have been discussed in the abstract so as to make the guide complete. In that case, do the letters really allow us to understand marriage practices among the regional aristocracy of that time, or does pure theory rear its head here and there? We cannot separate the real from the imaginary, but while allowing for the latter we may assume that the factual element predominates.

Of the thirty-one letters I have selected for examination, eleven deal with the behavior of husbands and twenty with the behavior of those who arrange marriages. Of the first group, four letters consider concubinage and seven adultery. Of the second group, eight are concerned with the *desponsatio* and twelve with incest. This rough classification brings out three remarkable features. First, the episcopal authorities are less interested in married life than in the formation of the couple; second, when the marriage contract is being drawn up, the decisions of the families involved generally take precedence over those of the individuals, especially those of the young women in each case; and lastly, incest is the great stumbling block.

Let us now examine the text more closely.

When the bishops were perplexed they turned to their colleague at Chartres.[17] They kept coming up against the problem of sin. For example, if a woman were already sharing someone's bed—sometimes she might even be pregnant—could the clergy do as the man in question wanted, and by employing certain rites transform this concubinage into lawful marriage? And what about the wife who was married according to the proper rites, but who gave birth to a child three months later? Was she to be deprived of the dignity of marriage? In what did the dignity of marriage consist? The bishops hesitated between conflicting canonical texts. Yves acted as their guide.

You must always, he said, take circumstance and social position into account: those supposed to set an example should be treated more severely. But as long as they are not cousins or adulterers, the first rule is to avoid separating men and women who have come together through their own common will and who have also been united sexually and "become one flesh." "This applies all the more where there is issue not of vice but of nature."

The social reality was clear: an enormous number of prenuptial relationships existed, and many couples who had come together without benefit of Church ritual now wanted their unions to be consecrated, just as those of kings and princes had been. The fact that the bishops were asked such questions suggests that the custom of seeking the Church's blessing on marriages was spreading, while concubinage was gradually becoming discredited among the aristocracy.

In answering these queries Yves of Chartres called on his correspondents to overcome their aversion and admit that the *commixtio sexuum* was not devoid of value; that without the sexual act "the duties of marriage were not fully accomplished," that the flesh is not entirely evil. But the answers he supplied put the emphasis on monogamy. For the great preoccupation of the prelates who consulted him was how to restrain that multitude of husbands and their cousins and brothers, all eager to change wives; how to make them take the marriage contract more seriously than the treaties of peace or alliance they were always so casually breaking.

The bishops also had to cope with adultery, a legitimate cause for divorce. Yves of Chartres's correspondence mentions female adultrery only, and it does so constantly, reflecting the frequency with which it was alleged by men always on the lookout for it. Guillaume, a knight, returns from an expedition to England after nine months' absence to find his wife giving birth to a child a week prematurely. His suspicions grow until he reaches the point of accusing another knight. But no, says Yves of Chartres,[18] it is not right to calculate so closely: "nature" may be either hasty or slow, as we see every year from the ripening of the harvest.

Then comes Jean of Soissons again, accusing his wife of infidelity. She has been seen "conversing in private" with her lover. Wait, says Yves; you must have at least three reliable witnesses.[19] On another occasion we see him dealing with a group of heirs whose interests are threatened by a widow's remarriage, and who allege that she is marrying a former lover. Yves tells them to hold their peace[20]: "If out of fear or favor they did not denounce the woman as a sinner while her first husband was still alive," they were accomplices in her adultery.

Women under suspicion, defended by a father or brother[21] anxious to protect the family honor, sometimes said they were ready to prove that "they had never been one flesh" with the man in question. They would swear their innocence, call on God to judge them, take the red-hot iron in their hands. Yves, like all his sex, believed women were by nature prone to sin and deception. So while he usually forbade judgment by ordeal, in certain cases, where an accusation had been made in due form and there was no contradictory witness, he felt there was no alternative.

But, whenever possible, Yves urged that the parties should be reconciled, that marriages should not be allowed to break up except as a last resort. And he insisted that great care must be taken to see that a divorced couple did not remarry.[22] For the words they pronounced at the *desponsatio* bound their souls together forever.

Since the *desponsatio* was of such capital importance, it must be closely supervised, controlled, and shielded from abuse. The correspondence highlights three points of variance between the model Yves was trying to perfect and the practices of matchmakers, and especially of those giving women in marriage.

First, the custom was for families to arrange matters too early and to marry children who were too young, still far below even the "age of reason," which, though fixed neither by human nor by Church law, everyone knew to be seven. Such matches were often arranged with good intentions—to promote peace and spread "charity." But what was the value of promises uttered by the fathers of the interested parties rather than themselves?[23]

The second abuse, a direct consequence of the first, was the easy breaking off of such arrangements. The more precocious the engagement the more likely it was that the matchmakers would change their minds before the actual nuptials could take place. Such casual attitudes proved that from the laymen's point of view what really concluded a marriage was the coming together of the two bodies, the mingling of blood, the nuptials. For example, it was commonly accepted that a bride could be replaced by one of her sisters, so that the friendship between the two families might not be harmed. If a match veered too close to incest, a substitute might be chosen from another family.[24]

Thirdly, the *desponsatio* might be broken by violence: abduction was not altogether a thing of the past. But it was becoming rare, and Yves deals with only one case of it.

In this case, a father had lodged a complaint.[25] His daughter, already promised to Galeran, one of the king's knights, had just been kidnapped by the nephew of the bishop of Troyes. No one thought of questioning the Church's right to dispense justice in the matter. The bishop of Paris was informed and convened his court. The girl was interrogated. Why had she resisted? She had already been promised, she said. She had been taken by force. She struggled and cried; her mother cried too. The abductor himself was also present, but after refusing to answer questions he vanished and was never seen again. The witnesses confirmed the victim's allegations, so she was immediately freed—not of the marriage but of the concubinage.

Concubinage could be broken off then? Yves seems to be contradicting himself. But in fact, from his point of view, only the bodies and not the wills had been involved in this case, and it was on the agreement of wills that the indissolubility of a union depended. So the woman could go to another man's bed without committing a sin; or, rather, the men of her kin could use her to make another marriage contract. Galeran did not want her anymore, but another lord had agreed to have her. However, the new bridegroom was afraid of being accused of bigamy, and it was to reassure him that Yves was writing to his bishop, the bishop of Auxerre.

For Yves, as he repeats elsewhere, anyone who had sworn to a marriage pact had performed the essential part of the "sacrament," or marriage rite. Was not Joseph the husband of Mary? This was the first reference to the Holy Family.[26] Similarly, anyone who had not undertaken the engagement with his own lips was not bound. Girls whose fathers had made promises in their stead were therefore entitled to oppose such arrangements.[27]

It was in the name of such principles that the advocates of reform fought the offending customs. They were making a frontal attack on one of the main buttresses of a society based on lineage: the right of the head of a family to dispose of its women.

The subject on which there are the most letters is incest. Yves expounded the relevant doctrine to Hildebert of Lavardin.[28] Because "marriage was consecrated from the beginning of the human condition, it is natural institution." (This passage shows the idea of "sacrament" gradually taking shape, and reveals Yves's assumption that, just as society was divided into three conditions, or orders, so the married state, the order of conjugality, was established *ab initio* and outside history.) Marriage cannot be broken off except on the grounds, i.e., fornication, provided for by the "law" and the Church. However, another cause for divorce was later added "in the development of the Christian religion." (This further ground thus belongs to history and to culture and not to nature. This is probably the best example to be found of the jurist's embarrassment at the contradiction between the insistence on monogamy and the ban on consanguinity.) The addition was made because "according to apostolic doctrine the union must be honorable and without stain in all respects." Yves is referring to *honestas* and the notion of defilement.

He does not elaborate, makes no attempt to justify by clear arguments and reliable authorities what was an obstinate insistence on the part of the priests. The refinement of the Church's intellectual apparatus, the minute classification and rigorous criticism of texts—all efforts were futile when confronted with this immovable object. A monk from Saint-Bertin, compiling a genealogy for the count of Flanders in 1164, made his point loud and clear when commenting on Baudouin VI, who had been excommunicated along with his wife, the widow of one of his relatives: "Incest is worse than adultery."[29]

And yet incest was rife. Knights apparently felt far less horror than priests at the idea of mingling their blood with that of their relatives. But aversion to incest was not entirely absent. It was indeed sometimes linked to the fear of begetting monsters, a dread exploited by rigorist reformers like Peter Damian. In the *Romance of Thebes* (about 1150) the unknown author uses the story of Oedipus as a tragic backdrop to the story of the warring brothers.[30]

But the field of prohibition seems to have been much narrower when submitted to lay morality. When the bishops urged laymen to examine their lines of descent beyond the third degree and even as far as the seventh, princes and knights found it hard to understand why—especially when many ecclesiastics on the fringes of orthodoxy were always saying how unseemly it was for clerics to concern themselves with such essentially carnal matters. For the aristocracy themselves, genealogical inquiries, which could be counted on to uncover some sort of dubious relationship, were the surest means of ending marriages they had tired of.

Sometimes the initiative came from heads of families, as when old King Philip and his son Louis wanted to have a girl's divorce solemnly pronounced in a plenary court.[31] Sometimes the question was raised by the prelates, out to prevent a marriage that did not suit them.[32] In either case, "nobles born of the same line" as the family concerned were called together to swear an oath to serve the justice of the Church,[33] and publicly computed their degrees of consanguinity. Clerks took down the various declarations, producing innumerable tables of affiliation, which were used over and over again. We have already seen how Count Fouque Réchin invoked some of them to get rid of his wives. Yves of Chartres could "lay his hand on" a whole collection of such family trees, "which start with the trunk and branch out into degree after degree until they reach the people concerned" in the cases at issue. They were modeled on the genealogies in the Bible.

Such procedures stimulated ancestral memories, which were naturally keen to start with, as Pope Alexander II well knew. In 1059, to justify the extent of the Church's ban on consanguinity, he declared that *caritas*, or natural friendship, existed between relatives up to the seventh degree of kinship, and that within that limit there was no need to reinforce it by further marriages, for such family affiliations might be "recalled and kept up from memory."[34] Memory gained in clarity and solidity, too, as it passed from the oral to the written; and the countless court cases concerning incest at the end of the eleventh century helped to strengthen people's awareness of lineage relationships. These cases together with the evolution of social structures combined to change from horizontal to vertical the image aristocratic families had of their own kinship networks.

The sort of genealogical chart that Yves of Chartres set before the king of England to prevent "his royal majesty from authorizing what he ought to punish,"[35] i.e., consanguineous marriages, shows that such unions had been frequent in previous generations. It also shows that prelates had once been far less strict, and that those of them who became more severe did so only after 1075 and under the influence of the reform movement. Other charts show that great lords did not shrink from marrying the daughters King Henry of England had begotten out of wedlock; on the contrary, they fought over them.[36] In my view this proves that the higher aristocracy in eleventh-century Normandy, despite the objurgations of the reforming clergy, had no objection to "second-class" marriages, marriages in the Danish manner, or to their offspring.

Everyone knew that the children of such inferior unions could not aspire to inherit, but they did have their father's blood in their veins: and it was their royal blood that made Henry's daughters so sought after. It seems unlikely that this attitude was peculiar to Normandy. King Louis VI himself was preparing to marry an illegitimate daughter of the marquis Boniface; the agreement had already been concluded. But Yves of Chartres made him undertake to break it off out of respect for *majestas*[37]: a king must not stoop, against all "seemliness," to marry a girl who was "infamous" because of her illegitimate birth.

So those who wanted to lead Christian society back into the paths of what they regarded as righteousness were faced with practices that had been engaged in peacefully for centuries, and which formed an apparently insurmountable barrier. But gradually, wielding words and exclusions, the rigorist priests succeeded in dismantling that barrier. It took them a long time, though, to teach people to regard concubinage and illegitimacy as "unseemly." The battle to denigrate marriage to one's cousin met with even stronger resistance, for not only did such allegedly incestuous unions often add to a family's prestige, but, because of the promiscuity that reigned in many great houses, they often took place unwittingly. The *Decretum* of Bourchard of Worms spoke of the looseness of domestic morals, and three of Yves of Chartres's letters show that he was still worried about this.

One deals with a man who confessed to having slept with his wife's sister before his own lawful nuptials. What was to be done? Six people were ready to confirm his confession. Yves separated the couple, leaving the wife her dower as the "price of her maidenhead."[38]

In another letter Yves considers the case of a wife who allegedly had shared the bed of her husband's cousin. (She herself had not spoken; it was the cousin who raised the question.) Yves answered that others would have to back up the cousin's sworn statement; the wife could clear herself of the allegation by her own oath alone.[39]

Thirdly, a man confessed that before his marriage he had defiled his bride's mother by "external pollution." A similar case had been debated before Pope Urban II, who had refused to grant a divorce on such grounds. Indeed, the *disjunctio* of a marriage "badly begun or violated" could not be pronounced if there had been no physical intercourse. Here Yves adds a further particular of interest. He says that it is "by the mingling of bodies, the *commixtio carnis*, that a couple becomes one flesh in the mingling of sperm."[40]

There was a great deal of sexual liberty, we observe, within the family. So it was usually easy for a man who wanted to be legally separated from his wife to make charges to the clerics about such vagaries. He was sure to find witnesses ready to confirm his allegations. Who, in those houses devoid of private rooms,[41] had not seen, or thought he had seen, family affection turning into less than chaste embraces?

Another interesting aspect of this correspondence is that it shows how the more enlightened prelates were forced to mitigate their strictures. Yves was uncompromising on the subject of indissolubility. A canon in Paris had married. Let him resign his prebend, let him descend into the inferior order of the married, and let him stay there. What God has joined let not man put asunder.[42] But on another occasion Yves does vacillate. A husband had discovered that his wife was from a lower-class family. It seems like a good reason for repudiation: the blood of "nobles" and that of "serfs" was not to be mingled; moreover, those who gave the girl away had practiced deceit. Yves, however, is inflexible[43]: one may authorize the interruption of "nuptial knowledge" and separate the bodies, but one may not authorize a violation of the "sacrament"; one may not grant a divorce. But the correspondent's answer came back: had not Yves himself allowed free men to repudiate wives who were not free? Yves tried to wriggle out of the inconsistency[44]: what he had dissolved in the previous cases, he said, was not a marriage but a wicked concubinage. Similarly here. He quoted a decree of Pope Leo and insisted above all that the agreement concluding a real and indissoluble marriage must be contracted in good faith. If there has been deception, God cannot have tied the knot. It is men who have done so, and badly; there are loose ends, and it is permissible to undo them.

For all his efforts, the eminent canonist's arguments were unconvincing. But how could he go against the social structure, against the hierarchy of "orders," ranks, and classes; against the principle he himself appealed to when he advised that the married priest be downgraded from the jurisdiction of divine law to that of human law? Human law prescribes marriage. And, as Yves himself had written,[45] according to that "natural" law there are neither free men nor serfs. What then? Between the two levels of lay society a barrier had been raised by God himself. The theory of virtuous marriage could not fly in the face of another important theory, the theory of providential inequality.

Yves hesitated in this case and tried to feel his way out of his bind. But the difficulty he encountered led him to develop his ideas about marriage further. It was not coitus that made a marriage, he repeated, but the reciprocal engagement of wills; it was faith, good faith. Between partners who know they have been misled, that the blood of one can debase the blood of the other, and that one is reducing the other to servitude through concubinage—between any such partners there can be no real *dilectio*, only resentment and hate. And if the "precept of love" is not respected, the couple cannot embody the union of Christ and the Church; their marriage cannot be the "sacrament" that is the sign of that mystery.

We see here how the gradual working out of a legal argument on the basis of individual cases could lead to the creation of theological dogma, itself closely dependent on the gradual construction of a liturgy.

About 1100, when the purging of the upper clergy was proceeding apace, certain churchmen like Yves of Chartres were working to perfect a legal apparatus defining which marriages could be made and which could be unmade in the name of God—an apparatus subjecting matrimonial morals to the control of the clergy, thereby ensuring the supremacy of spiritual power over the temporal.

The same prelates, together with others, also worked to strengthen the ideology justifying that supremacy—an ideology that was also a theology of marriage. Around the cathedrals of Laon, Chartres, and Paris, meditation gradually became concentrated on the mystery of the Incarnation. The questions the law-making prelates asked themselves about marriage thus came to coincide with two questions the scholars asked when they were commenting on the Scriptures. The first of these concerned the motherhood and virginity of Mary; the second, the relationship between Christ and his Church.

The first was made more urgent by the spread of the cult of the Virgin. As is shown by the case of Guibert of Nogent, this movement was not unrelated, on the one hand, to the increasingly rigorous sexual restraints imposed on the priests and, on the other, to the strengthening of kinship structures, which accorded a special importance to motherhood. Mary offered an image of a woman who was a partner in a true marriage yet who gave birth to a son without being touched by evil. She was the model of the good wife. The scholars and teachers, building up their model of virtuous marriage, referred not only to the words of Christ as reported in the New Testament but also to a profusion of stories and canonical or apocryphal accounts that had grown up around Him.

The second question was also made more topical by the revival of anxiety about death and the afterlife. So long as this world lasted—and its end was not now thought to be so imminent—Christ was present in it in the guise of those who spread His word. But what was the nature of the *societas* between Him who sat at the right hand of God, those of His human brothers who broke bread in memory of Him, and those, much more numerous, who merely ate the bread and were lost for words? The inexpressible relationship between man and God could be apprehended only by analogy, by reference to man's experience of other deep and reverent relationships, such as that between a vassal and his lord or, more illuminating and of still greater metaphorical power, that between a wife and the husband who rules, corrects, and loves her.

This kind of thinking led to a more precise definition of the notion of sacrament. The scholars working in and around the cathedrals were engaged in the training of clerics, who propagated not only the Word but also grace. It was through their necessary mediation that this intangible good came down from heaven and was spread among the people. The scholars found the word *sacramentum* in the books with which the Carolingian renaissance had filled the episcopal libraries. Saint Augustine speaks of the "nuptial sacrament" and includes the "sacrament" among the three values contributing to the virtue of marriage. "That which is great in Christ and the Church," he writes, "is small in each husband and wife and yet is the sacrament of an inseparable union."

As a matter of fact the meaning of the word, inexact enough in the Latin of the Fathers, had become even more confused in the unregulated thinking of the early Middle Ages. In ordinary speech it meant first of all just the vow, the fact of a man and a woman joining together and taking God to witness, at the same time touching some sacred object, a cross or relic. In this connotation "sacrament" took its place naturally in the vocabulary of the marriage ritual.

But it was applied more generally still to all the acts and forms of words used on various occasions to bless different objects. So when the wedding ring or the marriage bed was blessed, the word *sacramentum* rose to people's lips bearing this very vague signification.

Lastly, what the scholars meant by *sacramentum* was "sign" or "symbol." In the middle of the eleventh century Bérenger, master of the school of Tours,[46] had been accused of heresy for reducing the word to this meaning alone. The great controversy his arguments aroused had led various teams of intellectuals to embark on the task of semantic refinement. They worked away diligently, but when Yves of Chartres compiled his canonical collections, an exact notion of what a sacrament was remained undecided. Did it belong more to marriage than, for example, to the vassalic oath? The persistent feeling that marriage was something physical and thus inevitably sinful prevented its being classified on a par with baptism and the Eucharist.

But this reluctance gradually faded as the custom spread of transferring the verbal and spiritual rites of marriage, those by which the contract was concluded, to the church door, in the presence of a priest. Developments in the legal apparatus were another factor in the change of attitude. Since the end of the eleventh century, texts from Italy had been finding their way into the canonical collections, and among them were precepts of Saint Ambrose concerning the *sponsalia* and others from Roman law concerning consent.

Yves of Chartres used these to draw a clear distinction between the promise of marriage—the "troth of agreement," a formula that might only have been spoken by those who had arranged the match—and the marriage proper, concluded by an agreement solemnly uttered by both the husband and the wife. Commentators belonging to the learned community at Laon referred to the preliminary and the definitive engagement as the *consensus de futuro* and *consensus de presenti*, respectively.

At the same time one of Yves's more frequent correspondents, Hildebert of Lavardin, went so far as to include marriage among the sacraments, and in a very eminent position too. "In the city of God," he began, "three sacraments preceded the others in the time of their institution, and are the most important for the redemption of the sons of God." Here the new meaning is beginning to emerge: the *sacramentum* not only as the sign but also as the channel or vehicle of efficient grace. Hildebert went on to name these three sacraments as "baptism, the Eucharist, and marriage. Of these three the first"—meaning the oldest—

"is marriage." Therefore—and this is what Hildebert was getting at—marriage came under ecclesiastical law and the jurisdiction of the prelates, despite the carnal connotation that still clung to it.

Between 1120 and 1150, the decades that followed Yves of Chartres's death, in the upsurge of creativity that led to the rebuilding of Saint-Denis and the sculpting of the spandrel at Chartres, the elaboration of Church doctrine also accelerated. Taking the word *sacramentum* in its most obvious sense and emphasizing the notion of a "sign," scholars developed the symbolical meaning of marriage. They started from the metaphor representing the Church as the bride of Christ. The two were joined together by a bond of charity; or, rather, the life-giving force emanating from the *sponsus* raised the *sponsa* up toward the light. This force was not *amor*, which comes from the body, but *dilectio*, a disincarnate and condescending solicitude operating within a necessary hierarchy, foundation of all terrestrial order, which places the male above the female.

Soon after 1124 Hildebert, who was good at rhetoric but somewhat lost in the labyrinths of dialectics, tried to define the part played by mutual agreement in the marriage contract.[47] According to Saint Matthew and Saint Paul, a husband and wife must remain united until death. Why? Because "neither Christ nor the Church dies": between them the ebb and flow of *caritas* cannot be interrupted; it is unimaginable that this "most holy and spiritual" marriage could ever end. It is this idea that signifies [*designat*] the stability of carnal marriage. Thus, "It is the stability in marriage that is the sacrament, because it is the sign of that which is sacred"; i.e., stability is a symbolic equivalent, a projection of the invisible onto the visible. Human marriage, if it is not broken off, if it is able to preserve charity until death, is itself a sacrament, belonging, with baptism and the Eucharist, among the holy practices instituted by God. Gérard of Cambrai, confronting the heretics exactly a century earlier, would have regarded such arguments as senseless or even sacrilegious.

This step taken, another still remained. If marriage really was a sign of the sacred, did that mean it was a vehicle of grace, able to contribute to the "redemption of the sons of God?" Hugues, a regular canon [living within a religious order] in the monastery of Saint-Victor just outside Paris, set about solving this problem. In his treatise *Concerning the Sacraments of the Christian Religion*, he examined all the ways in which the clergy should act upon society. His title is significant. Sacraments are more than signs. They are the means by which clerics are to perform their work of mediation. In Book II, chapter 11, paragraph 2 of his treatise, Hugues of Saint-Victor speaks of marriage as a medicine that it is the clergy's duty to administer to the laity. So marriage does possess "virtue," or saving grace—as long as it is dissociated from sex.

Hugues, like Yves, was an advocate of asceticism and attempted to make marriage entirely spiritual. Even more strongly than Yves, he stressed the importance of the mutual commitment pronounced at the *desponsatio*[48]: "When the man says, 'I receive you as mine so that you become my wife and I your husband,' and when the woman makes the same declaration . . . when they do and say this according to existing custom"—Hugues makes no stipulation about the surrounding ritual—"and are in agreement, it is then that I say that they are married." Whether they have made their declaration before witnesses, which it is important that they should do, or whether "by chance they have made it, as they should not, alone, apart, in secret, and with no witnesses present, yet in both cases they are well and truly married."

This was very daring. Hugues was answering the heretics' challenge and meeting Henry of Lausanne on his own ground. He was also freeing individuals from the power of their kin. His position ignored the interests of the families, preliminary negotiations, dowries, money, rings. Marriage was pared down to its essentials. Rites were of no importance.

When reduced to an exchange of vows, marriage was completely desocialized, losing its basic function of adding one more procreating couple to the rest of humanity. So it is not difficult to understand the cool reception Hugues's approach met with, the resistance put up by tradition and the defense mounted by society.

But there was something here even worse than the demoting of ritual. Hugues believed that a couple might—it was illicit, but they might nonetheless—become man and wife in the eyes of God without any benediction, without any priest taking part, and thus without any check or interrogation as to whether they were related and, if so, to what degree.

This suggestion may seem to have run counter to all the efforts previously made to incorporate the conclusive aspect of the marriage pact into the rites of the Church. It did sacrifice an enormous amount. But the sacrifice was necessary in order to obtain the essential result: to ensure that nuptials no longer mattered; that sex no longer mattered; that marriage, in its essence, in what gave it its curative value and enabled it, like baptism, to cleanse away sin, should be disincarnate, spiritual. Hugues's theories were in fact straying toward out-and-out spiritualism, in the philosophical sense of the word.

The research of Francesco Chiovaro[49] has led me to another work by Hugues, a treatise, *Concerning the Virginity of Mary*,[50] dating from about 1140. The author meditates on how the mother of God could have been a "real wife" while remaining a virgin. He goes on to pose the concrete and earthly problem involved in what was regarded as a true and exemplary story: can the vows Mary made in marriage, implying as they did submission to her partner in the performance of her marital duty, be reconciled with her virginity? Marriage is a lawful association established by common consent and imposing reciprocal obligations upon the contracting parties. Hugues, like Hildebert of Lavardin, sees in the principle of common consent the promise to preserve the bond until death, but, at a lower level, he also recognizes another consequence of the agreement: that of "reciprocally asking for and granting carnal intercourse."

This undertaking, as distinct from the first as the body is distinct from the soul, and consequently inferior, is for Hugues "the companion [*comes*] and not the creator [*effector*] of marriage." Its role [*officium*] is derivative, secondary; this is not the promise that secures the knot. Here again we see the decisive influence of the concept of hierarchy, subordinating the carnal to the spiritual, which is the cornerstone of the whole of "Gregorian" ideology. "If this [sexual] function ceases, we may not think that the truth or virtue of the marriage ceases, but on the contrary that the marriage is all the truer and more holy because it is based on the bond of charity alone and not on the lusts of the flesh or the ardor of desire."

Hugues goes on to comment on Genesis 2:24: "The man shall leave his father and mother." The husband should find again in his wife that which he has left behind for her. However, what bound him to his parents was obviously not the union of the sexes but "the affection of the heart and the bond of loving-kindness." "It is thus," says Hugues, "that we should think of the sacrament of marriage, which is of the spirit," like the love of a mother for her son.

So we see this virtuous canon, like the monk Guibert of Nogent, irresistibly drawn toward his mother, and through her toward the Virgin. He goes on to say that when it is written that a man "shall cleave unto his wife . . . this is to be considered the sacrament (i.e., sign) of the invisible and spiritual association between God and the soul." But in the latter part of the same verse, Hugues comes up against the inevitable obstacle of the body: "They shall be one flesh." He explains these words as the "sacrament (sign) of the invisible partaking which occurs in the flesh (i.e., the world) between Christ and the Church. The second sign (i.e., the second element in the metaphor) is great, but the first is greater: they shall be one heart, one single love in God and spirit." Physical intercourse is relegated to a secondary role. It may cease without breaking the marriage pact. Husbands would do well to follow the example of Joseph.

Hugues of Saint-Victor, withdrawn from the world, took to heart the life of Saint Simon of Crépy and the story of the emperor Henry, whom the pope was about to canonize. Indifferent to the fate of the great families, indifferent to the fate of mankind itself, he added his voice to all those, heretical and orthodox, persistently calling for virginity in marriage.

Those prelates who were anxious to exercise a practical influence, especially among the aristocracy, took care not to go as far as Hugues of Saint-Victor. When, ten years later in Paris, Peter Lombard provided a definition of "sacrament" that was received as definitive, he started from the distinction on which Hugues's teaching was based. His definition was: "A sacrament is an outward and efficient sign of grace," which adds to the idea of a sign and implies, in the case of marriage, indissolubility, the idea of a real transfer of virtue. Between husband and wife, says Peter,[51] there is a dual union, "one involving the consent of souls, and one involving the mingling of bodies." The Church is joined to Christ in the same way, by will and by "nature," the Church willing what Christ wills and Christ assuming human nature. "The wife is given to the husband both spiritually and physically, that is to say, both through charity and in conformity with nature. The *desponsatio*, or consent, is thus a symbol of the spiritual union of the Church and Christ, while the nuptials, or mingling of sexes, is a symbol of their corporeal union."

So a marriage that is not consummated is nevertheless holy, already "perfect" or complete. The *consensus de presenti*, the personal undertaking exchanged between husband and wife, "is enough in itself to conclude a marriage." The rest is mere appurtenance [*pertinencia*], whether it be the part played by the parents in giving away the bride or the part played by the priest in blessing. Neither of these elements adds anything to the validity of the sacrament; all they do is make it more "seemly."

Nevertheless, and this is of crucial importance, sex retains an essential role, especially within the context of human society, for it is sex alone that lends meaning to the other aspect of the mysterious union between the human and the divine, "that which through incarnation joins the members to the head."

Thus, nuptials and the flesh escape condemnation. But, having gone this far, Peter Lombard shrinks from saying that marriage transmits grace. Its virtue, conferred completely at the time of the *desponsatio*, is negative, defensive: it merely protects from sin. Marriage is admittedly a sacrament, but not a life-giving spring like the sacrament of ordination. Its action is only prophylactic. That is why, though it was then being officially included among the seven sacraments of the Church, the sacrament of marriage was still kept in the background, still tinged by vestiges of anxiety and repulsion regarding what went on at night in the marriage bed.

As the only one of the seven sacraments not instituted but only "re-stored" by Christ, marriage existed already in Paradise before the Fall. But the first sin plunged it into a state of corruption, and whatever effort was made to purify and elevate it, a trace still remained to remind us of its descent. Perhaps to make it fall again. Placed at the intersection of the spiritual and physical, it was the sacrament which most manifestly symbolized the mystery of the incarnation; it was trembling on the brink, in the middle ground, dangerous.

But the main thing is that by the middle of the twelfth century mar-riage had come to be sacralized without being disincarnated. The conflict between the ecclesiastical and lay models of marriage had become much less acute.

THE

WELFTH

CENTURY

CHAPTER X

THE ROYAL FAMILY

o place the battlefront in the conflict between Church and lay views on marriage and to get some idea of its ebb and flow in the second half of the twelfth century, the simplest method is to return to the most exalted of the families involved, the family of the king of France. By following the course of three royal marriages, we will best be able to pinpoint the parallels and contrasts beween knightly and priestly morality.

In 1152 Louis VII separated from his wife Aliénor, known in England as Eleanor of Aquitaine. She took with her her heritage, the duchy of Aquitaine, which was taken over by her new husband Henry Plantagenet. Because of its political consequences, this domestic event has been examined very closely by nineteenth- and twentieth-century historians. Even at the time it created a great stir. People talked about it, and also wrote about it, untiringly and at great length, producing a whole range of evidence that it is instructive to read now.

One account puts forward the version the French court would have had people believe. In 1171, perhaps earlier, a monk from Saint-Germain-des-Prés wrote a eulogy of the "most glorious king."[1] The occasion may have been the birth in 1165 of Philip, the male heir with whom God had at last rewarded Louis. According to the author, this special favor spared France the sorrow of seeing their country fought over by rival claimants, as England had been for so long. The implication was that God preferred France to England. The account, which was written in Paris, is chauvinistic from the outset, a bias that must be borne in mind in attempting to disentangle from it the real course of events.

Louis was already married to his third wife when Philip was born. He had married his first wife, Eleanor, in 1137, when he was sixteen and she somewhere between thirteen and fifteen. Eleanor had no brothers, and her father had just died; so she inherited his estate, and Louis became, through his marriage, head of the house of Aquitaine. To strengthen still further the alliance between the two families, he arranged a marriage between Eleanor's sister and Raoul of Vermandois, his father's first cousin, despite impediments of kinship. It was a long while before Eleanor had any children, but she gave birth to a daughter in 1145, and to another in 1149, when she and Louis were on their way home from the Holy Land. The official historian says nothing about what passed between them on the journey. He deals with their divorce in chapter fifteen. If we are to believe him, "Friends and relatives of the king came to him and joined together to tell him that he and Eleanor were more closely related than was seemly, and promised to confirm this upon oath." In fact, Louis and Eleanor were related in both the fourth and the fifth degrees. Apparently, after some twelve years, the relatives had suddenly discovered that the marriage was incestuous. The king, "surprised," could not endure to go on living in sin and turned for help to the archbishop of Paris, whose parishioner he was, and to the metropolitan archbishop of Sens. In March 1152, there was a meeting in Beaugency of the four archbishops whose authority extended over the heritages of the king and of his wife, together with many of their suffragans and of the "great ones and barons of the realm of France." In the presence of husband and wife, this assembly brought in a verdict of consanguinity, and as a necessary consequence the divorce of Louis and Eleanor was "celebrated."

The *History* shows Eleanor losing no time in remarrying. "In all haste" she went to Aquitaine. "Without delay" she married Henry, duke of Normandy. In fact, before marrying Henry, she had escaped the eager clutches of the count of Blois and of Geoffroi Plantagenet, Henry's brother. But it was Henry who finally captured her and, in May, installed her in his bed. In July, Louis, aided by Geoffroi, attacked Henry, and the ensuing war lasted until the following year.

As for Louis, we see him, as a good family head, busy marrying off his two daughters: the first—at the age of eight—to the count of Troyes, and the second—only three—to the count of Blois, consoling himself for having failed to marry her mother. Then Louis himself remarried.

There was no obstacle to his doing so. As his first marriage had been incestuous, it did not exist. All the same, the monk from Saint-Germain takes care to justify the second marriage with two arguments. First, Louis wanted to live "according to divine law," which recommended the married state to the laity. Secondly, mindful of his duty as head of his line, he was acting "in hopes of a successor who would govern the realm of France after him." And so, in 1154, the "emperor" of Spain gave Louis his daughter's hand, and soon afterward she bore him a daughter. Almost at once, in 1156, the infant was "joined" [*sociata*] in marriage to Henry, son of the king of England and Eleanor, a child born in 1155. The historian assures us that this marriage, so contrary to the clearest canonical precepts as regards both the age and the kinship of the couple, was concluded "by an arrangement [*dispositio*] obtained from the Roman Church."

Dispositio or *despensatio*—the terminology was still undetermined.

But the mechanism itself worked perfectly, making it possible to get round the law yet at the same time respect papal authority.

A second daughter was born to Louis VII in 1160, but the queen died giving birth and the king took another wife. Very fast. A fortnight later, according to English historian Raoul of Dicet; but in fact Louis waited a full five weeks. But no longer, for time was passing and he was growing older. The panegyric explains this haste. First of all, the king decided to remarry "counseled and urged by the archbishops, bishops, and other 'barons' of the kingdom," for his marriage was not just his own affair but that of his whole family, in this case of the entire network of vassalic bonds stretching over the whole of northern France. Louis was also acting "for his own salvation," since it was better to marry than to "burn." (Could he really have been burning so ardently still?) Finally we are given his real motive: "He was afraid the kingdom of France might not be ruled by an heir of his own seed."

A daughter of Thibaud of Blois was chosen to provide Louis with the necessary heir. Her father was not a king, and she had brothers and thus no hope of inheriting. But what counted in her favor was blood—the blood of Charlemagne—and her youth, a gage of fertility. All this caused the kinship question to be overlooked, close as the kinship was: Louis was marrying his son-in-law's sister. Five years later Philip was born.

The *Historia pontificalis*,[2] written closer to the event, in 1160–1161, and by John of Salisbury, a reliable witness, shows the divorce of Louis and Eleanor in a completely different light. The author had seen the couple brought before Pope Eugene III in 1149, as they were traveling across the Roman Campagna on their way back from the Second Crusade. The pope "completely resolved the discord that had arisen in Antioch between the king and queen, having heard the complaints of both. . . . He forbade any further mention of consanguinity between them; he affirmed the marriage; and orally and in writing, and on pain of anathema, he forbade anyone to engage in or credit attacks on the marriage or suggestions that it be dissolved. . . . Lastly, he arranged for them to sleep together in the same bed, which he had decked with his own most costly trappings."

This interesting episode brings onto the stage the supreme pontiff in person, the ruler whose decisions counted more than all others in the legal apparatus the Church had adopted in the course of its reform. And the pope unhesitatingly set the law of indissolubility above that of exogamy. He did not deny the incest; he merely forbade anyone to talk about it. He threw a spanner in the judicial machinery: there would be no divorce for any reason whatsoever. And then he affirmed the marriage; he even celebrated fresh nuptials, since he not only ended what in the life of Godelive was called the "spiritual discord" but also brought the bodies into the same bed, sumptuously hung like a kind of altar in a rite in which he himself played the father, blessing the couple and exhorting them to live in "charity."

What had happened was that the pope, after hearing the complaints of both parties, had pronounced judgment by virtue of his own pastoral responsibility and had brought about a reconciliation, as a bishop was supposed to do. Under what circumstances? This was a case of suspected adultery, and, according to the collections of canon law dating from that period, fornication was a ground for divorce. But if a marriage was ended for that reason, the parties were not allowed to remarry.

The trouble was that at this point Louis had only one daughter, and he was a king. The Church had somehow to make him stay married to his wife. We now see that the Parisian version of the story carefully disguised the fact that the royal marriage was not invalidated by the ban on incest alone. The *Historia pontificalis* is more informative: centralization ensured that every rumor found its way to the Roman Curia. So we learn from the *Historia* that it all started in Antioch, where the king and queen had stopped over because the army was in need of reorganization. Louis and Eleanor were the guests of Prince Raymond, Eleanor's uncle. "The prince's familiarity with the queen, their earnest and almost ceaseless conversations, aroused the king's suspicions." Conversation was the first stage in the ritual of courtly love, and the prelude to other pleasures.

When Louis decided to press on to Jerusalem, Eleanor refused to go with him. How are we to interpret the behavior of Raymond of Antioch? Was he just amusing himself? But as Eleanor's uncle, was he not rather trying to bring his niece and her handsome heritage under his power, so that he might marry her off to someone else for his own advantage? For this to be possible she had to be divorced from her husband. But not on grounds of fornication; on grounds of incest. And it was in Antioch that the question of kinship was raised—not, as the Capetian account tries to make us believe, by the king's family but on the initiative of the queen. Eleanor "mentioned her kin, saying that it was unlawful for her and her husband to remain together any longer, for they were related in the fourth and fifth degrees." She was speaking the truth, and John of Salisbury adds: "This [problem] had already been raised in France before they went away, when the late Barthélemy, bishop of Laon, calculated the degrees of consanguinity, but without being able to guarantee whether or not the *supputatio* was just."

The revelation, if it really was one, would presumably have troubled Louis VII. But, in fact, he was already worried—by fears of his wife's infidelity. A letter from Abbot Suger urged him to suppress his "rancor" until their return,[3] but the king "loved the queen with an almost immoderate affection. . . . He loved her vehemently, almost childishly." This was not *dilectio* or *caritas* but the carnal and earthly love that led to sin. According to John of Salisbury, the king's fault was that he was not behaving as a *senior* should; his grandfather, Philip, had been criticized for the same weakness. Evil entered into a marriage when the husband surrendered to passion and fell under the power of the wife.

Louis agreed to a divorce, but he consulted his household first. So here, brought in on a matrimonial matter, were not only the king's blood relations but also those connected with him as vassals. In the twelfth century the latest fashion among young men was to lay seige to their lord's lady and play at taking her away from him. But it was also their duty to watch over her—and to watch over her lord; to make sure that he did not leave her and take another wife without consulting his "friends." If the head of a family lost control of it by turning childish over love, the family would be divided. Eleanor had her supporters and laughed at the other factions, calling one of the king's most loyal friends a eunuch. Which he was, in fact, in spirit, being a Knight Templar.[4] Like one of the *"losengiers,"* the jealous characters in tales of courtly love, he retaliated by advising the king to take his wife away, and speedily. But on no account to divorce her, since "because of her kin, it could bring down lasting opprobrium on the kingdom of France if, among other misfortunes, it was said of the king that his wife had been stolen away or had left him."

The danger was shame, that King Louis might be "dishonored through his wife," as Ysengrin had been when he was deceived by Renard le Goupil.[5] The shame would be "lasting" because of the possibility of her bearing a child not his own.

At all events, Louis and Eleanor set off again together, each nursing his or her resentment. Had Pope Eugene III managed to reconcile them? He spoke not of *amor* but of *caritas*. But he too wanted to avoid the scandal of any tinge of illegitimacy and provided the pair with a bed for the purposes of lawful procreation.

Still, despite the pope's prohibition, Louis and Eleanor were divorced three years later at Beaugency.

Other contemporary chroniclers confirm almost all John of Salisbury says.[6] Lambert of Wattrelos,[7] who may have been one of the first to write about the divorce, also accuses the king of "childishness." William of Tyre,[8] meditating on the failure of the Second Crusade, sees the blame in the sinfulness of princes. Their worst sin was lust: Raymond of Antioch tried to carry off [*rapere*] the king's wife "by violence and occult machinations." It was not difficult. Eleanor was "one of those foolish women" who liked amusement. She was imprudent, and "by neglecting the law of marriage harmed the royal dignity"; she was "unfaithful to the marriage bed." William, weighing his words, reveals what everyone was thinking in Antioch and Tyre: it was just a commonplace matter of female adultery.

English historians at the end of the twelfth century took a harsher view. Whether they were for or against Henry II, they all condemned Eleanor. William of Newburgh attributed the defeat in the Holy Land to King Louis's passion[9]: he set a bad example by taking his wife with him on what was supposed to be a holy pilgrimage. The army should have remained chaste and without women; Crusaders, like any other warriors who wanted to win battles, needed to be continent. So it was the queen, a modern Eve, a temptress and a deceiver, who was responsible for the disaster. For William, as for Gervaise of Canterbury,[10] she was an adulteress. She was dissatisfied with the king's way of life and complained of having married a monk. She dreamed of other "nuptials" "more suited to her own morals," i.e., to her amorous disposition. She obtained her divorce through cunning.

Giraldus Cambrensis[11] saw Eleanor as Melusine, the wicked fairy, corrupting the whole race of English kings. Henry Plantagenet was less blameworthy: he was not child*ish* like Louis, but child*like* in the favorable sense of the term, as in the tales of chivalry and adventure. He valiantly abducted the wife of the king of France, and out of "knightly love" nobly avenged his grandfather, Fouque Réchin. The sin in the matter was Eleanor's, twice an adulteress, for Henry's father, "Geoffroi Plantagenet, when he was seneschal of France, had used her." He had expressly forbidden his son to have anything to do with her, for two reasons—"because she was the wife of his lord; and because his father had known her before him. So it was due to extreme licentiousness that King Henry, as it is said, made bold to besmirch the queen of France by an adulterous union."

Eleanor "behaved not like a queen but like a whore." That was all the Cistercian Hélinand of Froimont thought it necessary to say on the subject.[12]

These vicissitudes show the great respect paid to legal forms by the highest levels of society, though the hierarchical Church that applied these rules was extremely flexible in practice. The contemporary accounts tell us above all how, thirty years after the death of Yves of Chartres, the impediment of consanguinity was made use of.

The ecclesiastical authorities held the ban on incest in reserve to use in case of later need. William of Newburgh says that the nuptials of

Eleanor and Henry were precipitate. This may well have been because the prelates in the West, at the behest of the king of France, were getting ready to prevent the marriage on the entirely justifiable grounds of consanguinity. Perhaps it was more usual for a presumption of incest to pave the way for a dispensation, a favor that always had to be paid for in one way or another. Nevertheless it was a device serving first and foremost the interests of the laity. Eleanor and Louis VII in turn made use of it. Did they really believe that defilement was the issue? At any rate I doubt whether Pope Eugene III did. Reading between the lines of the various accounts of the affair—almost all of them written by men familiar with the courts of princes—we catch a glimpse of the game of love with its ritual dances and displays, and of the way people of fashion now set about attracting one another. What comes across even more clearly is how freely men could gain access to the lady in princely houses. Eleanor does not seem to have been given much protection at Antioch; and, according to the perhaps apocryphal story of her relations with Geoffroi Plantagenet, she was equally accessible in Paris.

Such domestic arrangements were bound to foster suspicions, which seem always to have been poised to fall upon the wife. They also made seduction a recognized weapon in the plotting for inheritances, and especially for heiresses, though the ladies were aware of this and played their own games. In any event, in the circles with which we are concerned female adultery was not just a fearful figment of husbands' imaginations but a feature of high society. The *losengiers* in the romances knew this and took advantage of it. It was a ground for divorce, though the husband might hesitate to use it because of the shame it brought on him.

One thing everyone agreed upon was that fornication by the wife destroyed the marital union of the flesh. So when Church leaders managed to reconcile a couple where this had occurred, they had to repeat the nuptial rite. Louis VII, though all the courts and courtiers laughed at him, was certainly a virtuous husband according to the Church, to which he was perhaps all too obedient for his wife's taste. But even he seems to have put the law of lineage first. After fifteen years of marriage, and the delivery of another daughter, he heeded heaven's warning, disregarded the injunctions of the pope, and divorced Eleanor. If she had gone on failing to produce a son, he would have lost Aquitaine anyway. Eleanor was of no further use to the line of the kings of France; in fact she was positively harmful. So with the approval of the French bishops, and in accordance with canon law, Louis divorced her.

The divorce of Raoul of Vermandois (see page 190) had not been nearly so easy and had dragged on for six years. In 1142, in order to marry Eleanor's sister, Raoul had dismissed his previous wife on the grounds that she was too closely related to him. His brother, the bishop of Tournai, together with Barthélemy, bishop of Laon, and the bishop of Senlis, all had shown up to calculate and swear to the degrees of consanguinity. But the relationship had not been so close as that between Raoul and the wife he was now proposing to marry. "A rumor of perjury," says Hermann of Tournai,[13] "spread through the region and was carried to the apostolic court by Count Thibaud of Champagne: the wife Raoul had dismissed was Thibaud's niece, and he resented this dishonor."

Thibaud, defending the prestige that was part of his family heritage, appealed to Rome for justice, for this was where princely cases were decided. The pope welcomed Thibaud's complaint: as a threatened obstacle to the king of France's new marriage, it might be used to make Louis give way on the subject of episcopal elections.[14] Innocent II supported the Cistercians. Saint Bernard, abbot of Clairvaux, had given his full backing to the count of Champagne, his benefactor, and was agitating and calling for action. Like the correspondence of Yves of Chartres, the letters of St. Bernard elucidate a national concern from an ecclesiastical point of view.

"What the Church has joined, how can the chamber [camera] put asunder?" Bernard wrote to the pope.[15] As far as I know he was the first to declare quite clearly that the Church did have the power to join. In 1084, for Godelive's biographer, it had been God who joined people in marriage. And according to the Scriptures it was God. Now here was someone saying that it was the priests. According to Saint Bernard they not only blessed but also effected the union. It was the expansion of the Church's jurisdiction that had brought about this astonishing change.

By using the word *camera* Bernard was being deliberately ambiguous. The "chamber" was the room where a lord made love, and it suggested the bed, which in turn suggested sin and the flesh. But in all the great houses, including that of the pope, the chamber was also where the money was kept. And it was by money that things spiritual were corrupted. Thus, money came upon the scene, a factor that was to loom ever larger, making social relationships in general and marriage relationships in particular increasingly flexible, and also changing people's mental attitudes. Gradually, while still masked by a thirst for prestige, the thirst for material gain began to enter into the motives influencing men of noble birth to take or leave a wife. Bernard warned the pope against selling a dispensation that would legitimize Raoul's marriage.

But the warning was unnecessary. At Lagny, in the territory belonging to the count of Champagne but quite near that of the Capetians, a papal legate was presiding over a council. Its decision was similar to that given a century and a half earlier against Robert the Pious. Raoul must take back his first wife on pain of excommunication. The three bishops who had acted as swearers in his divorce were suspended. Louis VII, who had arranged the proposed marriage to Eleanor's sister, was also disgraced.

Louis took up arms against the count of Champagne, and won. Thibaud gave in. Not so Bernard of Clairvaux: the power of the Church was at stake, together with the whole Gregorian structure subordinating the temporal to the spiritual. He wrote to the pope urging him not to weaken. He pressed Thibaud to fight back, which he did through other marriages: he planned to marry his eldest son into the house of Flanders, and his daughter into the house of the count of Soissons.

The king immediately protested that he ought to have been consulted: these matrimonial projects affected the future of the fief the count of Champagne held from him. The quarrel gives us a glimpse of a feudal lord's pretensions: he wanted to join with his vassals' kinsmen in supervising the marriage arrangements of his vassals' families. His pretext was that the fief was hereditary, passing from generation to generation, from the hands of one man to the hands of another. If both men were of the same blood it might be supposed that birth and education would predispose them to continue the old amity and serve out their tenure loyally. But if the successor was a son-in-law, a member of a different line, there was no guarantee that he would be a "friend." So the lord of the property wanted to have a say in the matter before his vassals' daughters were promised in marriage.

It was as part of the hard-fought game he was playing against the intrigues of the clerics that Louis VII challenged the validity of the two betrothals arranged by the count of Champagne. Hermann of Tournai tells us that Louis alleged incest as one objection and feudal custom as another.[16] Then Saint Bernard shifted his ground and tried to invalidate the charge of consanguinity, arguing, as had Henry of Lausanne, that it was a merely corporeal matter.

Here we see the strength of the current that, at the time Hugues of Saint-Victor was writing, was slowly, and in the name of spirituality, depriving the ban on incest of the supremacy it had enjoyed among the reformers of Christian society in the days of Yves of Chartres. Now, because of its close connection with the body and the blood, it was being relegated to the background.

The marriage bond united souls. Saint Bernard had already proclaimed that the bond was tied by the Church; now he was proclaiming that the Church, when its power was at stake, might pass over proximity of blood and refuse to untie the marriage bond on such grounds. Writing of the proposed marriages between the houses of Champagne, Flanders, and Soissons, he said, "Whether there is consanguinity I know not. I have never consciously approved illicit marriages, and do not now." Precisely. He did not want to know. "But I tell you that if you prevent these marriages you disarm the Church and deprive it of much of its strength." Nowhere else do we see so clearly the fundamental link between, on the one hand, the principle leading to the idea of marriage as an indissoluble sacrament, and, on the other, the unwillingness of the Church to yield any of its power.

In the end Thibaud abandoned his projects. But Raoul and the king of France did not achieve their ends until 1148. John of Salisbury, who was then present in the entourage of Pope Eugene III, explains in the *Historia pontificalis* how this came about.[17] Raoul had realized he needed friends in the college of cardinals, the place where decisions were made. "The intervention of money," wrote John of Salisbury sardonically, "is not excluded." Everything was privily arranged. All that remained were the public ceremonies.

On the appointed day, Raoul appeared before the pope's consistory in Reims. Raoul was confident and had promised to obey the pope's instructions. His first wife was there: just as mutual consent clearly pronounced by the interested parties themselves was necessary to make a marriage, so the husband and wife had to speak and be heard face to face for it to be unmade. Pope Eugene was about to quash a verdict arrived at by all his predecessors in turn, a verdict that for many years had rarely been challenged. He opened the case, first addressing the wife, and through her all the men of her family present to support her. As the defender of repudiated wives, the bishop of Rome promised to be kind to her: "You complain that you have been refused a hearing, that you have suffered violence, that your enemies have injured you; I bring you back into the realm of justice, so that you and yours, and likewise the count for his part, may adduce whatever you please."

The wife—the only lawful one for the moment—then made it clear that she did not wish to return to a husband whose *animus* had been taken away from her. But she thanked the pope and said she would be glad to listen to what her adversaries had to say.

Then Raoul's supporters came forward "to swear, with their hand on the Gospels, to the kinship they had on another occasion falsified." At their head was Barthélemy, bishop of Laon, a very saintly man himself and a friend of Saint Norbert and Saint Bernard. The pope prudently stopped him when he was about to lay his hand on the Bible to swear his oath. But the evidence was accepted and the divorce immediately pronounced. The marriage had been incestuous; it was null and void; husband and wife had permission to marry again.

But it was agreed that the count of Vermandois should give his wife back her dowry. It was then learned with some surprise that count Thibaud had already received compensation. The whole ceremonial was revealed as a put-up job. Some people were outraged, including Saint Bernard. Furious at the triumph of Raoul, "who for so long had scandalized the Church," he prophesied that "no good will come out of his bed."

His prediction, continued John of Salisbury, came true in part. His second wife soon died, leaving three children, including a son who contracted leprosy, a sure sign of corruption. The two daughters, who thus became heiresses, were well married, one to the count of Flanders and the other to the count of Nevers. Both proved to be barren. Heaven was punishing adultery through its offspring.

Raoul took a third wife and soon afterward fell ill. His doctor forbade him to make love: he was *uxorius*, under his wife's thumb, the prisoner of his libido. He disobeyed instructions—and three days later was dead.

The story has a twofold moral. John of Salisbury does not seem to have believed that Raoul's blood had been corrupted by incest: few people now believed that kinship ties were harmful beyond the third degree. No, Raoul had been punished for two other main offenses: first, for concupiscence, for failing to control himself or perhaps rather to control his wife; secondly, for having "scandalized the Church." Herein lay the second moral of the story: a sinner who submitted to the authority of the clergy would be pardoned. A good Christian had to join in the game, a subtle game complicated not only by the "cupidity" now invading the highest levels of the ecclesiastical hierarchy but also by the contradictions in the texts used as references. Appealing to these texts, Eugene III could dissolve a marriage in Reims and then restore it a year later in Tusculum, both judgments being arrived at in terms of its "utility" to the Church. All that mattered was that the Church's authority should be recognized.

This authority was recognized more and more in the second half of the twelfth century. The popes were now scholars, like Alexander III (1159–1180), formerly Master Roland, an eminent jurist. After being driven from Rome by Frederick Barbarossa, he lived for a long while in France as a friend of Louis VII. It was in France, taking over from Yves of Chartres but more majestically, that he answered the bishops' questions about marriage, making decisions and pronouncing judgments, more concerned than any of his predecessors had been with matters relating to matrimony.

Alexander stood firm on two principles: the indissolubility of marriage from the time vows were exchanged, and the need for a solemn ceremony at the church door in the presence of a priest. At the same time he reserved the right to be liberal and flexible, and to grant divorces or dispensations according to the circumstances and individuals involved. His pontificate saw an acceleration, on the marriage front as on others, of the movement tending to reconcile the morality preached by the Church with that supported by the heads of noble houses. But, after Alexander, there occurred in the house of the Capetians another crisis inextricably linked to the convolutions of politics.

The young Philip, son of Louis VII, was married on April 28, 1180. His father, who was to die later the same year and was no longer competent to govern, had since his last remarriage favored the Champagne faction. Philip, by a natural opposition, inclined toward Baudouin, count of Flanders. Baudouin was of Carolingian descent, and aware of the prophecy that was the talk of the region: seven generations after Hugues Capet—Philip's generation was the seventh—the crown of France would return to the direct line of Charlemagne.[18] Baudouin himself had no children: his wife was being punished for the disobedience of her father, Raoul of Vermandois (see pages 190 and 198). But Baudouin did not divorce her. His reluctance to repudiate her, a solution that half a century earlier would have been thought not only permissible but necessary, shows the effectiveness of the pressure brought to bear on the behavior of the nobles by the morality of the priests.

But Baudouin did have a niece, Elizabeth, whom he loved and treated as a daughter and whose father, the count of Hainaut and also of Carolingian descent, was even more fascinated by the legend of Charlemagne. In 1179 Elizabeth had been solemnly promised to the son of the count of Champagne. This pact was now canceled. Elizabeth, aged nine, became the *sponsa* of Philip, who was fifteen. The nuptials were to take place when she was nubile. In 1184 she was judged to be so; but meanwhile there had been a reversal of alliances. Philip had by now fallen under the influence of his maternal uncles from Champagne, who were trying to break off the match before it was consummated. A council was summoned at Senlis for this purpose. At first its theme was consanguinity. The chroniclers of Flanders and Hainaut recount that during the council the young Elizabeth went barefoot through the streets of the city, followed by lepers and the poor, all of whom joined her in demanding her rights outside the palace.

Philip took her back but "out of marital duty and without communicating with her in bed." She was very young, but many girls were married and pregnant at her age. She waited, and in 1187 gave birth to a son, Louis. But three years later she was dying, perhaps because of having had a child when she was still too young. She had served her purpose. Her uncle and aunt had been generous with her dowry, and her widower, in the name of her son, held on to the handsome *maritagium*.

Philip then went off to the Crusades. When he came back, ailing, he was anxious to marry again, as his father had done twice and for the same reasons. He was "burning"; and, besides, his dynastic duty required his remarriage, for young Louis was sickly, and many people's thoughts turned to the prophecy. What Philip needed was a king's daughter, someone of good blood, and on August 14, 1193, he married Ingeborg of Denmark. Everything was made ready for her to be crowned queen the day after the nuptials. But by the morning the king had had enough of her: all of a sudden, during the wedding night, just as in the case of Saint Godelive, the love in the husband's heart had changed to repulsion.

The monk Rigord explains that, like Guibert of Nogent's father,

Philip had been "prevented by a spell" from fulfilling his part of the bargain. But the king could not wait seven years for the magic "knot" to be untied. In Compiègne, before an assembly of barons and bishops presided over by the archbishop of Reims, fifteen duly sworn witnesses, twelve of them from the king's family, solemnly calculated the degrees of consanguinity and showed that Philip and Ingeborg were fourth cousins.

This had seemed the simplest solution. But Ingeborg's brother, the king of Denmark, was no more prepared to be shamed in this fashion than Thibaud of Champagne had been. As Thibaud had done, he appealed to the pope, claiming that the calculations were wrong and producing what he claimed were correct genealogies. Pope Celestine III issued a warning to Philip, but prudently left it at that.

In June 1196 Philip took another wife: Agnès, daughter of the duke of Méranie. But Ingeborg was still alive, so he was committing bigamy. A new pope, Innocent III, on coming to power in 1198 flexed his theocratic muscles by urging Philip to drive the *"superducta"* from his bed and thus put an end not only to the adultery but also to the incest, for Agnès's sister was married to a nephew of Philip's.

The legate, Peter of Capua, did not go so far as excommunication, but he did lay France under an interdict, which meant that all religious services were to be suspended. Negotiations lasted for fifteen years, severity alternating with leniency, depending on whether the pope felt himself in a position of strength or weakness. In any case, the prelates did not apply the interdict. It was the time of the great Cathar upsurge, and as the Church was then confronted with the much more serious problem of heresy, Philip had only to go through the motions of submitting and to accept the judgment of the cardinals, and the interdict was lifted. The case opened in Soissons in 1201 before two legates: one, a kinsman of the king, was prepared to be accommodating; the other, a former Benedictine, was obdurate. For a fortnight the jurists battled with one another. Then one day Philip bolted, taking Ingeborg with him. According to Rigord, "He was escaping from the Romans' clutches."

The pope now had more need than ever of the Capetians' friendship, and the king's envoys kept hammering away at the Curia. In August,

Agnès died. Ingeborg still survived: as Philip would have nothing to do with her, she was spared the perils of childbearing. Philip was no longer a bigamist, but he was living in sin: in 1205 a "damsel from Arras" bore him a bastard son. Could the child's soul be left at risk? Philip protested: he was being treated more harshly than Frederick Barbarossa or Jean sans Terre, or his own father, Louis VII.

His officials drew up marriage plans designed to satisfy Innocent III, and the pope was beginning to weaken. In November 1201, he had legitimized the son and daughter Agnès of Méranie had borne the king, defending his decision with the argument that he was acting in the public interest and making the succession to the throne less hazardous. Besides, was Philip as culpable as all that? He had come to Compiègne, and he had recognized the authority of the Church.

Step by step they approached a compromise. The pretext of incest could no longer be used, but they chose another: the marriage between Philip and Ingeborg had not been consummated. They recalled a decision by Alexander III in which he authorized the remarriage of a fifteen-year-old boy who had irreparably damaged his twelve-year-old bride on their wedding night. But Ingeborg put an obstacle in the way here: she obstinately refused to admit that she had not had intercourse with Philip. The casuists did their best, suggesting a distinction between the "mingling of sexes" and the "mingling of sperm in the female vessel." But it began to look as if there was nothing for it but the last resort: the queen would have to agree to take the veil.

But, in April 1213, Philip, who with the pope's approval was preparing to invade England, announced that he was taking his wife back. His son Louis had just had an heir. The matter was closed.

Philip's differences with the Church had lasted a long time and, in the course of his ups and downs, given the doctors of the Church much food for thought. Let us try to imagine the immense intellectual effort of the period: the canonists trying to reconcile the contradictions in the authoritative texts; the lawyers in every large city called on to resolve concrete difficulties; and in Paris the biblical commentators, addressing the metaphor of marriage and trying to develop the notion of the relationship between the Church and its divine inspiration.

This line of thought was now culminating in the image of the coronation of the Virgin, the great spectacle with which sculptors were decorating the spandrel at Senlis just when Philip was rejecting Ingeborg. To represent the Virgin-Church beside Christ the bridegroom, and on the same level, was to signify the equality of husband and wife in marriage. But this act of crowning, while incidentally doing away with the usual subordination of a son to his mother, at the same time authorized the idea that the husband is the "head" of his wife, who—endowed with his gifts and wanting only what he wants—is necessarily subordinate to him. In any event, marriage was magnified by this display of symbols; and, as Guy Lobrichon has pointed out to me,[19] we find nothing in the glosses on the Apocalypse after the beginning of the thirteenth century that accords the married state any less dignity.

But already the masters in the Paris schools, whose object was to turn their pupils into effective preachers, were slanting their *leçon*, the annotated reading of the *divina pagina*, so as to draw moral lessons from it. They used edifying anecdotes to relate sacred text to everyday life and social reality.

Many of these scholars were connected with the chapel royal and had been directly involved in the divorce of Louis and Eleanor and the proceedings resorted to in it. One such was Peter, cantor of the chapter of Notre-Dame.[20] From those of his teaching notes that survive, we can see how preoccupied he was with the institution of marriage and the laxity and uncertainty it had fallen into. "Marriage is the chief sacrament of the Church. It is so through the authority of Him who founded it and by reason of the place, Paradise, where it was instituted. . . . I am amazed therefore that it should be subject to so many variations: no other sacrament varies so much."[21] It was the arbitrary power of the pope that was responsible for this state of affairs; he had become master of the law. "It is in his power to issue decrees, to interpret them, and to abrogate them."

Jean Bellesmains, archbishop of Lyons (1182–1193), had said the same to clerics from Paris on their way to Rome: they must be careful; they were going among men used to juggling texts. This trickery was profitable. It made it easier to grant dispensations, and to sell them even to third cousins [wishing to marry].

Another teacher, Robert de Courçon, takes the case of Eleanor as an example.[22] Recalling the indulgence that allowed her first to remain with Louis VII and then to marry Henry Plantagenet, he wondered whether papal power, in permitting such departures from the law, was really acting for the "utility" of the Christian community. For the answer one had only to look at the wars that ensued.

But for such moralists, those responsible for all this uncertainty were above all the *curiales*, the officials of the Roman Curia and of all the minor episcopal courts. These writers denounced the lawyers' greed and the financial transactions that allowed cases to be sent back from the papal tribunal to local and more indulgent courts. Peter the Cantor tells of a case from his own experience.

Two of his kinsfolk came to consult him. They knew they were married "within the seventh degree" and were unhappy about it; the rapid rise of preaching and private confession had sensitized lay consciences. What were they to do to set their minds at rest? "Go to Rome," Peter told them, "but do not give up until you have obtained a clear verdict of either confirmation or divorce." But try as they might, they were sent back to the archbishop of Sens, who passed them on to the bishop of Paris, who confirmed their marriage.

This was wise enough, but scarcely in accordance with the principles Yves of Chartres had worked so hard to establish; not to mention the waste of time involved, and all the money consumed in expenses and gifts.

Robert de Courçon thundered against the men "who, through the Church of the Gauls, are paid to celebrate divorces"—i.e., to swear to findings of incest—"and who break the marriage bond as if it were something of no account."[23] He pointed out the shocking contrast between such casualness and the sacred character the Church was trying to attach to the wedding ceremony.

Stephen Langton reports an anecdote from England.[24] The king, like his predecessor Henry I, wanted to "arrange a marriage between unlawful partners." He wrote to the pope for a dispensation, and a cardinal saw the letters. "I thought the king knew better," he said: there were other and shorter methods. And Langton draws the moral that "the Church allows many things, and conceals what it does not approve." Misappropriation, hypocrisy, perjury, the clink of gold being counted— all these made a mockery of the laws of marriage. Something was wrong —and it was this that brought the law of indissolubility and the need for exogamy into conflict.

Peter the Cantor heard a knight about to get married say of his future wife, "I like her because she has a large dowry. She is probably related to me by an affinity of the third degree, but that is not close enough to require me to repudiate her. Still, if I find I do not like her anymore, because of that affinity I could be granted a divorce."[25] As this *exemplum* shows quite unashamedly, "The tangled links of consanguinity and affinity make for endless transgressions." And the poor were at a disadvantage. Everything was being corrupted by money.

People needed to look again at Leviticus 18 and 20, the only sacred text that could justify the prohibition against marriage between relatives. They would see that it was very limited in scope, forbidding only ten categories of people to marry each other.[26] Why extend the ban? To spread affection more widely? Everyone knew that affection was no longer natural beyond the fourth degree of consanguinity [direct blood relation], and the second degree of affinity [relation by marriage]. To create and maintain it beyond, people linked by those more distant relationships must be allowed to marry.

Everything combined to restrict the notion of incest, to lower the threshold by three degrees. To the great distress of the cardinals, the lawyers, and the professional oath-takers, this conciliatory proposal was adopted by the Fathers of the Church at the Lateran Council of 1215.

CHAPTER XI
LITERATURE

After 1150 the mists which before that date hid marriage practices from us begin to disappear. There is still a veil between them and us—all the evidence comes from churchmen—but it is not so thick, and above all it distorts less. Among the writings that have come down to us are many that were intended to please the nobility, to amuse, reassure, and educate them all at once. Of course they do not show us how people really behaved, but rather how their authors wished people would behave. They back up a system of values still strongly marked by clerical ideology: what we hear is not what the aristocracy said about itself but what the priests said to the nobles. It was a discourse subject to pressure from two opposing models, the ecclesiastical and the secular, each of which prevailed, depending on which literary genre was involved.

Clerical ideology is at its weightiest in the sermon, several of which have survived from this period. Jacques Le Goff has brought to my attention three unpublished ones written by Jacques of Vitry at the end of the reign of Philip Augustus.[1] They were composed in Latin as models for the author's fellow preachers, who translated them into the vernacular and delivered them to a congregation of men and women ranged before them in segregated groups.

But the sermons were really addressed to the men and laid stress on certain points. One constantly recurring theme dominating everything was that women were wicked, lewd as vipers and slippery as eels; not to mention inquisitive, indiscreet, and cantankerous. This was just what husbands liked to hear. Some of them had daughters: well, let them prepare their girls carefully for the estate to which they were called, i.e., marriage, and steer them away from love songs and games of slap and tickle, which encouraged a taste for pleasure. When fathers came to drawing up the marriage contract, let them obey the rules: everything must be open and aboveboard; there must be no hole-and-corner marriages with just a scribe presiding; "priestesses" were instruments of the Devil. Marriage was instituted in Paradise and the Church was its image, so it must be concluded at the church door. As for other members of the congregation, who had not yet taken a wife, let them make haste and thus avoid the sins of fornication, homosexuality, and bestiality.

Having acquired a wife, a man must learn to rule her. Eve was not made from Adam's feet: wives must not be trampled on. But neither was she taken from his head: wives must not command. On one plane alone were husband and wife equal, and that was the plane of marital duties. The husband must respond to his wife's requests; but it was his duty to exercise ultimate control. It was this precise point that constituted the "rule" of the order of marriage, and obedience to it was more of a problem than obedience in any other order of the Church. A husband must refuse his wife's demands at forbidden times. He must be moderate; the Flood had been a punishment for sexual excess. And when he did obey his wife he must be careful not to deviate from the rules of nature: misuse of sex was one of the perils of marriage. But much worse than this was adultery—on the part of the wife, of course.

In adultery, sin took many forms: an oath was broken; the priestly benediction was spurned. A wife who went astray committed a theft— "The lover has the white bread, the husband the black." And the consequences were terrible. Who was the child's father? Would an illegitimate child not be likely to usurp the rights of the true heirs? Might he not take his sister as his wife unawares? So a husband's first duty was vigilance. He must not let his wife dress too attractively lest she inflame the desire of another. At the slightest suspicion, he must cast off the sin by casting off the woman.

It seems a very crude message. Which was why it struck home.

A more effective way of putting across the message about adultery was to dramatize it. A major innovation in the period we are considering was the use of the stage and its various devices for conveying moral lessons in the vernacular.

We do not know for sure where and when the *Jeu d'Adam*, or *Play of Adam*,[2] was composed. A sort of Christmas para-liturgy, it was probably first set down between 1150 and 1170 near the court of Henry Plantagenet, then the most outstanding center of literary creativeness. What is certain is that it was addressed to an aristocratic audience and performed in a church; the stage directions in the manuscript show that it called upon a set of already well-established technical resources. The main subject is original sin, i.e., marriage. The scene is Paradise, where the sacrament of marriage was instituted, and there are four characters: Adam, the husband; Eve, the wife; God, or good; and Satan, or evil. The text, a commentary on the Book of Genesis, is transmitted through these four voices, and with the help of versification indoctrinates the lay mind with the Church's matrimonial morality.

The play begins by setting out God's intentions and the form he originally meant marriage to take and to which it is necessary to refer if subsequent fallings-away are to be corrected. As Maurice Accarie has pointed out,[3] this model is feudal in structure. The princes and knights in the audience are shown Adam as a vassal of God, bound and subject to Him as they themselves were bound by homage and fealty. He possessed a fief the Lord would confiscate if he were guilty of a felony. But the hierarchy consisted of three levels: beneath man was woman, the vassal of man and under-vassal of God. As a good suzerain, the Almighty urged Adam to rule Eve through reason, and Eve to serve Adam with goodwill so that she in turn might be rewarded: "If you help Adam as you ought, I will set you beside him in my glory."

The vocabulary makes the marriage contract parallel to the vassalic one: both unite two parties equal in nature but necessarily unequal in power, so that one must serve the other. The relationship between husband and wife reflects at a lower level the primal relationship between the Creator and his creatures. This brings out the true nature of our first parents' sin. Satan insinuated himself in order to break the rule and introduce parity between husband and wife, and in consequence between God and man—parity in this case being synonymous with disorder. He suggests to Adam: "You will be the Creator's peer."

The author, treating his scriptural original with some freedom, represents Adam as the first to be subjected to temptation. Twice he is tempted, but he holds out through the strength of his reason. Satan then decides to appeal to the senses, and turns to the woman. Eve describes the taste and brightness of the apple he holds out to her, and the sensual pleasure it imparts. She represents the weakness in human nature, its irrational and sensuous aspect. She yields, and if Adam too is lost, that is because for a moment he agrees to regard his wife as his equal: "I will believe you because you are my peer." His sin is to abdicate, and fall from, his own superiority.

He is immediately filled with resentment. He hides from God, offering the feeble excuse: "I yielded to the wicked counsels of my wicked wife; she betrayed me." Even after he has been driven out of Paradise, he goes on blaming Eve. But she, in the long monologue that ends this part of the play, gives an example of redeeming humility, recalling that of Mary, the new Eve. She puts herself into the hands of God, her suzerain. It is for Him to judge, not for her husband, who failed in his seigneurial duties, insulting her and withholding his aid. She is therefore no longer bound in fealty to him; her faith is transferred to the superior lord. Eve also admits her guilt, and this example of contrition was very important at a time when the Church's teaching tended to center on the sacrament of penance, carrying with it obedience to the priests and acceptance of the grace they dispensed. Moreover, Eve gives an example of hope: one day someone will come to take away the sins of the world. That was the meaning of the work as a whole; Adam and Eve figure, as they were soon to do on many a cathedral porch, as the head of a long procession of prophetic characters foretelling the coming of the Messiah. Morality and theology were inseparable.

Marriage thus occupied a key position in the Church's ideology and its image of a perfect society. Together with the theory of the three functional orders, it formed the cornerstone of the social edifice. The whole universe was hierarchical, with order maintained throughout all levels by the presumption that every superior could expect reverence and obedience from his subordinate, while owing him aid and comfort in return. This relationship of necessary inequality was expressed in the symbolism of the *desponsatio*, offering a striking parallel to the symbolism of homage. Both rites included an exchange of vows between equals, the kneeling of the one who was to serve before the one who was to be served, and, in the husband's giving of the ring and the lord's giving of the straw of investiture, the same sign of magnanimous condescension. Both rites were a barrier against disorder, a bulwark of public peace. Both were instituted in Paradise, in the state of perfection where *ratio* ruled over *sensus*. It was considered necessary constantly to remind people of these origins, because, ever since the Fall, sensuality had been striving to get the upper hand. Rebellion was continually awaiting its chance, among women and vassals alike.

The *Jeu* seems to have been presented at a time when, deep down among the populace, there were signs of unrest, with heresy rampant. Heresy, in its diabolical way, suggested that women should be treated as equals, and against this danger Saint Bernard had revived all the accusations of debauchery bruited about by Guibert of Nogent. Monasteries for men and women, where male superiority was called into question, were condemned. New forms of spiritual life were suggested to take care of all the nubile women without husbands, to steer them away from the deviant sects: convents were one alternative, though there were harsher methods of exclusion, of putting them, like lepers, where they could do no harm.

I wonder whether the strong wave of reaction against the trend toward female emancipation was not partly responsible for the reversal of attitude that was first observable among noble families in the last third of the twelfth century: more young men were allowed to marry, perhaps because it seemed best to place one's daughters under the control of a husband.

For high society was still wary. It liked to hear the institutions of both feudalism and marriage being associated with the actual Creation. A satisfactory distribution of power rested on this dual foundation. Bishop Etienne of Fougères, delivering a sermon in his own dialect, recommended that women be kept under strict constraint: he was referring, of course, to high-born ladies; the others did not count. If they were left to their own devices their perversity would be unbounded: they would seek pleasure even among the servants, or with one another.

As well as being anti-feminist, anti-heretical, and in general anti-egalitarian, such outbursts were also directed against courtly love. They condemned the worldly pastimes in which men pretended to abase themselves before women, simulating mutual love and scandalously playing at serving ladies as they ought to serve only their lord. The last words of the *Jeu d'Adam* warned its audience to beware of poets.

But certain clerics were beginning to be much more tolerant of secular ideology. André le Chapelain, who worked in the chancellery of the young King Philip, wrote a treatise *On Love* between 1186 and 1190.[4] It was about *amor*, not about the *dilectio* and reverence felt for each other by virtuous husbands and wives. So it dealt not with marriage but with the game that less easy-going churchmen condemned, though admittedly it ends on a note of reprobation, saying that love is better avoided altogether. It was a didactic work, written in Latin and in a scholastic style, and dedicated to a layman as yet unmarried. It sets out to teach lovers how to behave in an orderly and "seemly" fashion. I do not think its conclusion is artificial: the whole argument moves from the physical to the spiritual, and thus leads farther and farther away from women. But it would be wrong not to allow for the irony contained in this Parisian essay, the main part of which treats in dialogue form the elegance and good manners of courtly love, a game then triumphing over the traditions of austerity in the royal household.

André, defending this pastime, distinguishes it from common love, love that is popular and crude. The love he is talking about has its own laws, and, far from undermining moral and social order, it helps to strengthen it by virtue of its remaining outside the neighboring but strictly separate realm of marriage. "Love cannot develop in its true forms between husbands and wives, because lovers grant one another everything freely and without constraint, whereas husbands and wives are duty bound to obey one another and refuse nothing." We should note in passing that the love André is talking about is not platonic.

But, for all its liberality and largess, courtly love was gratuitous, ludic, something apart from the serious things of life. For that reason, this treatise only skirts round our subject of marriage; but in doing so it defines it negatively, showing what it ought to be according to the morality of courtly love. André presents a man of very noble degree and a woman less noble,[5] the first instructing the second from a position of social superiority. When the woman asks whether conjugal love, which is without stain, is not better than courtly love, the man answers that it is not. If love—not charity, but strong, ardent, physical love—springs up within marriage, it can lead to excessive pleasure, which is sin. "Moreover, when people defile something sacred by abusing it, they are more severely punished than when they commit ordinary excesses. And the sin is more serious when committed with a married woman than with an unmarried one, for as the law of the Church teaches, anyone who loves his wife too ardently is considered guilty of adultery."

That indeed had been the doctrine formulated by Saint Jerome, and later by Peter Lombard: "The act of procreation is permitted in marriage, but whorish pleasures are condemned."[6] In the words of Alain of Lille: "An extreme *amator* of his wife is an adulterer."[7] While we must remember that our authors must sometimes have smiled, they were nevertheless convinced that marriage was not a game: if people wanted to play, they should do so outside marriage. Marriage was an order and therefore subject to discipline, and it was outside that order, on the wilder shores of life, that amorous adventures belonged, together with prostitution. Courtly love and prostitution both performed a useful function by siphoning excessive ardor from marriage, thus helping to preserve its proper state of moderation.

André was speaking here as a priest and chaplain. He was sure of a hearing not only from the bachelors, jealous of those who were not celibate, but also from the *seniores*, the heads of families who did not want to see marriage become licentious: you did not treat your wife [*uxor*] as you treated your lady-friend [*amica*].

Freedom and adventure were for men only. The sixth dialogue in Book II of *On Love* draws a clear distinction between male and female morality.[8] Men, even married men, could stray, as long as they did not go too far and destroy noble marriages in their quest for pleasure. "This is tolerated in men because it is customary and also a privilege of their sex to do everything that in this world is unseemly by nature." Women, on the other hand, were expected to be modest and reserved. If they took more than one lover, they were breaking the rules and would be excluded from the company of respectable ladies.

What difference is there, fundamentally, between the teaching of the treatise *On Love* and that of the *Jeu d'Adam* or of Etienne of Fougères? In all of them, man is the dominant figure and takes the lead. All put forth a male morality based on a primal fear of women and a determination to treat them as objects.

André was really writing for the prince, Philip Augustus, using his knowledge and literary skill to serve his patron, turning phrases to instruct and delight the court. At the end of the twelfth century, princes wanted to domesticate their knights, to attract them to their courts and keep them there. So Philip's court had to be agreeable, dispensing not only the physical pleasures as it always had but also the pleasures of the mind. These too were now part of the largess expected of a patron. The court had an educational function, one element of its political one of contributing to public order by bringing young men up under the prince's eye and teaching them to live according to the rules of *honestas*, thus strengthening the foundations of a whole system of values.

Any such small, closed society was full of young men learning to become knights, and such works as André's were primarily addressed to the "*jeunesse*," that youthful and most turbulent part of the courtly community. The young "bachelors" learned from their elders how to fight and hunt, but in the intervals between physical exercises they also learned how to behave, by listening to the tales and anecdotes that illustrated high society's dream of itself. The dream might be reflected on one of two planes: outside reality, on the plane of fiction and the imagination; or within reality, through experience, memory, history.

All the stories of the period showed, among other things, how men ought to behave toward women. The purely fictional accounts tended to treat the *game* of love, describing marriage from the outside, according it a lesser importance that varied in scope according to the literary genre involved. Epics celebrating military valor and feudal loyalty made women marginal figures, the wives of heroes, with very minor roles whichever side of the conflict they belonged to. Some were excellent mates and "helpers"—provident, supportive, just what they ought to be. Others were witches or immodest creatures full of the evil that threatened marriage. In either case, all this was ephemeral, lightly sketched and relegated to the background.

More was said about wives through the vehicle of comic short stories. What did people laugh at in them? Deceived husbands. But when people laugh at themselves they laugh ruefully, and so the objects of ridicule in the *fabliaux* rarely belonged to the gentry itself; instead, they were usually burghers, officials, peasants, or animals.[9] But sometimes the court was used as a setting, as it was in all the romances.

Few husbands escaped misfortune in these works. The backgrounds to the plots show how easily conditions in a noble household lent themselves to its mistress's adultery. She could easily meet her lover in the orchard or in the chamber. In the lai, or tale, of *Ignauré* there are no walls to prevent a lord from having his way with the wives of each of his twelve peers in turn. In fact the trouble was that there was nowhere safe to hide. A wife could be spied on from all sides—by those who envied her, by the chosen suitor's rivals, by the ladies he had spurned, and by her husband, who might fall prey to morbid jealousy as he grew older. Sometimes the errant pair were caught red-handed, at which point the wife and her accomplice might be bound just as they were while witnesses were called in from far and wide—"raising the cry through the city," as King Mark did when he discovered Isolde's infidelity.

The shame had to be public and established in order to be legitimately avenged. The husband had the right to kill. Despite the fact that Tristan asked to be put to "the ordeal,"[10] offering to fight three barons in a trial by combat, Mark prepared, as had Fouque Nerra, to burn both his wife and her lover. That was the natural ending to the story. In order to lengthen it, the authors of the romances elaborated upon the suspicion of adultery. They then described the legal procedures. Isolde offered to submit to the ordeal, but was let off, as the bishops required. She then took a purgatory oath and escaped by means of a trick. What is interesting about such details is that they show to what extent such infractions of the marriage laws were viewed as matters of secular justice, and did not fall within the jurisdiction of the Church.

I would say they were more than secular: they were private and domestic. It was for the members of the household involved to observe the effect of the red-hot iron and to hear the wife swear her innocence, taking God as her witness and laying her hand on the Gospels or some holy relic. Certainly it was not a matter for the husband to decide on his own. He had to heed counsel. But that counsel did not have to come from outside his own household or family; and the priests did not enter into it.

Of course, the husband's own escapades did not give rise to any such proceedings; nor were they a fit subject for romances. For it was honor that was at stake, and honor, though it was the business of men, depended on the behavior of women. The women were not always consenting parties: there was a good deal of rape in noble houses. When

Geoffroi Plantagenet took Eleanor, the very young wife of his lord, did he not take her by force? And look at the case of Queen Lionne in the *Roman de Renard*: Renard slipped into her bed and made love to her against her will, yet she was found guilty. Whether she had been raped or not, she had had pleasure outside marriage. The people who laughed at these tales were on the side of the rapists, who embodied the power of aggressive virility. For there is no doubt about it: what these works called "love," whether in Latin or in various dialects of the vernacular, was quite simply desire, the desire of men, and men's sexual exploits.

This is true even of the tales of so-called courtly love. Their theme was violent, sudden "love," which, like a flame, once kindled was irresistible. It heated the blood, inciting a man to attain at no matter what cost what Marie de France calls the "surplus."[11] This desire encountered obstacles that had to be removed one after the other. Lovers were always star-crossed, and the man had to submit to a series of tests. This was an educational process. A knight, in order fully to become a man, had to pursue this course throughout his *jeunesse* until he too joined the ranks of the heads of families.

A married woman was usually both his initiator and the object of his desire. She was the wife of his lord, who was often his uncle. Love grew out of the domestic propinquity Bourchard of Worms and Yves of Chartres thought dangerously propitious to adultery and incest. The bachelor hero, like most of his contemporaries among the nobility, left his father's house as a boy to be a kind of apprentice in the house of another, very often that of his mother's brother. This practice arose out of the customary inequality of rank between husbands and wives in the aristocracy. The maternal and usually superior line, by taking these boys in as soon as they reached the age of reason, strengthened its hold on the bearers of the ancestral blood born of a different family. In every noble household the head would maintain year after year such of his sisters' sons as were not dedicated to the service of God. He educated them, armed them, married them off, acted toward them as a father. (In the case of Charlemagne and ˙Roland, myth attributes this affective paternity to an incestuous paternity of blood.) And while his nephews served the lord as sons, at the same time they desired his wife. She, like the Virgin Mary in other cases, took the place in their hearts of the mother from whom they had been exiled so young. Thus do the plots of courtly romance reflect real relationships of conviviality as it existed in those days. If love is never depicted as arising between an uncle and his nephew's wife, it is because, as soon as the nephew married, he set up house elsewhere.

So the seed of love was sown in the friendship whose natural setting was kinship. I fell in love with you, says Isolde to Tristan, "because you were his nephew, and you did more for his glory than all the rest." The uncle's wife was bound to cherish his nephew because of the very reverence she owed her husband. Her role was to help in the nephew's education. As a teacher, and also because she was older than he—not much, but always to some extent—she was in a position of superiority. So she was the "lord" to his "vassal," and we see how easily the words and gestures of the rites of vassalage could be incorporated into the ritual of courtly love. This inverted the hierarchy of the sexes: Eve was above Adam and bore the responsibility for his sin. The romances tell the story of his fall. But adultery, though consummated, was barren. Bastardy was too serious a matter to be treated lightly even in literature. People were too afraid of it to use it as a subject for a tale.

So the lady, herself a victim of desire, yielded, offering herself to the lover. But she was likely to find that, like Potiphar's wife, she was left with nothing but a piece of his garment in her hand. Then she would become jealous and lie, saying the hero had pursued and ravished her. Occasionally the young man did put up some resistance, out of loyalty to his lord or holding out for a lawful and requited love that would earn him a wife. Then he would have to flee the uncle's wrath and set off in search of adventure.

Reality breaks through in the tales of adventure, too. In the twelfth century most youths were obliged to seek their fortune. They would roam from tournament to tournament, displaying their prowess and risking their lives in the hope of winning fame and perhaps, if they outdid their rivals, a wife. Transposed into works of the imagination, this perilous journey took place in two worlds.

One was like the real world, depicting knights-errant sheltered for the night by worthy country gentlemen, each with a houseful of meek and willing "virgins" skilled at massaging a weary warrior until dawn if need be.[12] If the hero was attractive, the maidens would fall in love—after all, they were women—and be very free with their favors:

So did they dally and embrace
That Gawain her deflower'd,
But she gave in with willing grace,
And never said a word.[13]

These easy-going damsels did not bother their heads about kinship. Arol[14] discovered one morning that the hand that had strayed as far as his "maiselle" belonged to a cousin, and he thanked heaven he had restrained himself. Such considerations apart, this sort of diversion was less culpable because the young ladies involved were not thinking of marriage. But they did run the risk referred to by Marie de France in *Milon*: the wrath of the bridegroom, finding out on his wedding night that his bride's maidenhead was already gone. Was this just a novelist's exaggeration? Did respectable men keep a more jealous watch on their daughters' virginity?

But sometimes the travels of the knight-errant took him across invisible frontiers into a different world, one full of marvels where he encountered beautiful white-skinned damsels bathing naked in clear springs. They were unknown, nameless, and therefore dangerous: they might be the knight's kinswomen—the clerical writers of romances lost no opportunity to arouse their audience's fear of incest. Or the ladies might be fairies, in which case they were usually raped. Despite their being victims of brutal male desire, they would then attach themselves to their ravishers, generously bestowing on them wealth and offspring. And yet they remained distant, inaccessible and mysterious, mining their lovers' paths to them with all sorts of prohibitions that, if disregarded, meant disaster. These fabulous creatures are probably best understood as further substitutes for the knight's lost mother. What the Virgin Mary was to Guibert of Nogent, the fairies were to many frustrated knights, who were often younger sons handed over to wet nurses as soon as they were born and, to all intents and purposes, orphaned of their mothers. When they imagined themselves winning, by violent and dangerous means, these enticing, elusive, dominating fays, they must have felt they were conquering their anxieties and returning to the warm bosom of their earliest infancy.

Like André le Chapelain's essay on the art of love, the literature of invention seems to skirt round the subject of marriage. But it tends irresistibly, though implicitly, toward it. For in the minds of the "young men" who enjoyed reading these works, there were two conflicting impulses. They dreamed of undermining the institution of marriage from which they were excluded, but at the same time they hoped to get married in spite of all the obstacles in their way. A mirage shimmered at the end of every adventure: the perfect woman, whom the knight would capture and upon whom he would beget splendid sons. The values of marriage itself were deeply embedded in these classic tales of romance.

The *Conte du Manteau*, or Tale of the Cloak, relates the story of a magic garment with the power to reveal the infidelity of every wife present at a courtly gathering—every wife except one. Her husband represents the hope that is the goal of every uncertain quest. In the poems attributed to Marie de France, ideal love is that which leads to marriage. She was writing in the last third of the twelfth century.

It was after the sixties of that century that a new trend emerged in fashionable circles in northern France, in the courts that set the tone and launched new fashions in dressing and speaking and showing off. People wanted to bring the fantasies of amorous pursuit and the responsibilities of marriage closer together. Chrétien de Troyes was trying to cater to the taste of his public, one of the most elegant and refined of its day, and perhaps by looking more closely at the way he intertwined love and marriage in the stories he wrote between 1170 and 1180 we may learn how this feeling was growing.

Apart from the sudden sublimation in the *Conte du Graal*, where a vow of chastity covers the forced renunciations to which the "young men" were subjected throughout their long educations in chivalry, most literary compositions increasingly taught that love—the love of both body and heart—found its fulfillment in marriage, and in the procreation denied to faithless women and Guineveres too consumed by passion for their "sperm" to be fertile. Fidelity, painfully acquired self-mastery, all the virile virtues—these guaranteed, through unions made strong by the husband's authority, the establishment of families and the perpetuation of dynasties. The young hero of the *Roman de la Rose*, when he ventures into the garden, is tempted by a flower that is in bud—a virgin, not a lady. And it is with honorable intentions that he reaches out to pluck it: to make the chosen one his wife.

At the beginning of the thirteenth century, in a society that was gradually losing its inflexibility and where more and more men were allowed to marry, the poems and romances that gave expression to men's dreams still showed a clear distinction between the erotic extramarital games reflected in André le Chapelain and the charitable relationship that was supposed to exist between husband and wife. But these two male attitudes toward the opposite sex seemed now to coincide with two normally consecutive stages in the life of a man born into a family of distinction. He was allowed a predatory period, a time for prowess and pursuit, for what Georges Dumézil would call "secondary amours." But the time also came when the man must turn his back on adventure, become mature, and settle down "in peace and good behavior." The transition from one stage to the other was marked by rites of passage, of which marriage was one.

But all these works of fiction, intended to instruct while giving pleasure, had something in common: they did not depict the rites attendant on marriage in the forms required by the Church. There are no priests in these stories, except for the lewd or grotesque caricatures in the comic tales. There is only the occasional hermit or other recluse, who may or may not have taken orders for all we are told, but he is the only one to deliver the message of Christianity to lovers and married couples. Can we not interpret this indifference as proof that the old conflicts had died down? Nuptial benediction was now a generally accepted formality, belonging to that everyday life about which romance had nothing to say. By means of mutual concessions and a natural trend toward conformity, the clashes between the two moralities had been resolved. Courtly literature at the end of the reign of Philip Augustus seems to reflect the kind of peace and stability into which the forms of European marriage came to rest after so many upheavals.

But how seriously are we to take this escapist literature? We know that it distorted reality. But in what ways, and to what extent? It is time to compare it with the writings that related true stories; where, though the imagination still played a part, it did not stray so far from fact.

CHAPTER XII
THE LORDS OF AMBOISE

The eldest son of the count of Guines was waiting for his father to die. He had recently married, and for those days he was no longer very young. He was an open-air man, accustomed to physical exercise: he hunted, and frequented tournaments with his friends. When it rained too hard and for too long, he did not know what to do with himself; he and his band of young followers were bored. So to kill time when he was shut up indoors, he had his companions tell him stories. One of the youths knew the exploits of Charlemagne; another could tell of adventures in the Holy Land; a kinsman of the count's recounted the deeds of their ancestors. It was this cousin, the repository of the family history, who was asked to trace a genealogy if ever a marriage needed to be dissolved; but usually he delved into his memory merely for the amusement of his companions. He spoke to instruct them also, for just like Roland, Godefroi of Bouillon, and Gawain, ancestors were models of good and admirable conduct.

Accounts of ancestors' deeds naturally struck home in men who lived where they had lived; who were their descendants or their descendants' companions, and believed that when they rode, talked, prayed, or made love, their first duty was to follow the example of the valiant forebears who had once gathered together for pleasure and glory in the same surroundings. More than any other kind of narrative, family history kept alive in the lord's entourage the desire not to degenerate, not to let those ancient virtues, borne in the blood of old and young alike, lapse.

In the second half of the twelfth century, when chivalric culture ceased to be entirely oral and practical [as distinct from literary, abstract, intellectual], ancestral history, like the *chansons* and the stories, was consigned to writing. The task of setting it down was always given to a technician, a churchman who was either a member of the family concerned or attached to it as a domestic chaplain or a canon of one of the collegiate churches that adjoined every chateau of any importance in northern France. This specialist was expected to put the remembered past into a grandiose and monumental form, which is why all the texts of this kind that have survived from up to the beginning of the thirteenth century are in Latin, the language of learning and of solemn ceremonies, such as funerals, and very pompous in style, adorned with all the devices of rhetoric.

In the course of transcription, memory was not only made more definite and more ornate; it was also given added scope and depth. The writer based his text's structure on the genealogical trees drawn up for use as evidence in ecclesiastical courts when someone wanted to dissolve a marriage on grounds of consanguinity, and this initial framework meant that the narrative had to follow a similar pattern. In every generation we see the main thrust of the story carried forward through some lawful and prolific marriage pact: X begets Y upon Z, his wife. But the author could go back beyond the personal memories revived in the context of divorce procedures; he was able to supplement what he had seen and heard himself or learned from older men with what he read in old books and archives. Following much the same method as I am now using, he would go through ancient records in search of traces otherwise lost, and then seek to please his kinsmen and masters by working back to the origins of the family and its founding ancestor.

To play his part fully he had to remodel memory, which he was all the more at liberty to do because it was so vague. In the case of the most distant forebears, who could be traced only through a tomb, an epitaph, or a mention in some cartulary, he was quite free to attribute to them the sort of behavior his own contemporaries regarded as exemplary; to project onto these dim ghosts all the marvelous qualities prized by family ideology. This ideology also left its mark on accounts of more clearly remembered family members, for the patron who had commissioned the history wanted his father and grandfather to receive special treatment— as well as to see himself represented in a flattering light.

So compositions concerned with genealogy constitute our most useful source, not for what they tell us about what had happened in the past but for what they tell us about what was then the present, and the self-image of the great families of the period. There are not very many such texts in existence, but it is certain this was a very popular literary genre in northwestern France at the end of the twelfth century, when secular culture was beginning to flourish. The great princes were not the only ones who encouraged such writings; lesser lords followed their lead. The strengthening of the major political groupings was a threat to their autonomy, and to fend off such pressures they used genealogy as a defensive weapon to remind the world at large that they too came from ancient and glorious lines.

We do not know what use was made of such histories, nor when and to whom they were read. There are certain signs suggesting they may have been written or rewritten on the occasion of certain marriages. The point at which one couple took over from its predecessors would be a suitable occasion to implant in the new lord and his hoped-for progeny the refurbished memory of family glory. What is clear is that these narratives were designed for private and internal use, which is why most of them have been lost. A few were saved by chance, because later scions of great families still rich enough to be patrons had the manuscripts copied in the fourteenth and fifteenth centuries, when aristocratic houses were beginning to build up serious libraries.

The oldest of these surviving documents dates from 1155, and comes from Touraine, the home of fine rhetoric. It is a beautiful text, celebrating the virtues of the lords of Amboise.[1] The panegyric to which it may owe its survival, however, speaks of others besides them. The author, a canon of the collegiate church of Amboise, was writing not only for the descendants of the heroes of Amboise but also for the head of another family—Henry Plantagenet, count of Anjou, who had just been crowned king of England.

The tone of the work is one of lamentation: the family has been struck by misfortune and suffered the loss of its head. The latter, a faithful vassal of the counts of Anjou, had fought for them in the war that the king of France, together with the count of Blois, had been waging against Eleanor's new husband. In the course of the hostilities, the lord of Amboise was seized in an ambush and died in captivity. His sons were still children, and his chateaux had either been or were about to be taken. The family appealed to the lord of their fief, so that the text is an elegant combination of act of allegiance and plea for help. Its most urgent purpose was not to instruct the dead man's successors but to obtain the goodwill of their last hope, their lord.

With this in mind the skillful author, quoting freely from Cicero, fills page after page with praise of vassalic friendship. He begins by describing Amboise itself, the feudal tenure at the root of the long friendship, the gift that for generations had bound the two families together through the reciprocal duties of vassal and lord. There follows a parallel history of the two dynasties, in which out of respect for hierarchy the story of the counts of Anjou takes precedence. What receives most praise is their military valor: this would, it was hoped, be given renewed proof when the current incumbent came to the rescue of Amboise.

So the actors in this part of the account are all men: nothing is said of their daughters, and nothing or almost nothing of their wives. All the men are valiant, with the single exception of Fouque Réchin, who was once the sworn enemy of the house of Amboise and is therefore denigrated. He was quite a promising youth, but as he grew older he succumbed to his love of women and grew fat and lazy: in the documents of this period, noblemen who took too long to die were often accused of falling into sexual self-indulgence. Fouque's main fault was his excessive desire for Bertrade, represented as an ambitious slut who finally provoked King Philip into abducting her. This biased text is the main authority for all the accusations of abduction and lewdness historians have leveled against Philip right down to our own day.

After the exploits of the counts of Anjou come those of their vassals, the lords of Amboise. Their family structure is similar to that of the house of Anjou, but it was founded later, at the end of the tenth century, and its menfolk exhibit different virtues, being less fiery than the sons of Anjou but prudent, loyal, and sensible. Again, one stands out from all the rest: the last, Sulpice II, victim of his own greed and lack of moderation, for which he was severely punished. His fault was not that he was too fond of women, but that at a certain point he forgot the feudal obligations he assumed on paying homage. For the honor of the lords of Amboise lay in their never having broken their vassalic faith: it was this constancy that gave them the right, in adversity, to claim help and counsel from their lord.

Vassalic friendship sprang from the homage that, as its name implies, united men (Fr. *homme*, man). It was thus a masculine virtue, and knights are here the main characters: the chronicle of the lords of Amboise names seventy of them.

But it also names twenty-five women. Some of these are mere extras: they just come into the story as wives. But the special interest of this text resides in the fact that it places in the foreground some female characters who are not imaginary, and by describing the roles they played shows the image men then had of them. It is an idealized image, of course; the work in question is a panegyric. So the female ancestors, those highborn ladies and maidens who came virgin to the bed of the head of the family, were never deceitful or adulterous, and were never repudiated. On the contrary, they helped their husbands increase the family honor. All except one, the last, Agnès, wife of the lord who had just died.[2]

She was still alive, the mother of the boys in whom the family reposed its hopes. But she was a widow; perhaps she had moved out of the family home; in any event, certain people wanted to deprive her of her dower and send her away. She was from good family stock—that of the Donzy-Saint-Aignans, who were related to the royal family. But this only put her on the wrong side: in 1155 the Capetian king and his friends were the worst enemies of the count of Anjou and his vassals.

She alone is criticized here, accused of being flighty and cowardly and even suspected of treachery. At the height of the crisis, with her husband held captive, she released "without discernment . . . without taking counsel" two hundred prisoners who had been taken by the valiant foot soldiers attached to the chateau at Amboise and who might otherwise have been exchanged for their lord. So she had not played her part properly. As the mother of the family heirs it was her duty to find a replacement for the missing master, to take control of the estate, and hold on to it at all costs until the family produced some worthy representative to relieve her. She should have been like the heroines who appeared from time to time in such chronicles: virtuous ladies standing on the ramparts of besieged fortresses urging on the defenders.

Agnès serves as a foil, her weakness bringing out all the more clearly the virtue of her recently deceased mother-in-law, Elizabeth of Jaligny, a daughter of Count Fouque Réchin and thus the great-aunt of King Henry Plantagenet. Elizabeth was "fortunate," first because of her birth and what she derived from her father, but also because of the glory reflected on her by her husband and by her sons. Everything that did her honor came from men: from the man who fathered her, from the man who fathered her sons, and then from the sons themselves. She owed it to these reflected merits to be active; the text explicitly says that it was this "manly boldness" that made her free of feminine weaknesses.

She even achieved the extraordinary feat of behaving like a man. Soon after her marriage she set off for her mother's country—with her husband's permission, of course, but alone. Attacks were being made on her inheritance, and she defended it, preserving it for her sons. Thereafter it was in a "virile" manner that she faced various tribulations, as one of the strong-minded women in the Bible would have done. And she was still just as "manly," if not more so, when she grew older, lost her husband, and then had to stand up to her eldest son, Sulpice II. Perhaps undermined by his unfortunate union with the weak Agnès, Sulpice wanted to control his mother's dower, but she appealed for justice to the lord of the fief. The count of Anjou was bound as a virtuous prince to defend widows, but he was also only too glad of the chance to put down an unruly vassal, and used armed force to make the lord of Amboise respect his mother's rights. Elizabeth, now sure of herself, set off to the Bourbonnais again to settle her third son on the property she held in her own right. Later she returned to end her days as a virtuous and pious widow in a house she owned in Amboise, near the monastery of Saint-Thomas.

From this vantage point she lectured her eldest son and tried to keep him from the sin of pride. Old and "full of days," she acted as a good counselor, a substitute for the dead father, wise as befitted any *senior*. "Why did you get yourself involved in this war without consulting me? You could not have found a better adviser."[3] Before she died, paralyzed, she took under her wing the youngest of her grandsons, whose father had died, who had lost everything, and whose mother was useless. She made over to him her own heritage of Jaligny, left vacant by the death of the last of her sons.

Elizabeth, left paralyzed, alone yet unyielding among the wreckage of the family fortune, stands out as an exception in this gallery of exemplary portraits. She outdoes men, surviving the perils of motherhood, surviving her husband. She is a *virago*, respected by the men of that era as one of those rare women of courage who, divested of their femininity, almost became men's equals.

The virtues more usually expected of a wife are embodied in the portrait of Denise, another female forebear, who had died sixty years earlier. She was buried in the monastery of Pontlevoy, and every year on the anniversary of her death her memory was revived in special services. Eight Latin words sufficed to sum her up, incidentally defining what men then saw as womanly perfection: *pia filia, morigera conjunx, domina clemens, utilis mater.* As daughter, wife, mistress of a household, and mother, Denise was all her life subject to a man: father, husband, brother-in-law—whoever ruled over the house where she lived. Until she married she was a dutiful daughter [*pia*]; she accepted the husband chosen for her. Her destiny being that of a wife, she then became what all wives should be: meek, obedient, *morigera.* But she was also a *domina,* or a mistress of a household, endowed with considerable power, for her husband had come to live in her house, the house of her ancestors, and it was from her that he derived the greater part of his power. But marriage had placed Denise under him, and it was he who ruled in the chateau of Chaumont, where Denise's male ancestors had ruled before. She was relegated to an ancillary position, like the Virgin standing beside Christ as he sat in the seat of judgment; and there she was *clemens*, indulgent, introducing a little kindness into the seigneurial office. But she was only an assistant, though all the actual rights belonged to her. Did motherhood, then, give her some authority at last? No. As a mother she had to be *utilis.* "Useful" to whom? To other men, to her own sons.

Such was the role assigned to women in the great parade of this chivalric male society. A woman was an object, a valuable object carefully guarded because of all the advantages that could be obtained through her. So it was with Denise, widowed very young and left with small children. The men of her own family who had been frustrated by the marriage of the heiress now prepared to get hold of her and arrange a remarriage to suit themselves. But the dead husband's family tightened their own grip on this valuable prize: Denise and her daughters were kept locked up in the hall of the chateau, and the keeper of the fortress was ordered to watch over this treasure. But what was it he was supposed to watch over? Was what was being so jealously guarded a person, or merely a body, a womb, a secret place where blood might mingle to produce future knights and heirs?

This was why a woman's real throne was the bed where she gave birth. One night the followers of the lord of Amboise captured a stone tower. They got into the ground floor through the storeroom, and made a hole in the ceiling, through which they climbed up into the hall. In this place of safety they found the wife of the knight who was in charge of the tower; she had been left there because she was still recovering from giving birth to a child. The soldiers killed the watchman [in the service of the knight] and hoisted their own master's banner to the top of the tower; but then they carefully carried the young woman on a pallet—they did not let her walk, for she had not yet been churched—and bore her like a holy sacrament to the cottage where her husband had stationed himself in hopes of protecting the tower, and where he was now sleeping.[4]

It was another childbed, that of the Nativity, which—just before the text I have just been examining was written—the sculptors at Chartres depicted in triumph below the Virgin "in majesty" on one of the spandrels of the cathedral doors. A woman was an object of value because she would bring forth children. An object of exchange, rather; a pawn in a game where men were the players.

They might be divided into two sides: those who took and those who yielded the pawn. But the second of these groups was made up of several teams. Among the makers of marriages in the middle of the twelfth century, among the castle dwellers conspiring to win as much as possible from the game, the bride's parents or relatives were flanked on one side by their lord and on the other by their vassals.

The history of the lords of Amboise pays particular attention to the personal bond created by homage, that special kinship whose links intertwined with those of blood. It shows clearly one of the results of the rise of feudalism, i.e., that most aristocratic estates were now feudal tenures, and the rights that were transferred with marriage from one noble house to another were almost all part of the network of vassalic obligations. This explains why so many took part in preliminary marriage bargainings: not only the man to whom the fief was subinfeudated but also the vassals and feudatories, who were directly concerned by the dowry and the dower and by what kind of son might result from the projected union to become the lord of themselves or their own sons. On the one hand the chief owner of a fief, and on the other the minor lords belonging to it and sharing in its profits, all intended to have their say in the choice of the husband, the knight from whom the former would receive homage and service and to whom the latter would pay homage in return for certain advantages. Strategies were complicated, the traffic was unceasing: what was at stake was always a woman.

There is nothing surprising about the emphasis on female characters in the Amboise family history. Two considerations kept the memory of the ancestresses alive. First, it was through them that the family's connections with the main powers in the region, so useful in this time of crisis, had been established in the past. Secondly and even more important, the castles, land, and influence, absolutely all that made up the family "honor," had been brought into the family by them. Over a century and a half, throughout five generations, four successive marriages had built up the huge seigneurial estate that made the lord of Amboise one of the greatest powers in Touraine.

It was by the first of these marriages that the founding ancestor had established himself in the region. Through the second marriage Lisois, one of his younger sons, installed himself in the stone tower, one of the three chateaux of Amboise. The eldest brother, Sulpice, acquired control over the chateau of Chaumont by marrying Denise. To Hugues, son of Sulpice, Elizabeth brought a splendid *maritagium*: the remaining part of Amboise, given by her brother; and Jaligny, the Bourbonnais heritage that had come to her from her mother—or at least that part of it her male relatives had not succeeded in grabbing back.

But what comes out here in a striking manner is the important part played in all this by vassalic friendship. In 1155 the Amboise family liked to recall that all their ancestors, one after the other, had received their marvelous wives at the hands of their lords: each lady had been a reward for valor and devotion. This was a mark of the lord's power as well as of his generosity. On each occasion he had imposed his will on the man who had power over the woman in question by right of birth. The lord had taken this man's place: he himself had chosen the husband and then obliged the father or uncle of the bride to ratify his choice.

The chronicle tells us little about the earliest of these marriage pacts, the one contemporary with the great change that took place in the decades before and after the year one thousand, when kinship relationships in the highest ranks of the aristocracy gradually took on lineal form. It may be that family memory had blurred what actually happened, but in any case, one hundred fifty years after the event marriage was represented as having played a major part in the establishing of seigneurial dynasties.

Hugues I, the primal ancestor, was a *"fidèle,"* or loyal follower, of Hugues Capet, and perhaps, with that Capetian name, his godson; the fact that Hugues I called his own son "l'Orléanais"[5] shows he came from the Capetian region. "At the time when he gave a count to the people of Le Mans," Hugues Capet gave that godson, Hugues I, the daughter of the lord of Lavardin. It was a modest enough property arrangement, so Lisois, Hugues I's son, went off like his father to seek his fortune, attaching himself to Fouque Nerra, count of Anjou. Fouque, according to the chronicle, wanted to reward the faithful Lisois, who had made himself indispensable after long years of service, by giving him something that would bind him firmly to Geoffroi Martel, his own intended successor. Flush with victories, Fouque was able to force the owner of the tower of Amboise to give his niece in marriage. Lisois took possession of her, and of the tower, in about 1030.

And so it went on. The lord of Chaumont, conquered and perhaps taken prisoner by Geoffroi Martel, was obliged to give his niece to Lisois's eldest son, and to endow her with all his property. Count Fouque Réchin had the right to marry off his daughter Elizabeth, but this right was usurped by his own son, who was fighting against him. This son, desperate for allies, gave his half-sister to Hugues II to gain his friendship.

So at least three of the four brides in this series of marriages had been prizes of war, part of the booty the victor shared amongst his companions-in-arms. It should be noted that, to make sure of these captives and of the possessions they brought with them, the beneficiaries —first Lisois and then Sulpice—had to go and live in their wives' houses to try to overcome the opposition of a hostile family, to try to gain acceptance. Some even went so far as to ask that when they died they be laid to rest among the dead of this other family. The author of the chronicle does his best to conceal the part played by abduction in these very early marriages, gilding the image of the good feudal lord handing out heiresses to those of his young followers who have served him well.

This image, which kindled the ardor of all the young denizens of courts great or small who endeavored by their exploits to win a patron's favor, played an important part in the chivalric ideology of the second half of the twelfth century. It occurs again in one of the anecdotes later added to the original text of the chronicle.

This story tells how the house of Chateau-Renault was founded[6] but we can tell it is a fiction, for it does not square with various facts found scattered in the archives. In 1044 Count Geoffroi Martel captured Touraine and replaced those he had vanquished, as at Chaumont, with his own followers. According to the legend, he had "with him," among these followers, a couple of brothers, "two noble youths . . . one called Renault after his father, and the other Geoffroi after the count, whose godson he was." The count of Anjou, taking full advantage of both the bonds arising out of baptism and those arising out of the giving of the accolade, dubbed Renault a knight and sent him back to his father.

Here we see one of the main functions of princely households. In them, young soldiers received a military education and its symbolical insignia. Such households also served as safety valves, taking in sons for whom there was no place in their own homes and who possessed nothing while their fathers remained alive. In these courts, as in a crucible, were forged the loyalty, the almost filial submission, and the almost paternal benevolence on which the political system we call feudalism was based.

Renault, being the elder brother, found himself satisfactorily placed: he soon succeeded his father, who had gone off to Jerusalem to make way for him. But his brother, Geoffroi, was jealous: he too wanted to be made a knight and, above all, to be given some land. Fortunately for him, it so happened that Count Geoffroi Martel needed someone he could rely on to build a castle in the region he had just conquered. So "the young man" was in his own turn dubbed a knight and given a dowery; the count "also gave him his wife's niece in marriage, a most noble and lovely maiden." She was one of several girls at his disposal, and as she was not of the count's own blood there was no risk of her ever laying claim to some part of his heritage. The bridegroom built the fortress and set about begetting children. Soon a son was born, and the castle *and* the heir, completed at the same time, were both named Renault. This story offers a good example of the close connection there was at that time between marriage, loyal service, dynastic ambition, and the stronghold from which the family tree took root.

No doubt memory and imagination are inextricably mixed here. The story of the lords of Amboise elucidates for us the dream of marriage as envisioned by the knightly aristocracy during the reign of Louis VII, a time when many of them were forced by family discipline to remain unmarried. Should we dismiss such evidence out of hand? Should we refuse to see the earliest ancestor the knights could remember as a successful adventurer, given a bride by the warrior-chief whom he had served faithfully? Canon Lambert of Wattrelos, author of the *Annals of Cambrai*, wrote his own genealogy at about the same time. According to him, the founder of the house whose name he bore was a brother of his great-grandfather, who had lived a hundred years earlier. He was a vassal of the bishop of Cambrai and had apparently been established and married off by his lord. Whatever the truth may be about the early days of feudalism, it is a fact that in the middle of the twelfth century knights prided themselves on ancestors who were abductors and on ancestresses of higher rank who had been handed over to them by victorious leaders repaying those who had supported their rise to power.

One of the best illustrations of this dream, and at the same time of contemporary matrimonial reality, is to be found in a little story[7] the monk Jean de Marmoutier told to amuse and instruct Henry Plantagenet. It was added in about 1170 to the part of our genealogical text that dealt not with the lords of Amboise but with the counts of Anjou. It was an *exemplum*, instructing the then head of the family on what and what not to do via a eulogy on the family's most distant recorded ancestor. The house of Anjou, as well as being more powerful, was also much older than the house of Amboise, and Enjeuger, the hero of Jean de Marmoutier's story, had lived at the beginning of the tenth century. Jean was at liberty to embroider at will on this figure shrouded in the mists of time, attributing to him whatever words and actions he pleased. He decided to make him a "young man," a blithe knight owing his fortune to nothing beyond his own virtues. Jean took a single phrase as his point of departure. The manuscript he worked from tried to explain the links between the count of Anjou and the Gâtinais region by this ancestor's valor: he had defended the honor of a Gâtinais woman, and so "had become very dear to her kin and to nearly all the nobles [of that region]."

Jean's imagination naturally seized upon the lady as a pivot for his plot; but Jean was a monk, so he speaks not of love but of marriage. He starts off with three characters: a king of France, whom he calls Louis since he does not know his name; Louis's vassal, the count of Gâtinais, who dies leaving an only daughter; and the king's handsome and valiant chamberlain. The king wanted to give the chamberlain the heiress as a reward for his services. In 1170 a feudal lord had the right to give the daughters of his deceased vassals in marriage, and Henry Plantagenet liked to be reminded of this prerogative. The obstacle in this case came not from the family but from the girl herself. The chamberlain had sworn homage to the count, and she objected that "it is neither fitting nor just to impose upon me my own man and vassal."

But her consent was necessary, as all Jean de Marmoutier's audience would now agree, and in the end she did give in, after being reprimanded by the queen and shut up in the ladies' chamber—which, contrary to the usual representations of it, could be a private little world of terrorism. But still the king had to get the "advice" and assent of "friends," i.e., the whole "family" of vassals connected to the count of Gâtinais. These gave their consent, and nothing now remained but to prepare for the wedding ceremonies.

It should be noted that in Touraine, when this story was written, the procedure no longer involved just two phases but three: between the "confirmation of the gift" (the exchange of "present" words, of promises uttered personally by both husband and wife) and the "celebration of the nuptials" (the joyous *deductio* of the bride to her new home), there now was interposed the "benediction." The author of this text was a cleric, but he addressed it to the most courtly lords of his day in obvious understanding that these distinguished aristocrats now completely accepted the participation of a priest in the matrimonial rite of passage. The Church had gained its point.

Through this duly blessed union the chamberlain, now his wife's superior despite his earlier submission to her father as a vassal, took over the estate. But in ten years of marriage he did not succeed in begetting a child on his consort and one morning was found smothered in his bed. Although he had been ill, there was an immediate rumor that his wife had killed him. Where was her lover? The accusation was naturally spread by the dead man's entourage, primarily by his second-in-command, the seneschal, who raised the alarm. (He played the part of the *losengier* in the courtly romances of the day.) The uproar among the dead man's retainers was not surprising. They had come to live in this house at the same time as their master, and it belonged not to him but to the lady. Now that she was a widow, she would remarry and bring in a new master who would install his own retinue and drive the others out. To prevent the lady from doing any such harm to their security she must be stopped from ever marrying again. It was not enough to convict her of infidelity. A surer method would be to add to the private and domestic charge of adultery the crime of "sudden death," which fell under public law.

Such an accusation could be and was brought before the royal court, and there the lady offered to swear her innocence. Her appeal to the judgment of God would have been enough if it had been a matter of mere fornication, but there was a charge of murder to consider as well. The court ordered a trial by combat. The accuser, famous throughout those parts for his prowess, declared himself ready to fight. Who would dare oppose him? The widow appealed to the men of her family, but they were all afraid, so strong was the suspicion that fell on a wife in such circumstances.

Widowed, who knew how; abandoned by all her male relatives—was not this proof enough of her guilt? Enter Enjeuger. He was sixteen years old, as yet hardly accustomed to bearing arms. He was not a kinsman of the lady, but her godson: so the bond between them was spiritual, superior to that of blood. He had been living in the count's house, serving him day and night; he knew the count had been ill and was certain that his death had been a natural one. So, sure of himself, Enjeuger fought and won. David triumphed over Goliath.

Though she had been shown to be innocent, the lady decided to live out her days in a convent. What would become of the inheritance? Who would take over the fief? The cousins who had not dared to fight for her, or the young man "who was not her kin in flesh but in spirit?" The king of course decided to disinherit the faint-hearted family and, sitting in his own court, declared Enjeuger to be a "mother's son." Henry Plantagenet was no doubt delighted to hear that the king's decision in itself was enough to overrule "nature." What had happened was that an earthly prince, interpreting the will of God, had consecrated the superiority of the spiritual over the physical.

Enjeuger, still a lad and a bachelor, had not acquired his fief through his sexual prowess, by sleeping with an heiress, but through the greatness of his heart and the power, with God's help, of his unskilled hand. Even in his youth the founding father of the house of Anjou performed one of the royal functions, that of defending the rights of widows.

This story would have thrilled all the young men at court. But their *senior* would have enjoyed it too, remembering his own youth and secure in his own power.

The unknown author of the first version of the dual genealogy on which this chapter is based does not say how Sulpice II, the bad lord who had just died, came to get married. It may well be that after playing the two lords of his two fiefs off against one another—the count of Anjou and the count of Blois—he was given a wife by the count of Blois, a point that did not bear·mentioning too overtly in this appeal to the Plantagenet.

But already in 1155 and then in 1170, when Jean de Marmoutier was writing, the violence of earlier days had died down, and feudal princes could no longer seize by armed force the ladies they gave to their vassals as wives. The wife bestowed on Enjeuger was not obtained by force. And we have seen how, in the *exemplum* (reflecting what was supposed to be ideal conduct), the king disposed of the Gâtinais lady's hand not by force but through his seigneurial power.

At the end of the twelfth century, when the heads of principalities large and small had exhausted their resources by early disposing of their daughters, nieces, and illegitimate daughters, they were obliged to rely on their prerogatives, claiming their regalian duty to protect widows and orphans as well as their inherent paternalistic rights, which they used to persuade relatives of deceased vassals to let them give the womenfolk left "desolate," virgin or otherwise, a husband of the prince's own choosing.

The relatives resisted as much as they could. At this period, custom allowed the duke of Normandy the "gift" of his vassal's daughters when they inherited the fief. But he was not allowed to give them in marriage without the counsel and approval of the male "friends" of the woman's family.[8] It was a matter of power, of bargaining, of money. "In the provinces of Gaul and England," wrote Robert de Courçon,[9] the prince of the region helped himself to the heritage of orphans; "he gives girls and widows in marriage to lesser nobles in return for money, thus selling the *generositas* of these young women."

Did the lords of Amboise, feudatories of the counts of Anjou, manage to marry off their own daughters as they pleased? They did marry them all off, and apparently quite freely. There were not very many of them, as it happened, for the wives bestowed by the counts were only moderately fertile. Lisois had five children, including three daughters who lived to be adults. Sulpice I had three, two of whom were girls. Hugues had four, including one daughter. That made six daughters in all.

The lords of Amboise did not give their daughters to vassals but to equals, rivals, owners of neighboring chateaux, potential enemies; their object was to gain these men's friendship, or at least reduce the possibilities of aggression. Marriage, as the Church moralists kept insisting in order to explain the need for exogamy, spread "charity" and love. What those who gave their womenfolk in marriage were hoping for was peace.

Did they get it? Did they achieve even more? This text gives us a glimpse of something to be seen practically nowhere else: the additional advantages the head of a family might look for when he married off his daughters. Sulpice I's brothers-in-law were powerful lords. One of them, the owner of the chateau of Les Roches-Corbon, was a faithful friend, and when Sulpice fell ill he chose to go and die in this man's house. This alliance, close and unshakable, was still alive in 1155: right down to the third generation, the cousins went on helping and consulting one another and coming to one another's aid in war.

But between Sulpice and the husbands of his other two sisters—the lord of La Motte-Foucois and the lord of Montrichard—relationship by marriage did not preclude, and perhaps even exacerbated, hatred. These two brothers-in-law had hoped to be able to exploit fully their wives' rights, and thus saw the ladies' brother not as a friend but as an obstacle. They stopped at nothing in their efforts to destroy him. But as chance would have it they came off the losers in the battle. Foucois, one of the two, was taken prisoner and beheaded—accidentally, according to the chronicler: the lord of Amboise knew nothing about it; some of his rustic foot soldiers were responsible.

Sulpice himself ran the same risk. A sister's marriage was obviously no guarantee of her husband's friendship. Could one then, at least, count on love's growing out of kinship, and hope for friendly relations with one's nephews?

It was in the second generation, after the two bloods had mingled, that a marriage alliance bore fruit—when the nephews, brought up by their maternal uncle in his own house, grew fond of him. That is, if the sister concerned, the boys' mother, survived her series of confinements long enough; or if the brother-in-law, her husband and widowed early, did not take another wife; or if this stepmother did not, as stepmothers were inclined to do, try to disinherit the sons of the previous marriage. It happened twice that the wives, exhausted by childbirth, died early. Then Hugues II, the story's real hero, the paragon of dynastic virtue, was torn between two conflicting duties. It was up to him to watch over the interests of his dead sister's sons and, if necessary, fight to defend them, "for fear that the children of the second wife might take the estate from his nephews." On the other hand, because of the friendship he owed his sister's husband, "He long remained silent, refusing to war against Archimbaud because he was his brother-in-law."

In 1155 the same problem arose again. The sister of Sulpice II died, leaving two small sons who had been born in the chateau of Déols. As a matter of fact, there was less danger this time. The mother, Denise— who had served her family as well as the revered ancestress whose name she bore—"had shown so many and various beauties and virtues that the widower, although he was still young, desired no other companion." It was expected of young women, when they were transplanted into another family, either that they bring forth healthy children and not die too young—or else that the charms they had inherited be so powerful they could hold their husbands captive from beyond the grave.

What happened when the offspring of these marriages were daughters, and the orphans heiresses? When Foucois, Sulpice I's brother-in-law, was beheaded, he left an only daughter, Corba, whose sad story is related in our text. She inherited one of the three chateaux of Amboise from her grandfather. The building itself had been destroyed but the site remained, together with the right to rebuild the fortress and to enjoy all the powers that came with it. At the death of her father, the orphan naturally came under the thumb of her nearest male relative, who was Sulpice, her mother's brother. He was in no hurry at all to give her in marriage, but Fouque Réchin, count of Anjou, had his eye on her. His Amboise vassals were getting above themselves, and he was trying to keep them in their place. La Motte-Foucois was a fief in his gift, but then, at the end of the eleventh century, the rights of a feudal lord did not yet take precedence over those of family. However, the early death of Sulpice I and the fact that Hugues II was still a minor placed the count in a position of strength. He bargained with Sulpice's brother, the temporary head of the family, and got him to agree that Corba should be given in marriage to a knight who was a friend of Fouque's and who took care of the third chateau of Amboise for him.

This was at the time of the Council of Clermont and the preaching of the Crusades, and Corba's husband, together with the young Hugues, set off for the Holy Land. When news came that the husband had been killed at the siege of Nicaea, Fouque married off the widow to a very old man, Achard de Saintes, who had taken the dead man's place as keeper of the third chateau of Amboise.[10] Achard thus received his predecessor's wife as an additional charge, but of course not for nothing: the text says he paid a very high price. The vendor, the count, did not bother to consult Corba's family: she had been his follower's wife, it was his duty to look after her, and her kinsmen had no say in the matter. Moreover, the only scion of the lords of Amboise was away at war; would he ever come back? Hugues did return: ill, but still alive. "Achard, terrified, took Corba his wife to Tours, to the house of his brother, the cellarer of Saint-Martin." A canon's house was a safe refuge, but the lady had to go out every day to perform her devotions. Fortunately the church was not far away, and inside it men and women were restricted to separate parts of the nave; on the way there and back, Corba was well guarded. Nevertheless the young woman did manage to make contact in church with an "Amboise servant."

"She told him how she could be abducted, and one holy day, when she was at matins, Auger, the aforementioned servant, entered the church, leaving some comrades at the door. He led Corba to them, and they set her on horseback and carried her off. They hid her in the house of a blacksmith belonging to Chaumont, where Auger lived. One of Corba's kinsmen, apprised of all this, came with many knights and sergeants-at-arms and took her to Chaumont. Her husband, stricken by illness and the sorrow of having lost his wife, died soon after."

The family had won. Corba was soon married off again to a friend of the family, who in 1101 set off for the Holy Land with William of Aquitaine, the troubadour. But William never traveled far without women, and following his bad example Corba's new husband took her

with him. But God punished the sinful Crusaders who could not do
without their wives, and they were vanquished in Asia Minor. This
disaster may be the cause of William's bad reputation: a hundred thousand prisoners were taken, according to the text, and among them was
Corba, carried off by the Turks "together with many Frankish women."
Her relatives in Touraine consoled themselves with the thought that she
had no children. That meant there was no more danger of seeing the
inheritance slip through their fingers, no more risk of seeing yet another
husband, perhaps one that did not suit them, ensconced on the ruins of
the castle.

This story shows how anyone who married off his daughter might
hope, through her, to get hold of her husband's inheritance. But for his
dream to be translated into reality there had to be a favorable series of
events, watched with the closest vigilance.

In three generations six sons and the same number of daughters
grew to maturity in the house of Amboise. That was not many, but
it might have been enough to cause the branching out of the family
and the splitting up of its patrimony. This danger was avoided, and the
family tree remained smooth and devoid of adventitious branches. And
yet none of the legitimate sons went into the Church; none had to
become a monk or a canon. But from the time of the founding of the
dynasty, only one son in each generation, the eldest, was allowed to
marry.

Lisois lived to a very advanced age because, says the text for the
benefit of the young men of the family, he remained chaste during
his adolescence. He had two sons, and he divided his possessions between them—but unequally, the younger receiving only marginal and
not very secure ones. Nor did his father find him a wife, and he remained a bachelor, his acceptance of this role causing the storyteller to

represent him as a hero of brotherly friendship. Just as virtuous as his sibling Sulpice, he was his loyal supporter despite considerable temptation.

When Hugues II was still a child and held as a hostage at the court of the count of Anjou, his father, Sulpice, fell ill. Summoning all his men into the great hall at Chaumont, he made them swear to keep his son in possession of the family "honor" and estate. The main challenge was suspected to come from the child's uncle, who had to take a special oath promising that "he would not diminish the boy's honor, nor take his land, nor harm his life or limb." He kept his word and surprised everyone by acting as a worthy guardian. And when he died childless and was buried beside his brother, his abnegation allowed his nephew Hugues II to bring together again in his own hands the whole of his grandfather's inheritance and the huge fortune that came to him from his mother.

Hugues was an only son, but he himself had three boys. In 1128 he went with Count Fouque of Anjou to Jerusalem. He was by then in his sixties and had participated in the Crusades before; now he wanted to await the resurrection near the Valley of Jehoshaphat. So before setting out on his last journey he gave away his possessions as his father had done before him. Geoffroi Plantagenet was then count of Anjou, and Hugues persuaded him to accept the homage of his eldest son, Sulpice II, to whom he "gave all his lands and made his men swear to it." There was then another solemn ceremony, this time in the chateau of Montrichard, at which Hugues exhorted Sulpice and the vassals swore allegiance.

But there was still a danger, and it came in this case from the two frustrated brothers. The lord of Amboise had, somewhat prematurely, applied the right of primogeniture; but his second son, the third Hugues, claimed his share. He was then living at the court of Geoffroi Plantagenet, who had dubbed him a knight and who now supported his cause, as he was to support, and for the same reasons, that of Hugues's mother, Elizabeth, when she claimed her dower from Sulpice II. When a fief was too large it became dangerous, and it was in the lord's interest to break it up.

But Hugues III was also backed up by some of the knights of the chateau of Amboise, perhaps his childhood friends and in any event men who could hope to be rewarded if they took his side. Here we see quite clearly the dual intervention of both lord and vassals, and how the bonds of friendship arising out of feudal grants could intertwine with family links to complicate dynastic politics.

But Hugues II stuck to his guns and offered his second son Jaligny the property he ruled over in the name of his wife. This offer being refused, these lands in the Bourbonnais were used to buy off the third son. As for the second, he was made to "take the cross," the badge of the Crusader, a solution often used to relieve such family tensions. When he returned from the Holy Land he was given the hand of an heiress, probably through the good offices of the king of France, whose friend he had naturally become since his father was of the opposite party. "With this woman" his lord gave Hugues III a little estate in Touraine, so he was thus both married and established by the Capetians, much as his distant ancestor and namesake (who had also been a younger brother) had been a century and a half before.

All these arrangements meant that each of Hugues II's three sons managed to have his own house without posing any threat to the family heritage, which remained intact except for property that had come through their mother: there was, however, nothing wrong about granting this to a younger son. But, as it happened, only the eldest son had children: both his brothers were murdered and died without heirs.

Sulpice II soon set about marrying off his eldest son, and this time he acted quite independently of his lords, the counts of Anjou. He was in a hurry to get hold of a neighboring fortress, Chateau-Renault (see page 238), which had recently been inherited by an only daughter. Like her betrothed, she was very young, and she was given in marriage neither by her parents nor by her father's lord but by the knights of the chateau, standing in for her dead father. For the garrison there was linked to its head by complex bonds of vassalage, kinship, and marriage. So at Chateau-Renault the vassalic body itself chose the man who would later lead them into battle in his wife's name. Elsewhere we see them reject a new husband of whom they disapprove: the knights of Chaumont almost drove out Denise's brother-in-law, then his nephew's guardian. The knights of La Haye murdered a son-in-law and his brother, who cramped their style.

But the precocious betrothal concluded by Sulpice II was broken off on grounds of consanguinity. The lord of Roches-Corbon, a loyal kinsman but one who drew the line at perjury, came to calculate and swear to the degrees of kinship. In fact, it was the count of Blois, lord of the fief in question and opposed to a marriage that he had not arranged himself and that did not suit his convenience, who was acting behind the scenes through the lord of Roches-Corbon. The count of Blois invoked episcopal justice to prevent the marriage, and Sulpice II had to hand the girl back. To be on the safe side, he had kept her locked up in his own house.

Jean de Marmoutier separated the genealogy of the counts of Anjou from that of the lords of Amboise, and recast it. In about 1180 he wrote a whole book in honor of the most recently deceased of the Anjou line: the *History of Geoffroi, Duke of the Normans and Count of the Angevins.*[11] It was dedicated to the bishop of Le Mans, for the duke was buried in his cathedral, beneath an enamel plaque we can still see today. The bishop was in charge of the tomb, the raising of which he had organized, as he had the funeral and memorial services. It was the custom to keep accounts and panegyrics of the lives of saints and princes near their tombs to be read ritually on certain occasions. Geoffroi had not wanted to be buried in Rouen: his own house was not there, only his wife's. He might have chosen Angers, but instead he decided on Le Mans, for it was here that his adult life had begun: immediately after his marriage in 1128 he had gone to live there in his mother's house until his father vacated the palace in Angers.

It was with this marriage that Jean de Marmoutier began his story, and this is how he told it.

⊗ Like Eustache of Boulogne, Geoffroi earned a wife through his fame. Henry I, duke of Normandy and king of England, having lost his only son in a shipwreck, was left with an heiress, his daughter Mathilda, herself left a widow by the death of the emperor.[12] For a long time Henry had been looking for some way of regaining power over the *comté* of Maine, and hearing that Geoffroi was of good birth, valiant in battle, a rising star rather than one likely to "degenerate," he chose him as Mathilda's new husband. Negotiations were begun with the young hero's father, and vows, "words of the future," were exchanged. The final ceremonies approached. But Geoffroi was not yet old enough to have been made a knight, fitting though it was that the young husband should be one: he was going to rule over a household, and it was only right that he should do so with a sword in his hand—the sword of justice that Geoffroi brandishes forever in his funeral effigy. So Henry arranged that he himself should give the accolade to his future son-in-law—a means of getting a further hold over him through that kind of spiritual yet secular paternity accorded to a chivalric patron. The dubbing ceremony was to take place in Rouen just before the betrothal, at Whitsuntide. Knights were usually dubbed on that day, so that the Holy Spirit might descend on them. The young man arrived the day before, escorted by a group of his fellows who were to receive the "sacrament," or sign of their military dignity, at the same time as he.

They all came to the house of Geoffroi's future father-in-law, who awaited them seated in the hall. Henry rose, went up to the man he had chosen as the father of his grandsons, embraced him, kissed him several times on the face, then made him sit down beside him on the same seat, ranked as his equal: the same relationship as that of Godelive sitting side by side with her husband, of the lady and her lover in amorous conversation, of the Virgin and the Son about to crown her. I see this ritual, analogous to that of homage in its expression of a combination of equality and submission, as a kind of rite of adoption. According to the *History*, Geoffroi was received "as a son" in his wife's house.

He had been incorporated into it by the man who still ruled there and who set store by this ritual of integration: anyone who gave an heiress in marriage meant to ensure that he himself had power over the man about to take his place vis-à-vis the bride. There followed a sort of verbal test, a dialogue or *confabulatio* in which the elder man asked questions and the younger answered as well as he could but discreetly, showing that despite his lack of years he was skilled in words as well as in arms, and capable of wisdom, the virtue of the *seniores*. It was important that he should demonstrate this when, through his marriage, he was about to become the lord of the seigneury.

The marriage took place on the Sunday after the knighting, not in Rouen but in Le Mans, near the house belonging to Geoffroi where the couple were to lie together. The bride's father led them there; the bridegroom's father awaited them. Jean de Marmoutier makes no mention of any religious rite when he describes the knighting ceremony, but speaks of nothing else when he describes the wedding. He makes no reference to the bed or the chamber, but only to the Mass, the nuptial benediction, and the essential act that preceded them—the giving away of the bride by her father. After the bishop had made his routine inquiry—a mere formality, since the consanguinity between the bride and groom was obvious to everyone—the "words of the present" were exchanged at the church door. Here Jean makes a dogmatic assertion nowhere stated so clearly in any contemporary text: "The consent makes the marriage."

The *History* was dedicated to the bishop of Le Mans but addressed to Henry Plantagenet, Geoffroi's son. The fact that the marriage was presented to him in this way shows that, by then, fashionable society was applying the rules laid down by the Church. When Jean de Marmoutier wrote his *History*, around 1180, the secular and ecclesiastical models of marriage in northwestern France seem to have coincided, at least on the level of ritual.

CHAPTER XIII
THE COUNTS OF GUINES

s I draw to a close, I am going to shift our field of observation slightly, skipping over a couple of decades to the time of Philip Augustus's divorce, and moving to the region of Bouvines in the north of the kingdom. Here we can make use of a range of information supplied by the parallel history of two families: the counts of Guines and the seigneurs of Ardres.[1] It was completed between 1201 and 1206 by one Lambert, a cleric who worked in the chateau at Ardres and was a distant relation of its master. Although Lambert was a priest, he made no secret of being married, and he had at least two sons, both of whom became priests like himself. This was a century after the great Gregorian offensive against concubinage among the clergy, and demonstrates the distance between ecclesiastical theory and practice in the matter of morals. Lambert had married one of his daughters very honorably into an illegitimate branch of his lord's family. He was proud of being a "master" who had studied in the schools, one of the several such whom the count of Guines, his patron's father, fed and sheltered in his house, and who in return read to him, debated with him, and translated for him books from the ecclesiastical libraries, including the *Song of Songs*, Saint Augustine, and other works used as references by theologians specializing in marriage.

Lambert's work shows not only that he was an expert in rhetoric with a good knowledge of classical poetry but also that he was up to date in courtly literature. He writes in Latin, the language of the learned, but looks with a very secular eye on the facts he relates "to the glory of the great lords of Guines and of Ardres."[2] In celebrating the two families, he was dealing with a small *comté* wedged between Flanders and Boulogne, and with the powerful seigneury that had grown up around a strong chateau within the *comté*. When Lambert was writing, the two families had been linked together for about forty years. The original bond had been the marriage of the present Count Baudouin II, and the two estates were soon to be actually combined in the hands of Baudouin's eldest son, Arnoul. Arnoul was already in possession of his dead mother's inheritance, which he had wrested from his father, and had established himself in 1194 at Ardres with his wife, heiress to the neighboring chateau of Bourbourg.

Lambert explicitly states that it was on the occasion of this marriage that, to please Count Baudouin, he undertook to produce a literary work in praise of both the young couple's ancestors. The task was rightly his since he was a servant of Arnoul, his hero, and he lived in the company of the knight, a cousin of Arnoul's, who remembered best the exploits of the family ancestors. But since Lambert's master was the son of the count of Guines, in whose person two bloods, two groups of ancestors, came together, both lines had to be honored.

Respecting the rules of hierarchy as had the chronicler of the lords of Amboise, Lambert naturally started with the story of the Guines: they were counts; they received homage for the chateau of Ardres; and, above all, paternal ancestors came before maternal ones. Both accounts are based on the obligatory family tree, going from one marriage to another and structured in accordance not with dates, which are rare and usually wrong, but with successive acts of procreation. At every level we find a biography of the man who was the head of the family either because he was the first-born son of a lawful marriage or because he had lawfully married its eldest daughter.

Both the memory and the fate of the estates on which memory was focused depended on the institution of marriage. At the origin of both these families, as at the origin of the human race, there lay, mystical, in the dim distant past almost beyond time, an act of copulation. At the beginning of the dominating line of the counts of Guines, imagination placed the virile image of a man taking a wife, just as Baudouin had more recently taken the heiress of Ardres; in contrast, it is a woman, given passively to a man, who is supposed to have started the dominated line of the lords of Ardres. This symbolical arrangement of the sexes was what would be expected by a minor potentate who, even though he was illiterate, boasted of his culture. The mentality and values it suggests also reflect what was then the primary function of marriage in society.

Lambert describes his patron's house, the chateau of Ardes, marveling at its admirably modern internal organization. It had been rebuilt in wood in the first third of the twelfth century, but the living quarters were subdivided into an "inextricable layrinth." But—and this confirms the impression left by all the texts of the period—this complex house was designed to shelter only one pair of progenitors, only one of the conjugal cells that made up the basic structure of this society. No place within the chateau seems to have been provided for other couples. Only the master's union was legally and permanently established there. On the middle, or living, floor at Ardres the one room, or hall, was divided up. (Denise and her damsels had been shut up in a similar living area in the chateau of Chaumont, as had the newly delivered mother who lay in the tower at Amboise.) Isolated in the middle, just like a matrix for the fertilization and germination of seed, was "the great chamber of the lord and his wife, where they sleep together."[3] There was just one bed in which the future of the family was created in the night. The rest of the numerous household slept in odd corners; those who were married, like the priest Lambert himself, were lodged in huts in the yard, as the keeper of the chateau of Amboise had been. The other rooms in the house itself were reserved for the lawful children of the master and mistress. Next to the room where they had been conceived and born was a dormitory, or sort of incubator, for the babies and their nurses. On the top floor, that of the sentries and the last refuge, were the adolescents, those who had survived the dangers of early childhood to become the hope of the family. Here there were two separate rooms, one for the boys and one for the girls. The young men were in residence only "when they felt like it." Their place was really elsewhere, in the world of adventure and chivalric initiation, i.e., the forest and the court. But not their father's court. Instead, they learned how to behave in the house of their mother's brother or of their father's lord. The girls were kept shut up and watched over "as was right" until they were married.

No place was provided for the eldest son when he got married. The house was not designed to hold two couples. As long as the father was not dead, had not gone into a monastery, or had not set off for the Holy Land, thus leaving the bed and bedchamber vacant, the heir could not marry. If he did get himself a wife, he had also to get himself another house. Often, as at Le Mans and as here at Ardres, this was the house of his dead mother.

Such domestic arrangements naturally had repercussions on matrimonial practice.

First of all it led people to lengthen the interval between betrothal and nuptials. The agreement between the two families was often arrived at very early: the daughter of the aged count of Namur was not yet one year old when, in 1186, she was given in marriage to the son of the count of Champagne, who took her away to his father's house. Thus, little girls promised to the sons of great families would be sent from their homes to come and join other little girls in the nurseries where they had been cared for since they were born. As the newcomers grew older they were exposed to the desires of men, and first and foremost to the desires of their future fathers-in-law. Who can say how many girls were raped, especially when the families concerned changed their minds and broke their agreements? Those involved did not always bother, either, to hand the girls back or even to claim them, especially when, as was the case of the daughter of the count of Namur, they were heiresses to an estate that tempted some uncle or cousin. This "wife" disappeared into oblivion. How could she, at her tender age, have given the voluntary consent required by the Church and, in that social stratum, now thought necessary also by the laity?

But by betrothing young children, heads of families hoped to ensure a durable line of offspring, so they restored to this practice often and with many variations. The then count of Guines, Baudouin II, had been betrothed ten years before he was dubbed a knight by Thomas à Becket[4], when he was less than ten years old. His fiancée was even younger, and could not yet even talk. Lambert tells how she was brought before the two families so that the gathering might see her accept publicly and solemnly the boy who had been chosen to be her husband. She showed her agreement by her *hilaritas*: the baby smiled, and was acclaimed as *sponsa*.

Baudouin's father lived for some twenty years after that, but the young bridegroom did not wait that long to claim his wife, who had given him five children by the time he inherited the *comté*. But meanwhile his father-in-law had died and his mother-in-law had remarried, so the "great chamber" at Ardres was vacant for his nuptials.

Lambert describes at length the nuptials of Baudouin's eldest son, Arnoul.[5] Arnoul had been champing at the bit for a long while. He had been knighted in 1181, and for thirteen years had been looking for a wife. The principality of Guines had grown in importance and it was not so easy now to arrange a suitable marriage for the heir. The political situation in the region made wife hunting hazardous. After lengthy attempts that came to nothing, a possible prey was spotted: the sister of the young master of the chateau of Bourbourg, who had just died. Arnoul wasted no time.

He was already affianced to one of the daughters of the count of Saint-Pol, but there, though the family was good, the prospects were poor.

Without hesitation he broke off the first *desponsatio*. The *History* does not say how, though it could scarcely have been easy. Moreover, dispensations would be needed, for the Bourbourg girl was Arnoul's fourth cousin. Rome was not applied to, but at that social level the permission of the "ordinary," the bishop of Thérouanne, was not enough, so recourse was had to the archbishop. It was then possible for a pact to be concluded by the engaging of hearts, which, as laymen then agreed, made a marriage.

Arnoul "was united and joined in marriage to his lawful wife" by an exchange of vows and the granting of a dower. This *sponsalicium* was the chateau of Ardres, which Arnoul had inherited from his mother and which he was able to dispose of freely during his father's lifetime.

The story is especially interesting when it comes to the second phase of the marriage, the nuptials. Unlike Jean de Marmoutier, Lambert says practically nothing about religious formalities, though he does tell us how, as priest to the newly married couple's household, he was supposed to ring the bells. He refused because Arnoul had been excommunicated for having damaged a mill in the course of his excursions: it belonged to a widow, and came within the "truce of God."[6] But Arnoul had bought an absolution at Reims at the same time as the dispensation, and Lambert, not knowing this, brought down upon himself the terrible wrath of the count of Guines. It was to redeem this offense, Lambert tells us, that he wrote the *History*. No doubt this explains why he describes the wedding from the point of view of the laity.

For them the main thing was not what took place in church but what happened that night in the bridal chamber. When the couple were in bed, Lambert and three other priests—two of them his sons—went round it performing an exorcism, sprinkling the husband and wife with holy water, perfuming the bed and turning it into a kind of altar, calling a divine blessing down upon it. Their job was to drive away through these words and gestures some of the evil the sexual act was bound to produce.

But the priests' role was less important than that of the chief officiant, the bridegroom's father. It was the bride's father who had been chief protagonist in daylight and the open air, when he transferred his daughter from his own hand to that of another. Now, at night, in an enclosed space, a place of darkness and gestation, after the couple had been led into their house and the wife into the family that received her to ensure its perpetuation, it was the turn of the father of the husband and pro-creator.

Religion was not of course entirely absent from this layman's rites. Raising his eyes to heaven and using a formula borrowed from the apocryphal acts of the apostle Thomas, he prayed to God to bless his son and daughter-in-law, already, in his view, since the first exchange of vows, "joined together by the holy law of holy union and by the ritual of matrimony." He prayed that they might live in concord, in harmony of heart; and then, following consideration of the spirit with that of the body, that "their seed might spread throughout the length of days and down the ages." And this was really why they were lying there. No one expected them to observe three nights of continence: everyone hoped the bride would conceive that very night.

After soliciting God's blessing, Baudouin pronounced his own, just as Abraham had blessed Isaac, and Isaac Jacob. As patriarch he was handing on the family's charismatic powers. It was in the performance of this generative function that he wanted to be represented, and as such the docile Lambert represented him. This appeal to fertility, together with the central place accorded to it in the account of the wedding, gives us a clear picture of the secular idea of marriage, super-ficially sacralized yet still fundamentally carnal. The flesh was rehabili-tated and reconciled through the priests' benedictions, and everyone, relations, friends, and neighbors of both sexes, joined in the couple's pleasure "with games and revelry, in joy and exaltation."[7]

The *History of the Counts of Guines* tells us nothing or almost nothing about feminine perversity. Lambert praises the purity of the wives he writes of, declaring that they all came virgin to the marriage bed. The men he served and whose ideas he was expressing took great care to keep their daughters locked up in the high chamber until they got married, to make sure their value did not deteriorate. And as soon as such refuges became available, these noble houses used an even safer place of sequestration: a convenient little nunnery. The convent at Bourbourg was inside the chateau itself, while that at Guines, founded by a countess of Guines in 1117, was adjacent to the castle.

This kind of private female monastery took in the surplus women of the family—widows, girls too young to marry, girls who had not found a husband. Although the females occupied themselves with prayer, effective orisons came from male mouths only, and the main function of such houses was to keep a close watch over those who lived there and, to a lesser degree, to educate them. The girls were "initiated into liberal studies,"[8] and when they emerged to get married they were usually less "illiterate" than their husbands—another factor in feminine influence. In the chateau of Bourbourg it was an aunt who had not herself taken the veil who ruled over the little band of inmates, "both the servants and the nuns."

Such communities were a more sophisticated form of the gynaeceum, or women's quarters, divested of some of its sinister power by the influence of religion. As in the ordinary "ladies' chamber," the girls were ruled over by matrons who could be very formidable. Gertrude, the wife of Arnoul the Elder of Ardres, was of distinguished but turbulent blood, and all the more violent in her ways because she considered herself a cut above her husband. Lambert represents her as grasping and very hard on the cottagers. One poor mother, unable to pay her tax of an Easter lamb, was made to hand over her little girl, and as soon as the child was old enough Gertrude put her to the same profitable use as she would have done if she had been a sheep. She had her "covered by a male" in the hope of obtaining more serfs. Another woman, a "pretty little thing" according to Lambert, and frivolous like many another female in such noble households, found that she was pregnant and came before the chatelaine to accuse one of the men of having raped her. She was put "into service" and had to work "with her hands," thus becoming another member of Gertrude's flock. Her child would belong to Gertrude, while Gertrude frugally obliged the alleged father to marry the mother. This story sheds a small ray of light on a subject we know practically nothing about: what marriage was like among the lower orders.

Lambert's *History* illustrates André le Chapelain's theme, that there were two different moralities for the two sexes. The daughters of aristocratic families were supposed to be demure and reserved, while the sons were praised for their sexual irrepressibility. Chapter 88 of Lambert's panegyric speaks of the elder Count Baudouin's "prudence and negligence," pretending to be impartial in mentioning his vices as well as his virtues. But clearly his patron was proudest of his faults: "From his early adolescence to his old age, his passions were urged on by an intemperate and impatient libido." He especially liked very young girls, virgins. Was this a sin? No. The feigned reproach is really a compliment. Baudouin did "better than David, Samson, and even Jupiter."[9] And his scattered thunderbolts were not without effect. In the course of his account Lambert mentions five male bastards, of whom two became canons of the Church. He is being very discreet here, for, in recording the funeral of the frisky old gentleman in 1206, the chronicler of the abbey of Andres, where the counts of Guines were buried, says there were thirty-three of Baudouin's sons and daughters present, "born either of his wife or elsewhere." Only ten of the children Baudouin's wife had given him survived their father. That leaves a balance of twenty-three.

The members of that masculine society did not frown upon such excesses in their own sex. On the contrary, they applauded them as long as this ardor was not frittered away on servants or prostitutes. When Lambert speaks of the lady friends with whom the youths of the family briefly amused themselves, he always starts by describing them as "beautiful." This was regarded as an excuse: Alain of Lille's manual on confession suggests that a sinner should be asked whether the woman with whom the sin was committed was pretty. If so, the penance should be lightened.[10] According to Lambert, these girls were all "noble," too. This means their fathers were of good birth: either vassals or, more frequently, illegitimate sons belonging to the family. Nubile young women not yet married, living in or near the house and not so closely guarded as the master's daughters, offered an outlet for the legitimate youths' passions. As we see once more, consanguinity was not really an obstacle in sexual relations outside marriage.

Lambert, writing of Arnoul, the founder of the line of Ardres, attributes to him a couple of bastards born of different mothers. The second Arnoul, while in search of adventure in England in his youth, begot three sons and then a fourth with a "noble" woman; all four became excellent knights like their father. His lawful wife bore him two sons. The elder had to wait to get married, since the master's bed was not yet vacant, and in the meantime he fathered two bastards: Lambert's son-in-law was the son of one of them. The younger of Arnoul II's legitimate sons began his "career" by fathering a son upon the hitherto virgin daughter of the canon Raoul, one of Arnoul I's own bastards, who was thus the uncle of his grandson's father. Raoul sang the services in the collegiate church near the chateau of Ardres, which fulfilled a function similar to that of the small nunnery for the girls: it took in the surplus males, especially the illegitimate ones. But despite the efforts of the twelfth-century reforming clerics it was not a citadel of chastity. The same younger son who, unable to marry yet, had deflowered Canon Raoul's daughter, went on to have two more illegitimate children by a "noble" young woman he had conquered, the daughter of another canon.

Two children by the same mother: this was not a passing fancy, it was concubinage. So this form of conjugality, a stable kind of relationship, still existed, though it was excluded from full legitimacy so that any sons born of it would be similarly excluded and not go claiming the inheritance. Lambert tells us that one of these illegitimate children, a daughter, became very famous: she gave one son to Count Baudouin of Guine's brother, and another to a canon belonging to the chapter at Thérouanne.

So illegitimacy was a normal part of the structure of ordinary society —so normal that illegitimate children, especially males, were neither concealed nor rejected. They were just as noble as the other offspring, and their birth allowed them certain prerogatives. They had the right, "by the privilege of consanguinity," to *contubernium*, or bed and board, in their father's house.[11] That house was always open to them. One of the bastards of Arnoul the Elder turned apostate in the East; but though he was still a "Saracen" when he returned, he was nevertheless welcome. It was only when he insisted on eating meat on Friday that they had reluctantly to show him the door.

Illegitimate sons shared the lives of their legitimate half brothers. Sometimes, because they had no hopes of succeeding to the estate, they were less unruly and more sure of themselves than the younger sons of the lawful wife. They were not jealous of the eldest son and could be his close friends. But some of them were troublesome. Arnoul the Elder's other bastard, "noble by birth and by arms," joined with a "powerful" knight, a bastard like himself and the son of Canon Raoul, i.e., of his grandfather's brother. Together the young men ravaged part of the family estate. But this was an unusual case and bitterly remembered. Usually a worthy lord watched just as carefully over his illegitimate offspring as over the others, educating them, dubbing the young men knights. Arnoul II made all his sons knights, "those conceived in the pleasures of Venus as well as those who came forth from his wife's womb."[12] Baudouin is congratulated for having provided his illegitimate sons with an excellent education and his illegitimate daughters with excellent matches.

It should be noted, however, that, if we are to believe Lambert, the men of the two families with which he is concerned only enjoyed the "pleasures of Venus" when they were living as bachelors—"young" knights or canons—or widowers. We hear nothing of their sexual vagaries when they had a wife at their disposal. According to the morality put forward by the *History*, the realm of license began outside the enclosure of marriage. Here we may be allowed to doubt the veracity of this account. André le Chapelain depicted husbands as much freer in their ways, as did Gislebert de Mons, historian of the counts of Hainaut. Gislebert expresses surprise at the behavior of the then count, whom he did not like. He was married to a very devout young woman, and respected her desire for chastity without seeking consolation elsewhere. "Scorning all other women, he set himself to love her alone with a fervent *amor*"—actual love in marriage, but non-physical—"and, what is very rare in men, gave himself up to one woman and contented himself with her alone."

Gislebert clearly regards this fidelity as a weakness rather than a virtue, a laughable defect in such a highborn lord. Husbands had accepted the constraints imposed by the Church and no longer repudiated their wives. Did this not mean they were tacitly granted more liberty? At any rate, Lambert, less cynical and probably less free to speak the truth than Gislebert, depicts only virtuous husbands who loved their wives. One example was the gallant Baudouin II, who was fighting in England when he heard that his countess's pregnancy—her tenth at least—had taken a dangerous turn. He hurried home, taking eminent doctors with him. When the physicians said there was no hope and that nothing remained but to "console" the patient, Baudouin, says Lambert, took to his bed with sorrow and remained there ill and solitary for days.[13] Was this a ritual display of grief, or genuine mourning? At any rate it is part of a eulogy of the count as husband.

Lambert's eulogy of him as father is even more earnest, for the real value of marriage lay in its offspring. "In and above all, the count of Guines rejoiced in the glorious propagation of his children, and used all his power and affection to promote their good."

He did so chiefly by arranging their marriages.

It was no easy matter either to make a wise marriage oneself or to arrange wise marriages for one's children. Take the case of Count Manassé of Guines, who lived in the first third of the twelfth century. His own marriage had been a good one: services rendered in England had earned him a wife with a rich dowry. But she had borne him only daughters, and of these only one had married, and all she had produced was a "sickly and hunchbacked daughter." As his hair turned white the count grew anxious: "He was much afraid, since no seed had come from his own body, that he would have to beg from one of his sisters an heir of another seed, as all his brothers had died without heirs."[14] Observe that the seed is supposed to be transmitted by the males only;

also that Manassé's father had prudently sent his younger sons away so that they might not lay claim to the estate and thus split it up. One of them had gone to the Crusades and become count of Beirut; but he had had no sons. The other, a member of the Thérouanne chapter, had been prevented by his vows from begetting legitimate sons. The danger of escheat or default of heirs had caused him to leave the cloister and become a knight, but he died before having any sons.

Count Manassé's sisters had been fertile enough, but their children were "of another seed." This story illustrates the then common obsession with "seed," and the power of the two main elements in lineal ideology: the prime importance of male succession and the prime importance of the direct line. Even though a sister's son might be dearer and more familiar, a brother's son was preferable from the dynastic point of view. And every head of a family wanted to "survive" through the seed "of his own body." That was why he half killed himself trying to beget sons.

Though Manassé of Guines gave up expecting to have any more children by his wife, other lords, some of them even older than he, did not despair so easily and did not hesitate to change wives for the purpose. Count Henry of Namur, already advanced in years, had married Laure, widow of Raoul of Vermandois. He was her fourth, perhaps even her fifth husband, but just as all his predecessors had failed to make her pregnant, so too did Henry fail. So he put Laure in a convent and in 1168 married Agnès, daughter of the count of Gueldre. His brother-in-law, the count of Hainaut, who had his eye on Agnès's inheritance, made no objection: Henry was now too old to be a threat.

Henry kept Agnès "for four years without ever uniting himself with her in bed, and in the end gave her back to her father." Hainaut breathed easily again. But in the autumn of 1185 there was a sensation: "Agnès, whom he [Henry] had abandoned for fifteen years, he received again [she was his wife, although the marriage had not been consummated], and she immediately conceived a daughter whom she brought forth in the month of July." A daughter was better than nothing. Her father put her to good use straight away, marrying her off while she was still in her cradle to the heir to the *comté* of Champagne.

But, for his part, Manassé did not take another wife, and we see respect for indissolubility triumphing over the desire to see oneself survive in one's own seed. Was it a victory for ecclesiastical ideology, or for married love?

As a last resort, not wanting to have to "beg" a successor from the families his sisters had married into, Manassé tried to make use of his granddaughter, even though she was not attractive. And he did succeed in getting her married. Of course, the initiative did not come from the bride herself. Nor did it come from her father, the lord of Bourbourg. When the girl's mother died, he had remarried, thus losing the right of control over the property to which the girl was heiress; so he was only asked for his consent and "support." It was the grandmother who acted and probably found the husband, an Englishman. The property she had brought with her at the time of her own marriage helped to give the girl a good dowry and thus make her less unattractive, so the grandmother gave "counsel" in the matter. But it was the grandfather who actually arranged the marriage, for he was the head of the house and the eldest of the male members of the family: all its heritage of wealth and prestige and honor was in his hands.

Such was the rule, and it was followed again later when Arnoul, the hero of the *History*, took a wife.[15] Though he was no longer young he was biddable, and married "through the counsel" of his father. As for his wife, she had neither father, brother, nor uncle—it was this that made her so desirable—and she was given in marriage by a group of men. Not by the knights of the chateau of Bourbourg but by her maternal uncles, the four brothers of Béthune, one of whom was the poet Conon. They spoke in the name of a woman, their widowed sister, the dowager who was in present possession of the inheritance. They were accompanied by the son of the father's eldest sister, the male then at the head of the paternal line, who had a say in the matter because the property that was to change hands as a result of the marriage had been handed down from his ancestors. Clearly the right to arrange a marriage always belonged to a man, to the one who wielded power in the household; when it was his daughter who was to be given away, he required the participation of his wife, since the bride's dowry was often derived from the dotal property of her mother or aunt.

All heads of families had the same objective. Their dream was to marry off all their daughters. That was what the girls had been born for: "engendered that they themselves might procreate offspring of good stock,"[16] that they might carry the blood of their ancestors into other houses and thus bind them to their own line. So they had to be married, and married again if possible when they were widowed. The viscount of Merck, near Guines, managed to arrange marriages for all of his nine daughters. Count Baudouin II married off his as best he could, to knights vassal. The lord of Bourbourg found husbands for only three of his five daughters: the eldest made a good match, the second a less satisfactory one, and the third had to venture as far as the Rhineland; the two who were left grew old in the family convent, consoled by the belief that virginity came highest in the scale of virtues.[17]

The supply of women exceeded the demand in the marriage market. Fathers followed the policy of the lords of Amboise and prevented most of their sons from taking lawful wives. The same Henry of Bourbourg mentioned above had seven sons: he sent two into the Church; three fell victim to the real dangers of chivalry, one getting killed "when still a lad," another when he was "already a knight," and a third, "blinded in a tournament," was incapacitated as a candidate for head of the estate. The eldest son was married twice but died childless. The only son left was the last-born, still very young. When his father died he was married off to his brother's widow, disregarding the impediment of affinity, since it was essential to preserve the useful link with the house of Béthune.

This couple had a son, who did not live long, and a daughter. While his twelve children were still alive, Henry of Bourbourg had naturally thought the fate of his line assured, but because of the restrictions he imposed on his sons' marriages he caused his heritage to fall to the distaff side. Arnoul of Ardres snapped up Henry's orphan granddaughter. This story makes clear the dangers inherent in the sort of discipline Henry practiced; but the first consideration was generally to avoid undue branching of the family tree.

Heads of families wanted their seed to survive, but in only one branch. So there had to be some birth control. Did anyone resort to contraception? A reference in Hermann of Tournai suggests that such practices were not unknown[18]: Countess Clémence of Flanders, "having had three sons in three years and fearing, if more were born, that they might quarrel over Flanders, acted according to feminine practices [arte muliebri] so as not to breed any more." She would have used secrets closely guarded by the womenfolk, the mixtures described by Bourchard of Worms, which enabled unfaithful wives to remain barren as in the romances. Though Hermann did not suspect it, Clémence was punished: all her sons died without heir, and the "honor" of the family went to the son-in-law of Hainaut. But it is hard to believe that much use was made of such procedures among lawfully married couples when we remember Baudouin of Guines's ten grown-up children and Henry of Bourbourg's twelve. The usual way of restricting the number of possible heirs was to stop all but eldest sons from marrying.

The gist of these accounts needs to be checked against as many family genealogies as possible to see if this practice was as general among the aristocracy of northern France at large during the twelfth century (before that there is too little documentation on which to base a reliable answer) as it seems to have been among the knights in the neighborhood of Cluny. A recent study gives another example of this strategy, devious but effective.[19] Aswalo, lord of Seignelay, a contemporary of Manassé of Guines, had five sons. One died young, another became archbishop of Sens, and the three others were married, which seems to contradict my theory. But let us examine the circumstances.

The eldest son got married, which was quite normal. The second also married, on his own initiative, but only after his brother's death, when he himself was his nephews' guardian, responsible for the dynasty and for ensuring its survival should the nephews die, as frequently happened, in tournament or battle. Nor was the third brother married off by either father or brother: he trusted to his own luck and late in life unearthed an heiress; he settled down on his wife's estate and made no demands on the paternal inheritance.

The marriages of the two younger sons were fertile, providing Aswalo with five grandsons. But three of these went into the Church, where they did very well for themselves. The other two became knights and set out in 1189 on the Third Crusade, from which they never returned. The only shoot producing shoots of his own was the eldest son of the eldest son. He had four sons, one of whom fathered legitimate offspring, but the other three died with their father's cousins on the expedition to the Holy Land.

Chance played a part in the withering of these adventitious branches. The family was well placed for settling its sons in careers in cathedral chapters. And far be it from me to say it was not just religious enthusiasm that led all these young men to go to Jerusalem or into the Church. But would so many of them have done so if family heads, anxious to prevent their "honor" from being divided, had not urged them to it?

From the houses of Guines and Ardres, too, young men went forth either to occupy posts in the Church—canons who though they might be prolific produced no legitimate heirs—or to become knights and fight profitably in England or Palestine. But the two family trees drawn up by Lambert are very significant: they show several sons in nearly every new generation, but no new branches—the same pattern as that of the lords of Amboise. This supports the idea I have put forward, and suggests that, like the aristocracy in the region of Macon, the great families of northern France protected their social preeminence by controlling their own expansion, which they did by controlling their sons' marriages. The great noble families seem not to have multiplied in the course of the twelfth century. On the contrary, over-cautious restriction appears to have thinned them out and concentrated fortunes in fewer hands.

But during this period there were some changes in matrimonial policy, and these had repercussions on the history of family inheritances. Leaving aside the more distant ancestors to whom Lambert ascribes imaginary wives, since the year 1000 the eldest sons and probable future heads of the Guines and Ardres families had all married wives of high rank who came from far away. Count Baudouin I married a daughter of the count of Holland; his son Manassé married the daughter of the chamberlain of England. Arnoul, founder of the seigneury of

Ardres and seneschal to the count of Boulogne, was married first to the heiress of a chateau in the Boulonnais and then to the widow of the count of Saint-Pol: this enabled him to administer his stepsons' fortunes while they were still minors, helping himself liberally all the while to property that included the relics he donated to the collegiate church at Ardres.

All these men were in the service of powerful princes: Baudouin owed loyalty to the count of Flanders, Manassé to the duke of Normandy, and Arnoul to the count of Boulogne. And apparently, as was true for the ancestors of the lords of Amboise during the same period, they also owed their rich and far-flung wives to the intervention of their patrons. But after 1100 both the scope and the quality of the marriages dwindled. Baudouin II and Arnoul the Younger married less wealthy young women from places not so far away. I see this change as a result of such families' increased autonomy. Their heads could no longer count on the generosity of a feudal lord and had to find their daughters-in-law for themselves. Safe in their glorious ancestry, they concentrated on strengthening their seigneuries and thus on accumulating lands. They were always on the lookout for what could be acquired as close as possible to home. As mental attitudes changed and the desire for prestige gradually yielded to the desire for material wealth, they tended to pass over the region's many highborn ladies, some of them descendants of Charlemagne, and choose instead first-born daughters who had no brothers but who did have the prospect of large and conveniently situated estates. The advantages brought by such matches outweighed the disadvantage of taking a wife lower in rank than oneself.

The father of Baudouin II decided to condescend in this way, marrying his eldest son to the infant heiress of his vassal the seigneur of Ardres. For generations the married couples in the family had been unequal in rank, but now for the first time it was the husband who was more nobly born than the wife. This choice must therefore have been greeted with some surprise. At any rate, Lambert seeks to explain it[20]: Baudouin, he says, consented to lower himself [*inclinavit*]—though in fact the decision came from the father rather than from a boy of about ten years of age. "Following the example of many noblemen, dukes kings, and emperors," he married the daughter of one of his vassals. But the count of Guines, now a sort of minor emperor in his own right, was only lowering himself in order to consolidate his possessions: he was paving the way for his heir presumptive to take over the finest sub-infeudated fief in the *comté*. The case was similar to that of Louis VI of France, who a few years earlier had married his son to Eleanor of Aquitaine.

At that time, through the combined effect of the high death rate among young men, biological degeneration, and the obstacles put in the way of male reproduction, there was no shortage of good catches—young women who, if only they could be got hold of, might bring great wealth. The seigneury of Bourbourg was inherited by a woman. That of Ardres came first to the sister of Arnoul III and Baudouin, and then to Baudouin's only daughter. Three women inherited the seigneury of Guines, one after the other: Count Manassé's daughter, her daughter, then one of the count's sisters. Such windfalls were sometimes seized upon by younger sons, who thus escaped the celibacy to which their rank would otherwise have doomed them; but this seems not to have happened often in the twelfth century. Such bold knights as we know to have seized fortune by the forelock in this way were all of high rank, the sons of powerful lords. For merely getting hold of the girl was not enough: the husband had to get the upper hand of her relations, who resented seeing an interloper settled on their ancestors' lands. The chronicles show that such struggles could be severe.

When Manassé died miserably in the chateau at Guines his grand-daughter's husband, an English knight known as Albert the Wild Boar, told of the news by his father-in-law Henry of Bourbourg, hastened to pay homage to the count of Flanders for the important fief that now came to his sickly wife. But a man with the blood of the counts of Guines in his veins rose up to oppose him: Arnoul, one of Manassé's nephews, the son of his youngest sister and of the keeper of the chateau of Gand. This younger son was trying to improve his position in the world. As was customary among "young" knights, he had gone to live with his maternal uncle, whom he had urged to help him establish him-self. The uncle had no son and liked the youth, so finally he agreed to grant him the fief of a fortress dependent upon his own chateau.[21] Arnoul of Gand thus had a house and a marriage bed and was in a position to make a settlement upon a wife. So he got married. His wife was the daughter of the keeper of the chateau of Saint-Omer and a descendant of Charlemagne. And Lambert does not neglect to mention that she was his hero's grandmother. On the death of Manassé—his uncle, his benefactor, and the lord of his fief—Arnoul laid claim to the succession and took up arms against the seigneur of Bourbourg, who defended his daughter's rights on the spot while awaiting the arrival of his son-in-law.

Lambert describes this war as unjust, and so it was. But such conflicts were frequent because of the belief that male rights were superior to those of females. Hugues of Bourbourg himself had suffered because of it: he had married a daughter of the lord of Alost, thinking to make a profitable match, but the young woman's paternal uncle seized her dowry "by violence," leaving his niece only a "tiny portion" over which he had no claim because it had come to her through her mother.[22]

The chronicle of the monastery of Andres makes mention of some young orphans whom their guardian, their father's brother, stripped of their heritage in a similar fashion. A clear pattern emerges: maternal uncles were naturally protective; paternal uncles were rivals and naturally inclined to despoil.

War attracted adventurers from all over the region. Among those who joined Arnoul of Gand was Baudouin, a "youth," younger brother of the seigneur of Ardres and, like him, in search of fame and fortune. Baudouin was wounded in the course of a siege, an accident that rarely befell the knights in their heavy armor and was thus regarded as a sign that heaven disapproved of the side Baudouin had chosen. That at least was what the monks of La Capelle-Sainte-Marie kept telling him. They were casting covetous eyes on the collegiate church of Ardres and lost no opportunity of exacerbating its protectors' guilt feelings. Baudouin abandoned Arnoul and went over to his enemy, but only after some bargaining: he offered to fight for the lord of Bourbourg and his just cause on condition that the lord's daughter and her material prospects were put up as the stakes.

But the daughter was not a widow. Her husband, Albert the Wild Boar, was in good health. So she had to be taken away from him. To obtain a more effective ally than his distant son-in-law, Henry opened divorce proceedings and sent a mixed embassy to England composed, significantly, of both knights and priests. An arrangement was arrived at. "On the day appointed, in accordance with the rules of civil and ecclesiastical justice, the union was dissolved."[23] The divorce was granted legally and ceremonially because the wife was ill and "for other reasons." What other reasons? Was it alleged that the marriage had not been consummated? There is no mention of such grounds, though all around Lambert, as he wrote his *History*, people were talking of nothing but Philip Augustus and the series of pretexts he was resorting to.

Baudouin married the divorcée, ailing though she was, and set about claiming his rights. But the lady was really ill, and died. On the day of her death Arnoul of Gand happened to be in the chateau of Ardres, which he had seized,[24] and to ask one of his brothers, formerly a monk but now a knight, to expound the psalm "O Lord my God, in thee do I put my trust." His brother told him, "It means you are rich." An interesting example of communication between secular and scholastic culture: at that very moment Manassé's granddaughter was expiring, blighting the hopes of Baudouin of Ardres.

But a new obstacle arose in the form of a cousin—arriving in hot haste from Burgundy—whom Arnoul had never seen. He was Geoffroi, lord of Semur-en-Brionnais, and he claimed the succession by right of birth: his mother was another of Manassé's sisters and had married well, as had her sister, but far away. As she was older than Arnoul's mother, Geoffroi argued that he had the better claim. This time there was no fighting, only long discussions. The arbiters who had been called together produced a verdict in Arnoul's favor. "Because there no longer existed upon the land of Guines any seed issued from Manassé's body," the heritage came to the collaterals. Though Geoffroi's mother had seniority on her side, she was dead and so her rights were extinct; in any case they were superseded by those of her living sister. Thus, the laws of succession evolved, putting the living before the dead and direct descendants, even women, before collaterals.

Not long afterward, the chateau of Ardres was the center of a similar lawsuit. Baudouin had obtained possession of the castle by chance and not without some expense. The scullions had killed his elder brother, who had left a widow he had taken into his own house. She was still a child and played with the other little girls of the household, dividing her time between her dolls, church services, and lengthy dips in the fish-pond, where the knights of the chateau enjoyed watching her swim in her white shift. Pétronille, the young widow, was not yet nubile al-though she had already been married off; the seigneury was her dower. So Baudouin had to come to some agreement with her uncle, the count of Flanders, who would only agree to take his virginal niece back "in exchange for compensation for her dowry." This was extremely expen-sive, and to meet the demand Baudouin sold the collegiate church to the monks of La Capelle. They got the reliquaries; the seigneur of Ardres got some gold and silver, most of which he gave to Pétronille's relatives, using the rest to finance his own departure on the Crusades. He died in the Holy Land, and two of his nephews then claimed his property. The arbitration court awarded it to the nephew whose mother was still alive, although she was younger than her sister. But the beneficiary had to pay his rival compensation amounting to the considerable sum of one hun-dred silver marks.[25]

Matrimonial strategies underwent further changes during the next generation, that of Baudouin II, and this time the changes were con-siderable: the heads of families relaxed their control over their young men's marriages and allowed younger sons to found families.

The count of Guines did this during the last years of the century. He had six sons. One was a priest; another had been killed "in the flower of his youth," for these young man played with death. But of the others not only the eldest was married but the others as well. Just as their grand-father's uncle had done, their father gave them the dwelling without which they could not take a wife. What they were each given was a fortified house, the center of a neighboring seigneury, but each of these seigneuries was small, and above all marginal in relation to the family estate, being made up of recent acquisitions or land reclaimed from the marshes.[26] The same thing was happening in neighboring families: at about the same time, the seigneur of Fismes arranged marriages for his four sons.

Archives and archaelogy alike teach us that most aristocratic houses were then beginning to hive off. Around the old chateaux inhabited by eldest sons there grew up a number of smaller fortified and moated houses, reduced replicas of the strongholds where the great dynasties had set down their roots.

This branching out from the old trunks resulted in growth of population: the number of men of good birth who were or expected to be knights increased rapidly in the early decades of the thirteenth century. This was a profound change that overturned the very structure of the aristocracy, affecting its behavior, its rituals, and its position in society as a whole. We need to know why it no longer seemed so vital to maintain the strict discipline that for so long, or at least for as long as we can trace the histories of feudal families, had forced so many men to remain celibate, "youths," swelling the ranks of a large and unruly group who weighed heavily on the evolution of power, culture, and the economy.[27]

What happened was that the violent pressure of this group, whose members longed to escape from it and make legal marriages, finally made itself felt. But why did the barrier they railed against give way when it did? Why did the younger sons get what they wanted only as the year 1200 drew near? Was it because the knights and their lords, no less anxious than their fathers to maintain their prestige and spread the glory of their blood as far as possible, were now in a position to be more generous and treat all their own sons more equally, instead of staking everything on one and keeping the others down? All the evidence suggests that in fact their means were expanding, mainly through the concentration of fortunes that had resulted from their ancestors caution.

It is evident too that in the region with which I am concerned, the borders of the Boulonnais and Flanders, as everywhere in northern France, changes in social structure in the last decades of the twelfth century both increased the wealth of aristocratic families and made that wealth more mobile. Estates brought in more revenue because hitherto unused land was put under cultivation, because finances were better managed, and because—through tithes; taxes on the use of mills, forges, and ovens; and payments for exemption from service and for access to law and justice—ever larger dues were being levied on what was produced by the workers. Such levies came more and more to be paid in cash, whether in pennies or in pieces of silver. Above all, seigneuries were more profitable because they had more people living on them: this was a period of sturdy growth in the rural population. And this growth was reflected on the level of the landowners themselves, so that the brakes that for five or six generations had prevented great families from expanding could now be released.

This new flexibility derived also from a strengthening of large-scale political structures, which caused a much more rapid circulation of wealth among the ruling class: the great princes took with one hand and gave with the other: they collected death duties and fines, and sold exemptions from service; but they also dispensed wages, gifts, and stipends. Many of these transactions were in cash. Land now counted for less, inheritance was no longer so important. Until only recently, families had preserved their aristocratic preeminence by allowing only a few of their young men to marry, while the rest had to exist precariously on the fringe, literally sterilized by the dangerous life-style of gambling, inconsequence, and adventure they were forced into. But now the state itself guaranteed the nobles' preeminence, maintaining privilege in the name of the theory of the three orders,[28] while the circulation of money brought into social relationships a flexibility that was soon to affect matrimonial practices.

The concomitant development of the law must also be taken into account. Laws governing feudal tenures became fixed in the course of the twelfth century. It seemed less dangerous to break up the ancestral inheritance if the custom of parage was applied, by which younger sons held in fief from the eldest that portion of the estate granted to them so that they might found a family. This procedure was common by the end of the twelfth century. Lambert projected its use back into the distant past, the period where he was free to locate ideal forms of behavior. He tells[29] of an imaginary count of Ponthieu who, about the year 1000, divided his lands up among his four sons. The eldest got the *comté* itself, the ancestral house and its appurtenances. The second and third got Boulogne and Saint-Pol respectively but had to do homage for them to their brother. To his youngest son the count bequeathed an alleged right to the *comté* of Guines, but as the son could not make this claim good he was given the heiress to the *comté* of Saint-Valéry.

The arrangements ascribed to this imaginary father, are exactly the same as those actually made by Count Baudouin II. His younger brother was restive so he arranged for him to marry the granddaughter of the count of Saint-Pol and, to enable him to do so, granted him a small estate as fief, having obtained the consent of his own son Arnoul. Then with equal prudence he married off his other brothers to daughters of his vassals, thus making them his own feudatories as well as the feudatories of his heir. So the latter would in one way or another control the whole of the family heritage.

Such practices spread in the course of this period throughout the whole of northern France. So much so that King Philip, fearing they would undermine the foundations of feudal service, decided to call a halt to them. What we know of the testamentary dispositions of a few of the great lords of that time shows us how their sons' marriages were facilitated by joint recourse to money and to vassalic relationships. In 1190 Raoul I of Coucy was about to follow the king overseas, so he divided up his property among his sons and daughters. He applied the law of primogeniture strictly, so that the inheritance which had come to him from his father went in its entirety to his first-born son. Among the others, who were knights, he shared more recent acquisitions, including the "*villes-neuves*," or newly reclaimed areas. These young men were thus able to marry, although they had to do homage to the principal heir. As for those of his daughters who were already married, Raoul did nothing more for them: they had had their dowries. For the one daughter who was unmarried, he drew on his financial reserves to provide her with an income. He did the same for a son who was destined for the Church but who was as yet still a student. Count Baudouin V of

Hainaut dealt similarly with his heirs: his second son, who was married, was given his mother's inheritance in the form of a fief taken from the eldest son's estate; the youngest son, who was difficult and a haunter of tournaments, was given an income in cash, but on condition that he paid liege homage. This very flexible tenure, a sort of "financial" fief that could be easily confiscated, might help him to find a wife.

So the approach of the thirteenth century saw the beginning of a phase of relaxation. The great princes were probably not displeased to see the number of noble families increasing, dispersing the powers of which the old fortresses were the centers, reducing the distance between the barons and their under-vassals, swelling the ranks of the orders of chivalry, which the princes regarded as the main bastion of their own power. They saw that these new matrimonial policies encouraged the knights to sober down, for they helped to absorb the unruly mass of "young" knights hitherto treated hardly any better than bastards. These knights—who previously had often had to live as beggars, ready to abduct the wives otherwise forbidden them and compensating for their frustration with their own special morality of rapine and aggressive independence—now at last entered into the category assigned by the Church to all the laity—the category ruled by the disciplines of marriage and family life.

For most of them now, "youth" was no longer a state, or sort of *ordo*, in which they might remain confined until they died, but merely a phase that ended on their wedding day, when they settled down and became responsible for a family of their own.

But they all looked back on their youth with nostalgia, and Lambert took care to include an apologia for those days in his account. He knew it would please old Count Baudouin II to read about himself in his widowhood depicted as still chasing girls just as when he was a a lad. In addition to his eulogy of the fathers, ruling their households judiciously and making farsighted and profitable matches for such of their children as they permitted to marry, and in addition to his praise for all the pious, obedient daughters, Lambert includes a eulogy of the rampaging sons. He even goes so far as to praise what the morality of the heads of families condemned as a sin: abduction, which the morality of the "bachelors" ranked highest among acts of valor. But in a society growing daily less brutal, decorum required such exploits to be sublimated. A young knight no longer seized a noble lady by force; he won her favors by his bravery, by the fame he had won in the lists or in the courts of love.

This was the great period of jousting, which served not only as military training but also as an outlet for youthful energy. A tournament was a sort of traveling fair, an exhibition of possible husbands showing off in front of the ladies and above all for the benefit of matchmakers. All the heroes of this chronicle are portrayed as excellent jousters in their youth. One of them, the second Arnoul of Ardres, had to arrange his own marriage because his father was dead and he had no uncles; but he found a wife from the famous house of the lords of Alost because, says Lambert, echoes of his sporting prowess had reached the ears of the head of the family, who bestowed on Arnoul his sister's hand.[30]

But the ideology of youth is seen more clearly in Lambert's description of the rituals of courtly love. He depicts them twice, once at each end of the genealogical chain: in both these key positions he sets up the figure of a young and seductive knight-errant.

The authors of princely genealogies liked to start their stories with an adventurer come from none knew where to found a dynasty with a wife he had captured through his own efforts. Here, at the beginning of the tenth century, this part is played by Sicfridus from the land of the Vikings, the land of Ingeborg and primitive legend.[31] His wanderings brought him to the lands of the Guines family, which his ancestors had ravaged in days gone by. Sicfridus, young and brave, was welcomed into the house of the count of Flanders and became companion-in-arms of its heir. Lambert, quite anachronistically, depicts him as being knighted and granted a fief, as princes' comrades might have been much later. But it was to love he owed his good fortune.

He outshone all the other knights, and the count's sister fell in love with him. Like Eleanor, she let herself be drawn into "colloquies," and in the course of "play" her friend got her pregnant. It was usual in the twelfth century for the "young men" to amuse themselves in this way, but their partners were generally daughters of their fathers' vassals. Sicfridus, however, had infringed his lord's honor and was thus a felon. So he fled to Guines, where he died of love "like another André," i.e., le Chapelain.

The child was duly born, a bastard, but luckily for him his cousin, the new count of Flanders, stood as godfather to him, brought him up and knighted him, and finally granted him the fief of Guines which had been his father's freehold. And that was how the family was founded.

At the other end of the tale was Arnoul, Lambert's newly married patron.[32] Here the author did not need to use his imagination, for he could draw upon what he himself had witnessed and what the family he served was fond of boasting about. Following the custom, Count Baudouin sent his son on a jousting tour just after he was knighted, so that both Arnoul's personal prestige and that of the family could be displayed before the very eyes of noblemen looking for a worthy son-in-law. Arnoul set off escorted by two squires, two valets, and a priest to keep the accounts: the tour was meant to be impressive, but within reason. Time went by and the count stopped sending money: Arnoul had to live from hand to mouth. But he went on jousting, and in the end, after five years, he attracted the attention of an heiress.

She was rich—too rich; and of impossibly high birth too. Saint Ide, whose name she bore, was her great-great-grandmother; Godefroi of Bouillon was her great-great-uncle; like the late queen of France, she was a niece of Count Philip of Flanders; and she herself was countess of Boulogne through her mother. She had already been married and widowed twice; she was decidedly older than Arnoul; and she was not averse to amusing herself. She sent the young man messages and even found a pretext to visit him in his own house. Negotiations were begun with her uncle. Then along came Renaud of Dammartin, who snatched Ide from under Arnoul's nose and galloped her off to Touraine. Arnoul rode after in pursuit but was arrested with the connivance of the bishop of Verdun for having earlier, when he was hard up, helped himself to some of the taxes being raised to finance the Third Crusade. He was kept in custody long enough to be done out of his bride.

Let us examine the version his family history gives of the affair. Ide had loved Arnoul, or at least "out of feminine frivolity and deceit" she had pretended to. Arnoul, for his part, had loved Ide, or at least "out of masculine prudence and cunning" had acted the part. In fact, "he aspired, by winning the countess's favors through that genuine or simulated love, to the lands and dignity attached to the *comté* of Boulogne." It could hardly be put more clearly. Lambert had read the romances of courtly love, but what he says about love here places it right in the middle of concrete reality. He debunks "knightly, or chivalric, love" and shows it for what it was: fundamentally misogynous. Woman was an object, to be despised: the chosen lady is explicitly described as "fickle" and "perfidious." Courtly love, exalting pleasure and inciting men to break the triple ban on abduction, adultery, and fornication, seems to defy in one fell swoop the power of the matchmakers, the exhortations of the priests, and conjugal morality.

But this challenge was only an apparent one. In fact, the heads of families—Baudouin behind Arnoul and the count of Flanders behind Ide—were really pulling the strings. And the Church itself was not too exacting in sexual matters when marriage was not involved. In reality, as we see quite clearly here, amorous posturings were only the prelude to nuptial ceremonies, and beneath such displays were hidden the stern realities of dynastic politics.

Right at the end of the twelfth century, when the Church was becoming more moderate and social relationships more flexible, so that all young men might hope to marry, the behavior models held up to bachelors and married men were coming to be complementary. Youths were invited to prove their "virtue" in the outside world so that families with women to marry off might promote the charade that these young men were capturing their brides by their own efforts. Even after they were married they could still tourney for a while. But once they took over their fathers' seigneuries and became "new men"—like Baudouin of Guines when he inherited the *comté*, already the father of five children, and still *indissolutus*—then they had to settle down, installed in the family house beside their ladies and bound to them, as Hugues of Saint-Victor insisted, "singly and solely in requited love."[33]

Thus, throughout those two centuries the image sharpened. We can see fairly clearly how a knight took a wife and how he treated her by the time of the reign of Philip Augustus. Were these customs so very different four and half centuries later, in Molière's day, or six centuries later, at the time of the Abbot Fabre of Languedoc?[34] A few fragments of the ritual trappings survive even today: the marriage proposal, the drawing up of the marriage contract, the engagement, the nuptial mass, the groomsmen dividing up the bride's veil. What I have tried to discern, on the basis of texts that become increasingly informative with the passage of time, is the introduction of those main structures that are now being eroded before our eyes.

I use the word "introduction" advisedly; and the process was a difficult one. We have already noticed how the image changed at the same time as it grew more clear. After the year 1000, when the historian finds the first proclamations of the theory of society dividing mankind into three complementary functions, he also discovers two opposing conceptions of virtuous marriage, one that had guided the behavior of the knights and another that the priests had tried to impose on the laity. Then came a phase during which both positions hardened, with the conflict appearing to reach its height around the year 1100; thereafter it eased, and at the beginning of the thirteenth century, when the ideology of the three orders became one of the foundations of monarchical power, an accommodation was reached. Did the Church's model win? Had Christianity transformed society?

At the outset, and in the region and in the social group I have chosen to study, Christianity already permeated every nook and cranny of life. But it was a different kind of Christianity. I am sure all those knights feared God, even the greediest and most violent of them, even those inflamed with a desire for women, such as Count Jean of Soissons. All those I have mentioned contributed liberally to the funds that went to build the cathedrals; and it was not a hope of plunder or love of travel that made them press on month after month through danger and deprivation toward the tomb of Christ. But, like the heretics, many of them believed with Christ that the Kingdom is not of this world. So that they might sleep in peace in their graves and eventually reach Paradise, they—*unlike* the heretics—looked to the priests for the saving acts that would cleanse them of their sins. But at the same time they denied that the priests had any right to force change upon the earthly customs they had inherited from their ancestors. But, in the great shift that brought about the internalization of religion, they gradually learned that rites count for little when acts and intentions are not blameless. Society slowly became more accessible to the message of the Gospels. And, at the same time, so did the Church. The servants of God, meditating on the meaning of the Incarnation, imperceptibly became aware that the liturgy alone was not enough and that they could achieve their objectives better if they did not handle nature and social reality too roughly.

While the spirit evolved, the body did not remain unchanged. During the eleventh century, when ideological positions were hardening, the feudal mode of production was coming into existence amid tumult and a bitter struggle for power. Power could be preserved and extended only through its concentration. The knightly class crystallized into great families clinging to the land—and to the right to rule, punish, and exploit the peasants. The Church, in order to resist the aggression of temporal powers, crystallized into rigorous principles. Marriage was an instrument of control. The leaders of the Church used it as a means of holding their own against the laity, and in the hope even of subjugating it. The heads of families used it as a means of keeping their power intact.

The struggle in which matrimonial practices were at stake was at its height at the same time as the first effects of rural growth began to be seen. The towns were awakening from their torpor, the roads were coming alive with traffic, the use of money was spreading, states were beginning to form. Everything became more mobile and flexible in the great upsurge of the twelfth century. The ruling class, its power assured and suitably distributed, could relax. Christianity evolved toward what it became for Francis of Assisi at the end of the period with which we have been concerned, and the priests and knights, brought together under the authority of a prince, at last came to an agreement on what marriage ought to be if the established order was to be preserved. Society and Christianity had changed together. Neither one nor the other model had been vanquished: they merged.

But perhaps it is wrong to speak of two models and two sides. On the one hand, the young were opposed to the old. On the other, the heretics were opposed to the rigorists. And in between were the conciliators who eventually won the day. The "older" members of the aristocracy came to terms with the Church mediators, and this agreement made it possible for the two models of marriage to adapt to each other, setting up the basic framework for a new pattern of marriage that was to last for centuries. But the new structures were flanked by two complementary forms of control: on the one hand, the celibacy imposed on the servants of God so as to satisfy the rigorists and disarm the heretics; and, on the other, the rules of courtly love, designed to impose a degree of discipline on the passions of what remained of the "younger" aristocracy.

It all added up to a solid system. But amid the clamor of all these men asserting what they had done or wanted to do, we must not forget the women. Much has been said about them. But how much do we really know?

GENEALOGICAL TABLES

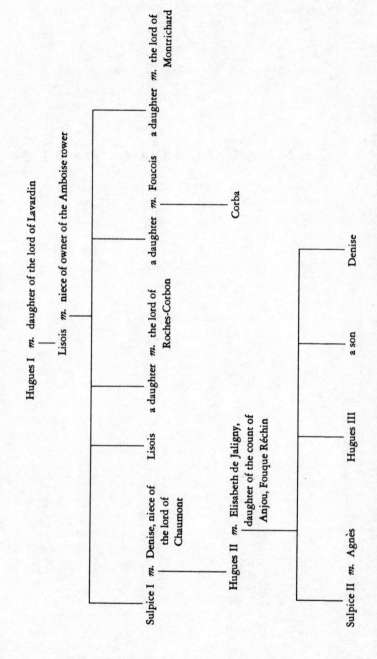

THE LORDS OF AMBOISE

Hugues I *m.* daughter of the lord of Lavardin

Lisois *m.* niece of owner of the Amboise tower

Sulpice I *m.* Denise, niece of the lord of Chaumont

Lisois

a daughter *m.* the lord of Roches-Corbon

a daughter *m.* Foucois

Corba

a daughter *m.* the lord of Montrichard

Hugues II *m.* Elisabeth de Jaligny, daughter of the count of Anjou, Fouque Réchin

Sulpice II *m.* Agnès

Hugues III

a son

Denise

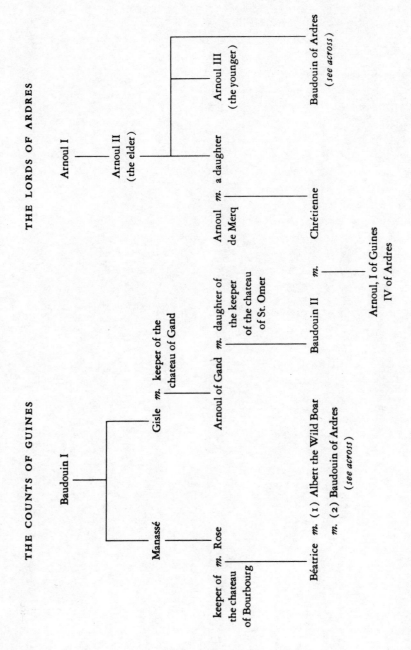

THE COUNTS OF GUINES

THE LORDS OF ARDRES

Baudouin I

Manassé · Gisle

Rose *m.* keeper of
the chateau
of Bourbourg

Arnoul of Gand *m.* daughter of
the keeper of
the chateau
of St. Omer

Béatrice *m.* (1) Albert the Wild Boar
m. (2) Baudouin of Ardres
(*see across*)

Baudouin II *m.*

Arnoul, I of Guines
IV of Ardres

Arnoul I

Arnoul II
(the elder)

Arnoul III
(the younger)

Baudouin of Ardres
(*see across*)

Arnoul *m.* a daughter
de Merq

Chrétienne

NOTES

ABBREVIATIONS

AASS—*Acta sanctorum.*
Anjou—*Chroniques des comtes d'Anjou et des seigneurs d'Amboise* [Chronicles of the counts of Anjou and the lords of Amboise], Paris, 1913.
BN—Bibliothèque Nationale [French National Library].
C.—*Recueil des chartes de l'abbaye de Cluny* [Collected documents from the abbey at Cluny], ed. Bernard de Bruel.
HF—*Recueil des Historiens de France* [A compilation of the works of historians of France].
M.—*Cartulaire de Saint-Vincent de Mâcon* [Cartulary of Saint Vincent of Macon], ed. Ragut.
MGH SS—*Monumenta Germaniae Historica. Scriptores.*
MGH Cap.—*Monumenta Germaniae Historica. Capitularia.*
MGH Ep.—*Monumenta Germaniae Historica. Epistolae.*
PL—*Patrologie Latine.*

1. At the end of the eleventh century, a hundred years after the Capetian dynasty came to power, the kings of France enjoyed great moral prestige throughout the kingdom, but their real power was confined to the northern half of France, between the *comté* of Flanders, the duchy of Burgundy, the duchy of Normandy, the *comté* of Anjou, and the north of the Massif Central.

2. MGH SS, VI, 367; V, 461, 463; *Recueil d'annales angevines et vendômoises* [Compilation of the annals of Anjou and Vendôme], ed. Halphen, p. 42.

3. Letter 212, PL 162.

4. *Cartulaire de Marmoutier pour le Dunois*, ed. Mabille, no. 60.

5. *Yves de Chartres: Lettres*, ed. Leclercq, Paris, 1962, Letter 13, p. 56.

6. *Ibid.*, Letter 15, p. 60.

7. *Ibid.*, Letter 23, p. 94.

8. HF, XIV, 791.

9. BN, Latin MS 11792, fol. 143.

10. Anjou, 232.

11. *Regesta pontificum romanorum*, ed. Jaffé, nos. 5636, 5637.

12. The War of the Investitures was the long quarrel, in the second half of the eleventh century, between the papacy, which was working for Church reform, and the ruling princes of Christendom. The pope fought to establish the superiority of spiritual over temporal power. He opposed simony, i.e., the trade in Church preferments, and so denied kings, including the emperor, the right to invest bishops with the insignia of the ring and the crozier, a ceremony that implied the submission of the prelate to the lay ruler.

13. The abbey of St. Denis (first bishop of Paris and patron saint of the French realm), north of the capital, was the traditional burying place of the kings of France, almost all of whom, from Dagobert to Louis XVIII, were interred there, thus symbolizing dynastic continuity.

14. *Vita Ludovici*, I.

15. *De gestis regum anglorum*, III, 235, 257.

16. *Historia ecclesiastica*, VIII, 387, 389, 390.

17. Anjou, 127.

18. *Vita Ludovici*, I.

19. HF, XIV, 745.

CHAPTER II

1. Regula Pastoralis, III, 27; PL 77, 102.

2. P. Toubert, "La Théorie du mariage chez les moralistes carolingiens," *Il matrimonio nella società alto medioevale* [Marriage in early medieval society], Spoleto, 1977.

3. MGH Cap., II, 1, 45, 46.

4. PL 125, 658.

5. PL 126, 655.

6. PL 126, 137, 138.

7. The False, or Forged, Decretals (genuine decretals constituted the second part of the canon law, containing the decrees and decisions of the early popes on disputed points) purported to be the decisions of some thirty popes of the first three centuries, supporting the claim of the papacy to temporal as well as spiritual authority. They were actually written in the ninth century.

8. PL 131, 87.

9. Every one of the seven joints in the arm stood for a generation.

10. Roman law counts the degrees starting from *ego*, or the self, going back to the ancestor and then returning to *ego* (descendants of the same grandfather, for example, are cousins four times removed. Medieval Church law calculates the degrees of relationship from *ego* also, but only in the one (returning) direction, so that to be cousins four times removed people had to have the same great-great-grandparent.

11. The others were murder, theft, and arson.

12. G. Dumézil, *Mariages indo-européens*, Paris, 1979.

13. PL 54, 1204.

14. In the Middle Ages, the term "honor" came to combine two ideas: the legal notion of all the property belonging to one lord, often consisting of several different manors, and the moral notion of the prestige arising out of such possessions and positions.

15. "Tenure" signified the terms on which a person enjoyed a tenement or holding, and thence the holding itself.

16. MGH Ep., V, 103, 115.

17. PL 122, 806.

18. PL 122, 893.

19. The Peace of God movement, which aimed at compensating for the weakening "king's peace," originated in the town of Le Puy, in Poitou (in the south of France), at the end of the tenth century, gradually spreading until it reached the region of Capetian influence during the third decade of the eleventh century.

Cf. G. Duby, *The Three Orders: Feudal Society Imagined*, trans. A. Goldhammer (Chicago: University of Chicago Press, 1980), pp. 134–139.

CHAPTER III

1. AASS, March 1, 280.
2. P. Fournier, "Le *Decretum* de Bourchard of Worms," *Revue d'Histoire ecclésiastique*, 1911.
3. G. Fransen, *Les collections canoniques*, Tournehout, 1973.
4. F. Chiovaro, "*Discretio pastoralis* et *scientia canonica* au XIème siècle," *Studia moralia*, 1977.
5. Marc Bloch, *La Société féodale*, Paris, 1968, 142. *Feudal Society*, 2d ed., trans. L. A. Manyon (Chicago: Chicago University Press, 1962).
6. PL 140, 573–579.
7. C. Vogel, *Le péché et la pénitence au Moyen Age* [Sin and penance in the Middle Ages], Paris, 1969.
8. PL 140, 828.
9. PL 140, 967.
10. PL 140, 968.
11. PL 140, 955.
12. PL 140, 975.
13. PL 140, 957.
14. PL 140, 784.
15. PL 140, 966.
16. PL 140, 961.
17. PL 140, 975.
18. PL 140, 958.
19. PL 140, 953.

CHAPTER IV

1. *Epitome vitae Roberti regis*, ed. Bautier and Labory.
2. Richer, *Histoires*, MGH SS, III, 651.
3. Pages 100–102.
4. On early eleventh-century heresies, cf. Duby, *Three Orders, op. cit.*, pp. 130–134.

5. HF, X, 535.

6. F. Lot, *Etudes sur la règne de Hugues Capet et la fin du Xème siècle* [Studies on the reign of Hugues Capet and the end of the eleventh century], Paris, 1903, p. 171, no. 1.

7. MGH SS, III, 694.

8. HF, X, 493.

9. HF, X, 211.

CHAPTER V

1. Adalbéron de Laon, *Poème au roi Robert*, ed. C. Carozzi, Paris, 1979, p. 30, line 390.

2. PL 141, 223.

3. Count of Anjou in the year 1000. He made the feudal principality of Anjou into one of the most powerful in France.

4. Ed. Marchegay, p. 64.

5. E. Searle, "Seignorial control of women's marriages," *Past and Present*, 1979.

6. PL 143, 797.

7. King of France, son of Robert the Pious.

8. H. Le Geherel, "Le parage en Touraine-Anjou au Moyen Age," *Revue historique de Droit français et étranger*, 1965.

9. K. Schmid, "Zur Problematik von Familie, Sippe und Geschlecht, Haus und Dynastie beim mittelalteslichen Adel," *Zeitschrift für die Geschichte des Oberrheins* (?), 1937.

10. On the "feudal revolution," cf. Duby, *Three Orders*, pp. 147–160.

11. *La Catalogne du milieu du Xème à la fin du XIIème siècle* [Catalonia from the middle of the tenth to the end of the twelfth centuries], Toulouse, 1976.

12. *Ibid.*, vol. 2, pp. 544–549.

13. See below, pp. 235–240, 255, 270, 280.

14. C., no. 1354 (974).

15. C., no. 2528.

16. C., no. 3032.

17. C., nos. 1415, 1425, 1426.

18. The *loi Gombette* was decreed by King Gondebaud at the end of the fifth century.

19. C., no. 2875 (1031–1060).

20. C., no. 2265.

21. C., no. 2875 (1031–1060); M., no. 463 (997–1031).

22. This entailed either ordeal by red-hot iron, often used in the case of a woman accused of adultery (she was deemed innocent if her skin did not burn); or ordeal by water (if the accused did not float on being thrown in, he was innocent); or trial by combat (the two claimants, or their champions, fought in an enclosed space and the victor was judged to be in the right).

23. *Cartulaire de l'église collégiale Notre-Dame de Beaujeu*, ed. Guigue, no. 12.

24. C., no. 2659.

25. C., nos. 2628, 2618, 2633.

26. C., no. 2605.

27. C., 2618 (1005); similarly, C., nos. 2628, 2633, 2659.

28. M., no. 463.

29. C., nos. 2022, 2867.

30. C., no. 2919.

31. C., no. 2412.

32. C., no. 3574.

33. C., no. 2493.

34. C., no. 2616.

35. M., no. 477.

36. C., no. 2036.

37. C., nos. 3874, 3821, 3654.

38. C., no. 3577.

39. "Roland" was not a family name, but that of the hero of a *chanson de geste*, or epic; "le Bressan" underlined the fact that he was a stranger, from another region.

40. C., no. 3744.

41. B. Guénée, "Les généalogies entre l'histoire et la politique. La fierté d'être Capétien, en France, au Moyen Age" [Genealogies as Influenced by History and Politics: Capetian Prestige in Medieval France], *Annales*, 1978.

42. J. Wollasch, "Parenté noble et monachisme réformateur: observations sur les 'conversions' à la vie monastique aux XIème et XIIème siècles" [Aristocratic Kinship and the Reforming Influence of the Monasteries: Observations on Conversions to the Monastic Life in the Eleventh and Twelfth Centuries], *Revue Historique*, 1980.

43. G. Duby, "Lignage, noblesse et chevalerie dans la région mâconnaise: Une révision," *Annales*, 1972. "Lineage, nobility, and knighthood," in *The Chivalrous Society*, trans. C. Postan, London, 1977. Also *Hommes et structures du Moyen Age* (Paris: Mouton, 1973).

CHAPTER VI

1. H. Taviani, "Le mariage dans l'hérésie de l'an mil," *Annales*, 1977 [Heresy and Marriage in the Year 1000]; G. Duby, *Les trois ordres, ou l'Imaginaire du féodalisme*, Paris, 1978, pp. 163–168.

2. Cf. G. Duby, *Three Orders*, pp. 133–134.

3. See pp. 50–51.

4. PL, 142, 1299, 1301.

5. Ed. Carozzi, lines 232, 244, 252.

6. B. Schimmelpfennig, "Zölibat und Lage des 'Priestersöhne' von ll. bis 14. Jahrhundert," *Historische Zeitschrift*, 1978.

7. Ecclesiastics supporting church reform, called the "Gregorian" reform after Pope Gregory VII.

8. P. Toubert, *Les structures du Latium médiéval*, Rome, 1973, p. 741.

9. P. Daudet, *Etudes sur l'histoire de la juridiction matrimoniale. L'établissement de la compétence de l'Eglise en matière de divorce et consanguinité* [Studies in the history of matrimonial jurisdiction. The establishment of the Church's competence on the subject of divorce and consanguinity], Paris, 1941.

CHAPTER VII

1. AASS, September VIII, 744–751.

2. MGH SS, XV², 877–881.

3. MGH SS, XV², 883–884.

4. PL 174, 1398–1399.

5. *Annalecta Bollandiana*, 1926.

6. AASS, July II, 403.

7. Mathilde, daughter and heiress of Eustache, count of Boulogne.

8. AASS, April I, 141–144.

9. Godefroi of Bouillon was one of the leaders of the First Crusade. He conquered Jerusalem in 1099. His brother Baudoin became the first king of Jerusalem. Their elder brother, Eustache, remained in France and succeeded his father as count of Boulogne.

CHAPTER VIII

1. *De vita sua*, ed. Bourgin.

2. J. Benton, *Self and Society in Medieval France*, New York, 1970; J. Kantor, "A Psychohistorical Source: The Memoirs of Abbot Guibert of Nogent," *Journal of Medieval History*, 1976.

3. *De vita sua*, I, 12.

4. *Ibid.*, I, 18.

5. *Ibid.*, I, 3.

6. *Ibid.*, I, 13.

7. *Purity and Danger*, London, 1966.

8. *De vita sua*, I, 14.

9. *Ibid.*, I, 7.

10. *Ibid.*, I, 2.

11. *Ibid.*, III, 19.

12. *Ibid.*, II, 5.

13. *Ibid.*, I, 12.

14. *Ibid.*, III, 14.

15. The name of Messalina, Nero's mother, has become a byword for lasciviousness.

16. *De vita sua*, III, 17.

17. In England, and probably in Normandy too, the debate on ecclesiastical celibacy was at its height between 1125 and 1130. See I. J. Flint, "The *Historia Regum Brittaniae* of Geoffrey of Monmouth: Parody or its Purpose. A suggestion," *Speculum*, 1979.

18. *De vita sua*, III, 13.

19. *Ibid.*, III, 14.

20. According to Y. Labande-Mailfert, *I laici nella società christiana dei secoli XI e XII*, Milan, 1968, pl. 3.

21. J.-B. Molin and P. Mutembé, *Le rituel du mariage en France du XIIème au XVIème siècle*, Paris, 1974.

22. Unpublished thesis, University of Paris IV, 1980.

23. *De vita sua*, III, 3.

24. *Ibid.*, III, 16.

25. Anjou, genealogies III and IV.

26. Anjou, genealogy V.

27. *Supra*, p. 11.

28. G. Burton Hicks, "The Impact of William Cliton upon the Continental Policies of Henry I of England," *Viator*, 1979.

29. *De vita sua*, III, 16.

30. *Ibid.*, III, 5.
31. *Ibid.*, III, 3.
32. *Ibid.*, III, 14.
33. Ed. Pétigny, *Bibliothèque de l'Ecole des Chartes*, 1853–1854.

CHAPTER IX

1. Y. Labonte, *Le mariage selon Yves de Chartres*, Bruges, 1965.
2. During the eleventh century the movement for Church reform was reflected by, among other things, the founding of clerical communities living according to a rule or canon. The most austere of these rules was that of St. Augustine.
3. Letter 16, ed. J. Leclercq, p. 69.
4. PL 161, *Panormia*, VI, 2 and 5.
5. *Ibid.*, 3 and 4.
6. *Ibid.*, 4.
7. *Ibid.*, 7 and 8.
8. PL 161, *Decretum*, VIII, 42.
9. *Ibid.*, 85 to 97.
10. PL 162, 608.
11. *Decretum*, VII, 59, 66.
12. *Decretum*, VIII, 140, 221–227, 230, 236, 239, 241, 255, 257–260, and most of Book VI of the *Panormia*.
13. *Decretum*, VIII, 238.
14. Bourchard of Worms, *Decretum*, VII, 41; Yves, *Decretum*, X, 169.
15. Letter 125, PL 162, col. 137.
16. Letter 239, PL 162, col. 246.
17. Letters 16, 148, 155, 188, PL 162, cols. 28, 153.
18. Letter 205, PL 162, col. 210.
19. Letter 280, PL 162, col. 281.
20. Letter 249, PL 162, col. 255.
21. Letter 252, PL 162, col. 257.
22. Letters 18, 222, PL 162, cols. 31, 226.
23. Letters 99, 134, 243, PL 162, cols. 118, 143, 250.
24. Letter 99, PL 162, col. 118.
25. Letter 166, PL 162, col. 169.
26. Letter 167, PL 162, col. 170.
27. Letter 183, PL 162, col. 184.

28. Letter 230, PL 162, col. 233.

29. MGH SS, IX, 320.

30. D. Poirion, "Edyppus et l'énigme du roman médiéval," *Sénéfiance*, 1980.

31. Letter 158, PL 162, col. 163.

32. Letter 45, PL 162, col. 57.

33. Letters 129, 130, 261, PL 162, cols. 139, 140, 265.

34. *Corpus juris canonici*, ed. Friedberg, I, 274.

35. Letter 261, PL 162, col. 265.

36. Letter of Saint Anselm, PL 159, 245.

37. Letter 209, PL 162, col. 214.

38. Letter 225, PL 162, col. 219.

39. Letter 229, PL 162, col. 232.

40. Letter 232, PL 162, col. 235.

41. The archaeology of human habitation in the feudal period shows that both the dwellings of the greatest princes and those of rich peasants had only two rooms, the hall and the chamber, both open and exposed. Though the chamber was more private than the hall, the individual was never alone in either.

42. Letter 218, ed. Leclercq.

43. Letter 221, ed. Leclercq.

44. Letter 242, ed. Leclercq.

45. Letter 221, ed. Leclercq.

46. In the early eleventh century, before Abelard gave the school of Paris its preeminence, the school of Laon, headed by Master Anselme, was the most active and famous of these centers of learning. Bérenger of Tours was declared a heretic because of his theory on the Eucharist.

47. PL 171, 963–964.

48. PL 176, 488.

49. I have made use here of an unpublished contribution by Francesco Chiovare to my seminar at the Collège de France.

50. PL 176, 859, 864.

51. *Livre des Sentences*, IV, 26.

CHAPTER X

1. Ed. Molinier.

2. MGH SS, XX.

3. HF, XV, 509–510.

4. The Templars took a vow of chastity.

5. Renard le Goupil (*goupil*=fox in old French) and Ysengrin the Wolf were the protagonists of the *Roman de Renard*, a satirical poem written in northern France in the twelfth century and continued in the thirteenth.

6. There are only two accounts that disagree: that of Robert du Mont, HF, XIII, 293, and that of Richard of Poitiers, HF, XII, 120. Richard was a Cluniac and a fierce enemy of the Cistercians, and therefore of Eugene III too.

7. HF, XIII, 507.

8. PL 201, 670.

9. HF, XIII, 101–102.

10. HF, XIII, 125.

11. HF, XVIII, 155–156.

12. PL 212, 1057–1058.

13. MGH SS, XIV, 343.

14. The king of France and the representatives of the pope were each supporting their own candidates for bishoprics then vacant.

15. Letter 214, PL 182.

16. Letters 182, 220, 224.

17. MGH SS, XX, 521.

18. K. F. Werner, "Die Legitimität der Karolinger und die Entstehung der *Reditus ad stirpem Karoli*," *Die Welt als Geschichte*, 1951.

20. J. Baldwin, *Masters, Princes and Merchants: The Social Views of Peter the Chanter and His Circle*, Princeton, 1970.

21. *Ibid.*, II, 226, n. 185.

22. *Ibid.*, II, 225, n. 182.

23. *Ibid.*, II, 225, n. 175.

24. *Ibid.*, II, 224, n. 169.

25. *Ibid.*, II, 225, n. 179.

26. Leviticus 18: 6–18 forbids a man to have relations with his mother, his father's wife, his sister, his son's daughter, his half-sister, his father's sister, his mother's sister, the wife of his paternal uncle, his daughter-in-law, his brother's wife, his wife's sister, his wife's daughter and granddaughter.

CHAPTER XI

1. BN, MS 17509, 3284; Cambrai, 534.

2. *Jeu d'Adam*, ed. Noomen, Paris, 1971.

3. Unpublished contribution by Maurice Accarie, professor of Romance literature at the University of Nice.

4. *Traité de l'amour courtois* [Treatise on Courtly Love], trans. Buridant, Paris, 1974.

5. *Ibid.*, p. 109.

6. *Livre des Sentences*, IV, 31, 6.

7. PL 210, 193.

8. Buridant, p. 160.

9. M. T. Lorcin, *Façons de penser et de sentir: les fabliaux français* [Ways of Thinking and of Feeling: The French Fabliau], Paris, 1978.

10. Tristan appeals to the judgment of God, i.e., trial by combat, to prove his innocence.

11. P. Menard, *Les lais de Marie de France*, Paris, 1978.

12. H. Oschinsky, *Der Ritter unterwegs und die Pflege der Gastfreundschaft im alten Frankreich*, Halle, 1900.

13. *Perceval*, lines 32191–32194.

14. *Ibid.*

CHAPTER XII

1. Anjou.

2. *Ibid.*, p. 128.

3. *Ibid.*, p. 127.

4. *Ibid.*, p. 99.

5. *Ibid.*, p. 75.

6. *Ibid.*, pp. 148–150.

7. *Ibid.*, pp. 135, 139.

8. B. Petot, "Le mariage des vassales," *Revue historique de Droit français et étranger*, 1978.

9. Baldwin, *op. cit.*, II, 178, n. 134.

10. Anjou, p. 101.

11. *Ibid.*, p. 172.

12. Henry V, king of Germany and emperor, who died in 1125.

CHAPTER XIII

1. MGH SS, XXIV.

2. *Ibid.*, p. 563.

3. *Ibid.*, Ch. 127.

4. *Ibid.*, Ch. 27.

5. *Ibid.*, Ch. 149.

6. The rules governing the Peace of God protected the defenseless against violence. These included members of religious orders, women, peasants, and above all widows and orphans.

7. MGH SS, XXIV, Ch. 123.

8. *Ibid.*, Ch. 122.

9. *Ibid.*, Ch. 89.

10. *Liber paenitentialis*, 1, 27.

11. MGH SS, XXIV, Ch. 113.

12. *Ibid.*, Ch. 126.

13. *Ibid.*, Ch. 84.

14. *Ibid.*, Ch. 43.

15. *Ibid.*, Ch. 149.

16. *Ibid.*, Ch. 66.

17. *Ibid.*, Ch. 127.

18. MGH SS, XIV, 282.

19. C. Bouchard, "The structure of a XIIth-Century French family: The Lords of Seignelay," *Viator*, 1979.

20. MGH SS, XIV, Ch. 67.

21. *Ibid.*, Ch. 144.

22. *Ibid.*, Ch. 122.

23. *Ibid.*, Ch. 60.

24. *Ibid.*

25. The *marc* was a unit of weight equal to half a *livre*, or pound. The silver *marc*, a multiple of the *denier*, was used in contracts in the twelfth century to signify large quantities of coins.

26. MGH SS, XIV, Chs. 72 and 79.

27. G. Duby, "Les 'jeunes' dans la société aristocratique," *Annales*, 1964. [Yonten in aristocratic society," in *The Chivalrous Society, op. cit.*] Also *Hommes et structures du Moyen Age* (Paris: Mouton, 1973).

28. The rulers adopted the originally ecclesiastical theory of the three orders (those who prayed, those who fought—both these orders were privileged—and those who worked). This ideological schema served as the basis for the French monarchy up to the Revolution. Cf. G. Duby, *Three Orders*, pp. 271–292 and 346–356.

29. MGH SS, XIV, Ch. 15.

30. *Ibid.*, Ch. 123. G. Duby, *Le dimanche de Bouvines*, Paris, 1973.

31. *Ibid.*, Chs. 11 and 12.

32. *Ibid.*, Chs. 93 and 94.

33. PL 176, 987.

34. Author of a story edited and commented on by Emmanuel le Roy Ladurie in *L'Argent, l'amour et la mort en pays d'Oc* (Paris, 1980). *Love, Death, and Money in the Pays d'Oc*, trans. Alan Sheridan (New York: Braziller, 1982).

Urban II, Pope, 6, 10, 12, 84, 120, 175
  clergy purged by, 3–4, 8
  Philip I's excommunication and, 4–5

vassalic friendship, 231, 236
virginity:
  early Church praise of, 26–28
  marriage and, 30, 57
  of Mary, 177, 182
  monasticism and, 51
  unlawful taking of, 70
Visio Wettini (Eginhard), 49

War of the Investitures, 13
Whitsuntide, knights dubbed at, 251
widows:
  meritorious state of, 144
  remarriage of, 73, 143–44, 170, 234
William, count of Arles, 78
William V (the Great), duke of Aquitaine, 91
William IX, duke of Aquitaine, 13, 123, 154, 158–59, 165, 246–47
William of Anjou, 16
William of Malmesbury, 14, 39, 155
William of Newburgh, 195–97
William of Volpiano, 77
William Rufus, king of England, 16–17
William the Conqueror, king of England, 10, 42, 43, 126–27, 155
witchcraft, 71
  virility robbed by, 141, 142

white magic of, 141–42
women:
  Biblical subjugation of, 24–26, 46
  Church protection of, 88
  creation of, 24, 50
  distrust of, 46, 65, 72, 106, 144, 147, 150, 218
  early Church subordination of, 28
  education of, 260
  hereditary property of, 90, 96, 99
  heresy and, 109–10
  ideal attributes of, 233–34
  lifetime estates of, 100–101
  marital property of, 97–104
  married names of, 44–45
  masturbation by, 69
  medieval subjugation of, 33, 46–47, 96, 106, 115, 137, 138, 143, 164, 212, 215–16
  moral weakness of, 46–47, 65–66, 72, 170, 212
  as prizes in war, 237
  sexual appetite of, 147, 157
  as subject to sin, 46–48
  witchcraft by, 71

Ysengrin, 195
Yves, bishop of Chartres, 6, 8–10, 13, 15, 16, 29, 52, 61, 84, 120, 129, 139, 144, 154, 161–80, 196, 198, 200, 203, 208, 221
  canon law compiled by, 161–66
  letters of, 166–72